LUCCA THE
WAR
DOG

LUCCA THE WAR DOG

The inspiring true story of the world's most heroic dog

MARIA GOODAVAGE

EBURY
PRESS

1 3 5 7 9 10 8 6 4 2

Ebury Press, an imprint of Ebury Publishing
20 Vauxhall Bridge Road
London SW1V 2SA

Ebury Press is part of the Penguin Random House
group of companies whose addresses can be found at
global.penguinrandomhouse.com

Penguin
Random House
UK

First published by Ebury Press in 2017
First published in the United States of America by Dutton,
a Penguin Random House Company, in 2017

www.penguin.co.uk

A CIP catalogue record for this book
is available from the British Library

ISBN 9781785035173

Designed by Katy Riegel

Printed and bound in Great Britain by Clays Ltd, St Ives PLC

*Dedicated to the military working dogs
and handlers who have faithfully served
our country since World War II.*

*To the ones who made the ultimate sacrifice,
you are missed.*

CONTENTS

CONTENTS

PART FOUR BACK TO WORK

PART ONE

Line of Duty

1

Thirty Feet Ahead

MARINE CORPORAL JUAN "Rod" Rodriguez crunched across the dry farm field, his right hand resting on the M4 strapped to his chest. He kept clear of the path that meandered through hard clumps of dirt that looked nothing like the rich soil of his New England roots. The road less traveled—ideally, no road at all—was the safest from homemade bombs sowed by the Taliban. This was the Nahri Saraj District, in southern Afghanistan's Helmand River valley, and a war unlike those of previous generations.

Rod watched his dog, a German shepherd–Belgian Malinois mix, who was thirty feet ahead and inspecting the land for IEDs. His eyes swept the area, keeping watch for anything suspicious. Unlike much of the agricultural land around here, this field was barren, not a sea of young poppies a month away from opium harvest. Furrows here and there hinted at past crops, but it was mostly flat, which made for easy maneuvering. In the distance, a compound, a tree line, and farther out, some worn-down old mountains.

Rod continued walking and observing. He could see his dog trotting with purpose, nose down, tail up, knowing just what to do. It was March 23, 2012, just one month shy of her sixth anniversary as a marine. With two deployments behind her, she was an old pro at the business of sniffing improvised explosive devices while off leash. "Good girl, Mama Lucca," he said under his breath.

Lucca Bear. Lucca Pie. Bearcat Jones. Mama Lucca. The twelve Special Forces soldiers had come to know military working dog Lucca K458 by all the nicknames Rod used for her—the terms of endearment she had inspired during her career. She had led more than four hundred missions, and no one had gotten hurt by an IED when they were with her.

Mama Lucca was the name that had stuck lately. She was the only one at their remote combat outpost the Green Berets felt comfortable hugging after a tough day or when they missed home. She was more experienced than some of the soldiers, and the maternal moniker was a natural fit.

Rod saw Lucca moving close to the narrow dirt path. "Lucca, come!" he called. She paused for a beat, looked at him, and kept sniffing. That wasn't normal. She almost always listened. But Rod could sense she was onto something. He didn't want to distract her, so he let her continue, watching her intently in case he needed to steer her clear of suspicious-looking spots. She walked back and forth, nose to the ground, and every few steps she turned more quickly, as she traced the scent to its point of origin.

Lucca's luxuriant tail gave a few high, quick wags, looking momentarily like a victory flag. She stopped and stared at Rod.

He got the message, automatically imagining her words. *Hey, Dad, got one right here.* He called her back and praised her with his voice an octave higher than normal. "Good girl, Lucca!" He patted her side a few times but left the Kong in his cargo pocket because throwing a rubber reward in a place like this was a bad idea.

"Ben," he called to the engineer, who was close behind. "Lucca just responded, right there." He pointed to the spot with four fingers extended together.

"'K, we'll take care of it," Ben said. "Nice work, Mama Lucca."

Rod shifted their course to the left to keep Lucca away from the IED and the trail. She trotted ahead for about twenty-five feet, spun around, and headed back toward him. Rod kept close watch, realizing she may have locked onto the scent of another explosive. Where there's one, there's often at least one more.

The cloud of gray smoke erupted before Rod heard the explosion. A scream pierced through the boom, and a sickening thud followed. Rod couldn't see Lucca through the thick mass that hung in the air. He shouted, "*No!*" and squeezed his helmet hard between his hands, hoping he'd wake up from every dog handler's worst nightmare. Radios around him buzzed into a frenzy, but he didn't hear words, just felt the surge of adrenaline that instantly made Lucca his sole focus.

As the curtain of debris curled away, he could make out his dog. She had dragged herself up and was standing, dazed, alive. Rod dashed toward her. He didn't think about the IEDs that could be between him and her. Lucca could take only a few unsteady steps before Rod reached her. He leaned down and swept her up in his arms, trying not to notice the smell of her burned fur and flesh.

Snipers struck at times like this. Rod wanted to run to the tree line with his dog to hide her from them, but the blood poured from her leg and he couldn't take a chance she would bleed out.

He laid her on the ground and ripped a combat application tourniquet from just inside his flak jacket. They were in easy reach. He could grab a tourniquet and apply it with one hand to save his own life or anyone else's.

The blood streamed, and the soil softened under Lucca. He saw clearly now that her left paw and a few inches above it had been torn away in the blast, exposing the bone, muscle, and tendons of her midleg. It was like something out of the dog anatomy images Rod and his classmates had studied in canine school, only with an alarming coat of red. Lucca panted hard, whimpering quietly every few breaths.

Focus, focus, Rod told himself. He wrapped the tourniquet strap around her shoulder, twisted the plastic stick. The bleeding slowed. Good. He picked her up again and cradled her close. She melted into him, relaxing as he ran with her to the tree line sixty feet away. He gently placed her down again, and the Green Berets pulled security around them, weapons and eyes facing outward, protecting the dog team.

Rod grabbed another tourniquet and positioned it closer to Lucca's injury. She had bled all over his pants as he carried her. "An extra tourniquet never killed anyone, right, Lucca?" He secured it.

Scott, an 18-Delta medic, ran over. Rod drew his first conscious breath since the explosion. Special Forces medics are some of the most experienced and efficient medical trauma technicians in the world, and veterinary care is one of their many areas of expertise. Scott checked the tourniquets and injected Lucca in the thigh with a dose of morphine. Her panting slowed, her body relaxed, but she remained aware, eyes open. They checked out the burns on her neck, chest, and face and bandaged her leg and shoulder. Scott took a Sharpie from his aid bag and wrote *1400* on the time tag of the upper tourniquet.

Lucca shifted her gaze to the sky. Rod looked and saw the medevac helicopter chopping its way toward them. The Black Hawk landed just far enough away that the wash didn't disturb Lucca. They loaded her up, and Rod got in.

Special Forces Sergeant Jake Parker turned around briefly from his lookout and gave his friend a thumbs-up. Rod returned it, and the Black Hawk rose straight up and headed east toward Camp Leatherneck.

Goddamned IEDs, Parker thought as the helicopter disappeared and the farmland became silent. *That dog had better not die.*

2

First in Class

THE FAMILIAR SMELL of dogs and disinfectant cleanser greeted Marine Staff Sergeant Chris Willingham as he and four other Americans walked into the kennel in Israel. From the dead silence just moments before, a cacophony of barks erupted and bounced off the concrete walls like something dangerous. Only it wasn't. Willingham liked the sound, the warm exuberance.

He was used to riotous canine greetings from his years at much larger military kennels stateside. Back at Lackland Air Force Base, the heart of the U.S. Military Working Dog Program, the barking came from dozens of dogs at a time—a heavy-metal band with treble and base on max volume. He had spent the last three years there training dogs and instructing handlers and before that was a dog handler at Camp Lejeune. The Israel-based canine ensemble, while far smaller than those he'd worked with in the U.S., still provided the rush he got from entering a military dog kennel.

April 23, 2006. This was the day he had been looking forward to since arriving in Tel Aviv a couple of weeks earlier. At his side was longtime dog handler Staff Sergeant Kristopher Knight, Willingham's close marine pal, who was also a trainer and instructor at Lackland and played a mean game of Texas Hold'em with him and the other handlers on Friday nights. Two other marine dog handlers, Sergeant Rob Bowker and Sergeant Christopher Baity, and the U.S. Marine Corps K-9 program manager, William Childress, rounded out the canine contingent that traveled halfway around the world to learn about off-leash dog handling from the people who did it best.

They had landed in Israel just before Passover week, which turned out to be a bad time to deal with the government documents and official paperwork required for their visit. Not that they had any complaints about a few extra days at the Isrotel Tower hotel, with its sweeping views of the Mediterranean and its beachfront location. The hotel was close to the U.S. Embassy, which was the reason they'd been booked there, but that wasn't high up on the handlers' list of favorite features.

As much as Willingham was enjoying Tel Aviv, he was ready to immerse himself in the world of dogs as soon as everything was good to go. He missed them. He'd been working with military dogs intensively for the last six years and he wasn't looking for a break. The drive to the headquarters of Oketz, the elite K-9 unit of the Israeli Defense Forces (IDF), would take only a half hour when they finally got the paperwork squared away. So close, yet so far. He was eager to get to a place where he could once again speak his native tongue: dog.

Oketz had been producing excellent bomb-detection dogs trained to work off leash. In the U.S., these canines, known as specialized search dogs (SSDs), were fairly new additions to the four-legged forces. The U.S. Department of Defense wanted a few top American handlers to learn how to train and work with these dogs. Childress had sought out four seasoned handlers to go to Israel for an intensive eight-month specialized search dog program designed specifically for the Americans. The handlers needed to be sergeant or above, with a solid foundation of military dog knowledge. This would make it easier to absorb and apply the techniques being taught and to go back to the U.S. and train other dog teams.

And now the handpicked marines were about to meet the dogs who would be at their sides for the next few years. Most likely, months at a time would be spent in the IED-infested streets, compounds, and rural areas of Iraq—just a few hundred miles east of here. Their lives and the lives of countless others could depend on these dogs and on the extensive training the teams would receive during the next eight months.

Willingham's heart rate amped up as their head instructor, an IDF dog trainer of Russian origin named Michael (*Mi-kie-el*), unfolded the paper that would reveal the results of his matchmaking.

"Knight, you've got Rocky. Baity, you have Rona. Bowker, Yona is yours. Willingham, you get Lucca."

Four simple sentences, the die cast.

"You've got five minutes. Go meet your dogs," he told them.

The men surveyed their new partners. Three barked in steady rhythms. The two loudest whirled round incessantly, pausing only briefly to catch eye contact with whoever glanced their way.

The fourth dog stood wagging a resplendent auburn tail, not

saying a word, her slightly open mouth set in what Willingham swore was a smile, as if pleased, even delighted.

"Lucca!" Willingham entered her kennel and knelt down beside her. Lucca wagged harder and her back half wriggled with excitement while she inspected the man before her. Taller than most she had met, muscular, shaved head, beaming smile.

Willingham stroked her head and neck while looking over his new partner. German shepherd and Belgian Malinois in one dog. The best of both worlds, if the mix settles right. Hard to tell where one breed began and the other ended, but she was a beaut. And those eyes. He'd never seen anything like them before on any breed. She seemed to have real eyebrows, small, dark, and deeply expressive while they danced over her large, calm eyes. A charcoal line went from the outside corners of her eyes all the way back to her ears, like a smoky cat eye in heavy pencil, and she had a little black beauty mark on each cheek. From each mark grew three long whiskers.

"All right, Lucca, you ready to do this thing? I'm Chris. We're about to start this journey. I have no idea what the future entails, what tomorrow is about, but I'm really excited you're my dog."

Her tail swept out widely, from side to side. He noticed that the very end of her tail was black. It reminded him of an old story his mamaw had once told him about a boy dipping a girl's braids in an inkwell.

"Sıt!"

"Zit!"

"Sitz!"

School began early the next morning. The dogs, it turned

out, hadn't received any training, at least none that was notice-able. Lucca couldn't even sit when Willingham asked her—no matter what language he tried.

IDF canine experts had purchased the dogs during a recent trip to Europe. The dogs were all about two years old and came from breeders known for producing quality working dogs. The U.S. Military Working Dog Program gets most of its dogs from Europe as well. In countries like the Netherlands, the Czech Republic, and Germany, working dog sports have been going strong for up to a century, so there's an abundance of dogs bred for the kind of work military and police dogs do every day. The breeders and the vendors who raise them don't generally put much into training the dogs. They figure that's best left to the countries that buy them.

Lucca's home country was the Netherlands. Even though the Dutch and German words for *sit*—*zit* and *sitz*, respectively—are almost twins to the English word, he tried both languages in case some nuance of the word made her recognize it. But Lucca, Willingham's little Dutch girl, just stood there wagging. The lack of training didn't surprise the Americans. It's often best when a dog is a blank slate. That's how the U.S. military buys them: more raw material than ready-to-wear. The tailoring is up to the trainers and handlers.

The first several days together would be all about building rapport. Standard procedure. The sergeants-turned-students knew that rapport was everything. Without it, a dog won't work, or at least won't work reliably. When you're searching for homemade bombs in war-torn countries, halfhearted detection doesn't cut it. The dog has to want to work, has to crave that K-9 paycheck—a combination of heartfelt praise from a handler and a rubber toy such as a Kong or tennis ball.

What struck the Americans as unusual was that this bond would initially be forged over food. "For the next week, you are going to feed the dogs by hand," Michael announced. Willingham and Knight looked at each other, eyebrows raised. This was a new tactic for making friends out of military dogs. In the U.S., using food to train military dogs was the sign of a lazy handler or an unmotivated dog. But they figured that if Oketz did it, there had to be something to it. So the handlers measured their dogs' kibble and doled it out on walks and during early training on basic skills.

Bonding wasn't all about chow. The marines spent hours every day playing with their dogs, petting them, grooming them, and just hanging out. "This is the best job in the world," Willingham told Lucca while brushing her long auburn and black coat after they'd chased each other around outside for an hour or so.

In a few days, the handlers introduced Kongs to their dogs. The hard red or black rubber toys, shaped in the fashion of small snowmen someone had squashed a bit from the top, are ubiquitous in the military dog world. They're the ultimate reward for many dogs—eminently chewable, virtually indestructible, and with an off-kilter bounce that resembles wild prey on the run.

Lucca quickly became obsessed with the Kong. When the toy appeared, everything else disappeared, including Willingham. She didn't seem to hear him or see him when she was chomping on the red rubber, eyes semiclosed in bliss. "Meet me halfway, Lucca," he implored one day when she was facing away from him with her jaws wrapped around the Kong, refusing to look at him. "We gotta get past this."

He had an idea. A chunk of her paycheck was guaranteed: his affection and enthusiastic praise. She could have that anytime she did something good, and it would last a long time. Even when the words died down, she could sense Willingham's pride and approval. But the Kong was a commodity that came and went quickly. She earned it, enjoyed it for less than a minute, and had to give it back. Who wants to give back a paycheck?

Willingham decided to stretch out Lucca's paycheck in hopes she wouldn't be so grabby with it. When it came time to take back the Kong, he tossed another Kong. She'd run for it, bring it back, and he'd throw the other Kong out. Revolving credit! Paychecks everywhere! The canine version of supply-side economics worked. With the Kong commodity less rare, Lucca learned that the guy throwing these toys was a valuable guy to know.

"LUCKY BASTARD, YOU'VE got the best dog here," Knight told Willingham a month later, as they settled into their cots in a room they shared near the kennel.

"My Shepinois is pretty amazing," Willingham replied, and smiled like a proud dad. After the bumpy start, Lucca was at the head of her class—excelling in basic obedience and some scent work.

Knight rubbed his neck in a vain attempt to keep a stress headache at bay. It had been another tough day. He had at least four years more military dog experience than the other handlers and was well-known as an exemplary trainer who could "talk dog." Naturally, Michael matched him with the most challenging dog of the four.

If dogs could have attention deficit disorder, Rocky—an angular Malinois with giant bat-like ears that looked like they belonged on another, much larger dog—had it bad. The behavior issue had come to a head earlier that day when Knight and his Malinois were training together in a field near the kennels. Spring was in the air, and butterflies occasionally winged by. When this happened, Rocky stopped whatever he was doing, turned his head toward the fluttering insect, and watched it as it looped about and eventually flew out of sight.

Getting through to Rocky during these reveries was futile. Rocky was in his own world. It took several minutes for Knight to get Rocky back on task after the butterfly left the scene. This would never do in combat. Not at all. Knight had a few months to get Rocky on board. It would be an intensive training challenge.

Butterflies were the least of it, though. What took Rocky out of the game for days were female dogs in heat. Female Oketz dogs don't get spayed, unlike American military dogs. The rationale is that the male Oketz dogs are going to be dealing with a lot of unspayed female dogs in third world countries. They have to learn to ignore those tempting calls of the wild. But when any of Rocky's three gal pals were in heat, he was a dog undone. He couldn't function. He drooled. His mouth chattered. He couldn't focus on Knight.

"You look like a fool, boy," Knight told him as he brought Rocky back to his kennel to chill.

If Rocky were the only dog Knight had to train, that would have been enough work. But he was just half the equation. Earlier that month, Michael told the marines that someone among them should take on another dog, in case one of theirs didn't pass the rigorous training standards.

"What about this one?" Knight said, pointing to a Belgian Tervuren, who looked like a very furry German shepherd with a dark head, in a kennel next to theirs. "He's already here in the kennel. I can take him on starting tomorrow."

"No, no, no! You don't want Bram [rhymes with *mom*]."

"What's wrong with him?"

"He's crazy! Craaazy," he said in his thick Russian accent. "He doesn't listen to anyone. He's one of the rare untrainable ones."

Bram, now standing at attention in his kennel, looked as if he were intent on listening to the conversation.

"Untrainable? No dog is untrainable," Knight said with a cocky chuckle. He gave a nod in the direction of Bram. "We'll take that dog."

A month later, Knight was having serious second thoughts about his proclamation.

Although Bram wasn't being trained as a protection dog, he liked to bite—people, the ceiling of his kennel, anything that moved and anything that didn't move. While searching, the dog bit chunks of grass out of the ground.

The bars of Tel Aviv provided Knight with the kind of setting he needed to talk Bram troubles with Willingham. One Saturday evening, after another challenging week with Bram, the two sat at the popular club, Whisky a Go Go, drinks in hand.

"He's pissed off for having to do what I command him to do versus what he wants to do," Knight said loudly, above the noise of the crowd. It felt good to shout about this dog.

"He's a tough one, man," Willingham said.

"Bram always thinks he knows what's best for Bram," Knight said, and took a long draft from his glass of Red Bull and vodka.

During detection exercises, instead of calmly walking or trotting to sniff out explosives, Bram raced counterclockwise full speed with his body tilted at a forty-five-degree angle. Sometimes he stopped, picked up a thick log or other fascinating object, and ran back to Knight with it.

One day after detecting an explosive, Bram scooped up the block of C-4 and, head raised high with pride in his find, galloped back to Knight. The explosive was falling apart from the pressure of his teeth when he delivered it to his handler.

"You hairy bastard!" Knight said, standing in disbelief as Bram dropped it at his feet. "Are you trying to kill me?"

Knight knew the explosive was a highly stable one that even Bram's mouth couldn't detonate, but he figured Bram didn't know that.

At least Bram didn't share Rocky's love of the ladies. He didn't even seem to notice when they went into heat. But he did have a one-track mind. "If you could read his thoughts," Knight told Willingham, "it would be 'Kong! Kong! Kong! Kong! Kong! Kong! Kong! Kong!'"

Knight often lay awake at night, trying to figure out ways to deal with this dog. He'd trained many dozens of dogs in his military career, but nothing had prepared him for Bram. Could Michael be right? Maybe. But he couldn't give up on Bram. He could just hear Michael, with his Russian accent, admonishing him. "You see? The dog is crazy! Craaazy! I told you so!"

Failure wasn't an option.

THE BEAUTY OF specialized search dogs is that they can follow their noses far more independently than leashed dogs. There's a wide consensus in the military that the noses of dogs, especially the long-snouted breeds commonly used for detection work, are unbeatable when it comes to finding bombs. A good nose on a well-trained dog who has bonded with a great handler is a formidable weapon against bad guys who plant IEDs in the fields and roadways of war. Being able to trust a dog to do the job off leash is a significant force multiplier.

In the years following Vietnam—a war in which dogs were put to use as sentries, scouts, and mine detectors, and then, tragically, left behind or euthanized when the war was over— bomb-dog work shifted focus. These dogs became used primarily for ensuring base safety, supporting the State Department and the Secret Service with special events, and being on call for emergency explosives-detection work.

But after the U.S. put boots on the ground in Iraq, all that changed. In 2003, the Defense Department announced that a young soldier, Army Private First Class Jeremiah D. Smith, died after his vehicle was "hit by unexploded ordnance." It was an unintentional oxymoron that revealed the military's lack of experience in this deadly new type of warfare that was about to unfold.

Soon after Smith's death, these explosives began taking a noticeable toll on U.S. troops. The term *improvised explosive device* and its acronym, IED, readily worked their way into military and civilian parlance. Al-Qaeda operatives saw that these relatively cheap and easy-to-make explosives could do the kind of damage to coalition forces that the operatives could never dream of doing in traditional combat. There was no predicting it at that time, but IEDs would become the number one killer of American troops in two wars, in Iraq and then Afghanistan.

The U.S. needed a weapon to combat these new killers.

The specialized off-leash bomb dogs got the call.

Experts usually concurred that no machine could compare with the nose of a dog for detecting IEDs. The combination of a trained dog handler's ability to spot potential danger areas on the ground and the dog's prowess at sniffing explosives would prove to be a formidable defense against these homemade bombs. With some extra training to acclimate them to new scents and the types of environments they'd encounter, bomb dogs were ready for the battlefield.

Most military dogs went to war on leash and still do. But a couple of years after the initial canine involvement in Iraq, leaders in the military dog world got a prototype of the specialized search dog program up and running.

Specialized search dogs learn commands like *forward, left,* and *right* and work in tandem with a handler. They listen to the handler, watch for hand and arm signals—well-trained dogs are aces at responding to these visual commands—and let their own noses take over when they're in the right spot. They can work at distances of a few hundred yards from their handlers when they wear radios in their harness pockets. At that distance handlers aren't able to scan the area the dog is working as well as they normally do. Signs of IEDs are more likely to go unnoticed by the human. But this distance work is a sometimes critical military dog tactic that requires unusual skill.

These canines have to be smart, dedicated, focused, and very well trained. If standard military working dogs have bachelor's degrees, specialized search dogs have PhDs.

After a few more months of SSD training, Lucca was still the clear top dog of her class. Sometimes she'd confuse right and left, but who doesn't? "No, Lucca, left," Willingham would tell her gently if she went off course to the right. And off to the left she'd go. She aced nearly every skill, quickly. Obedience, scent training, detection, off-leash work. Lucca made it look easy. And she remained unruffled regardless of the task.

Lucca excelled at off-leash detection. Whether in the dry hills covered with brown weeds and dotted with craggy rocks, the forests of tall trees with spindly trunks, on the hot roadsides, or around small structures reminiscent of what they'd find if they deployed to Iraq, she seemed happy and at ease doing her searches. Even on the hottest days, she had a spring in her gait that made her look like a dog enjoying a jaunt in a park. When she found an explosive, her tail went crazy, and Willingham could see that same smile she'd worn the day they met.

When other dogs might go off focus, Lucca always seemed to stay on task. She could find a small amount of explosives scent far from Willingham while he used subtle hand signals to direct her where he thought the explosive could be, based on environmental cues. A little mound of rocks here, a haystack there, some scrapes in the ground where scrapes shouldn't be. She never balked on strange surfaces or at loud noises, and she checked in frequently, turning around and glancing at Willingham to make sure she was going the way he intended and changing direction when she needed to. Willingham was in awe of her talents and dedication and felt the kind of pride he imagined fathers feel when their children excel.

But something was eating at Willingham. One reason the off-leash skills of specialized search dogs are so valuable is the standoff distance they create between the bomb and those out on a mission. If an off-leash dog accidentally sets off an IED while sniffing for one, the humans on the mission could well be safe from the blast. The dog, however, would likely perish.

Willingham understood the need to keep everyone out of

harm's way. One of the reasons he joined the marines was to keep others as safe as he could. He figured it was genetic. He came from a long line of military men. Lucca was becoming a fellow marine in his eyes, someone he would look out for as she looked out for him. "We're a team, Lucca," he told her as he sat next to her during a break one afternoon. He didn't tell her what he was thinking: *I hope you'll never have to take a bomb for me.*

BY THE TIME their six months of training in Israel wrapped up, all the dog teams had made significant progress. Even Rocky and Bram had moved out of remedial education and seemed to have a fairly bright future as specialized search dogs. They were still works in progress, but they were ready for the next step.

They flew off to the U.S. for more fine-tuned training. But first the dogs had to go through the canine equivalent of military induction at Lackland. They all got an operation called a gastropexy, in which the lining of the stomach is stitched to the abdominal wall in order to prevent fatal stomach twisting in cases of bloat. The female dogs were spayed, and all the dogs got identification numbers tattooed inside their left ear while they were still anesthetized. Lucca's was K458, a number that seared into Willingham's memory immediately. It was like her last name. Lucca Kilo 458.

After the dogs recovered, the teams headed to Yuma Proving Ground, in Arizona. One of the Oketz trainers met the dogs and handlers there for seventy-three days of training in an environment very similar to Iraq—from the climate to the terrain to mock Iraq-style buildings, and the loud gunfire, rocket, and mortar simulations.

The dogs and handlers polished skills they'd learned in Israel, taking them to the next level and building confidence while working in realistic scenarios. The teams may have done roadway searches a few dozen times each, but more practice meant they'd be ready for almost anything they faced in war. The handlers worked on tasks as seemingly simple as getting their dogs around a bend in the road and taking advantage of wind currents in a variety of settings. The skills had to be ingrained so they were second nature.

The marines stayed at the Best Western while their dogs stayed at the Yuma Proving Ground kennels, which were set up open-air fashion, with no walls, just a high roof. Sleeping in their kennels after a hard day's work, the dogs were vulnerable to dangerous critters that might crawl out of the desert, so the handlers had to take turns spending the night in the office beside the kennels. Every four hours, whoever had kennel duty would pry himself from his cot and check the dogs to make sure they weren't suffering from spider or snake bites. The four handlers were relieved when a class of about a dozen specialized search dog students came in from Lackland for their own training and took on their overnight shifts.

All five dogs from Israel were doing very well, but Lucca, working in perfect synch with Willingham, and dedicated to whatever he asked of her, was still the class star. So when it came time to do a demo for the Lackland students, Willingham figured his confidence in her was well placed. "We're gonna smash this, Lucca," he told her quietly. "You've been a freakin' robot at distances a lot farther than this."

The demo involved a detection problem that led to a dry creek bed. Lucca had to walk down the deeper part of the creek bed, which ran about four feet below the surrounding sand and dry dirt. The former creek was about eight feet wide, leaving plenty of room for a comfortable passage. Willingham's subtle voice commands and hand signals from no more than a hundred yards away would guide her through to the other side, where the creek bed disappeared and came back to ground level. It would be like threading a needle. As she approached the end, she would be greeted by an explosives scent that would make her day, and all the students would witness the kind of skill and teamwork they could aspire to if they kept at it.

At least that was the idea.

At first, Lucca moved perfectly to Willingham's signals for left, right, and forward. But when she approached the place where she had to follow the creek bed, instead of going straight in, she went left. She went right. She would not go forward into it. It was as if it was still filled with water and she was scared of water. (She wasn't, of course.) No matter what Willingham did, the needle would not be threaded.

He realized Lucca needed a little time to rest and reset. He didn't want her to get any more frustrated than she must have already been. He walked about fifty yards toward her and told her, gently, "Lucca, down." She lay down. A few minutes later, he told her, "Lucca, forward," signaled forward with his right hand, and waited to see what she'd do.

Much to Willingham's relief, this time she nailed it. She walked straight down the creek bed, and as she approached the other side, she caught the scent of the explosive and beelined her way toward it, sniffing the ground intently all the way. Her tail fanned fast, making it clear to everyone watching that she was over the moon about this latest discovery. She sniffed some more, lay down, and stared at the spot where the explosive was buried. The students from Lackland cheered; Willingham loved her up and gave her her Kong. He vowed to himself that if he ever started getting too big for his britches, he'd remember this demo.

All four handlers and five dogs passed the four-day certification test in mid-December. They had to do vehicle searches, roadway searches, and compound searches. Handlers had to show clearly that they could read their dogs, and dogs had to demonstrate commitment to the tasks and a certain focus, regardless of distance from their handlers. They had all finished by Friday, and that night they celebrated over steaks and beers.

The Lackland students were heading back by bus a couple of days before Willingham had planned to go home to San Antonio. He badly missed his wife, Jill, so he hitched a ride with them.

Jill hadn't started vacation yet from nursing school, but she cleared her schedule as well as she could to be with her husband as much as possible. As many years as she'd known him, she loved spending time with him. They had been together since high school, well before he was a marine. He was reserved back then, but she saw the change in him after he became a marine, and especially when he became a dog handler. "He found his calling, and he found his voice," she told a friend. "He's got the kind of personality that puts people at ease and just draws them in. I just love that about him."

He had two weeks off before going back to Lackland, where he would meet up with Lucca and keep her proficient, and only two months before heading to Camp Lejeune for predeployment preparations. During his time at home, Jill made him his favorite meal, spaghetti, as much as she could stomach. She tried to vary the sauces for her sake, but spaghetti with the same sauce could be on the menu every night and her husband would be content.

For Christmas, he surprised Jill with diamond earrings. They were simple three-quarter-carat stud earrings, princess cut. She put them in her ears and fell in love with the sparkle.

Nine months later, their first child would be born.

But Willingham wouldn't be there for the occasion. He would be several months into his deployment to Iraq with Lucca—his first deployment in his career. Knight would be heading over, too, for his first deployment, and had decided to take Bram instead of Rocky because he didn't think anyone else could handle Bram. He bequeathed Rocky to another handler.

Jill gave her husband a small cross made of two shiny silver nails, which she found at James Avery Jewelry in San Antonio. She liked it because it was both rugged and something she hoped might keep him safe. Willingham bought a chain for it so he could wear it around his neck every day in Iraq.

Shortly before he left for the war, his parents drove from Tuscaloosa and visited him at Camp Lejeune, where he was spending a few weeks preparing for deployment. His father presented him with the dog tags he had worn during his nightmarish time as a marine in Vietnam. Attached to the dog tags was a crucifix. Willingham's father had connected these two potent objects thirty-seven years earlier while in Vietnam.

"I wore these during every patrol, and I want you to have them for your deployment," his dad told him. "I came back in one piece with these. You will, too. Your dog will see to it."

3

A BADASS in Baghdad

THIS THING'S GONNA fly? Really?" Knight said to Willingham as they walked toward the hulking C-5 Galaxy transport plane at Marine Corps Air Station Cherry Point, North
Carolina. "All the way to Iraq?"

"That's what they tell me," Willingham said, squinting into
the sun as he checked out the huge gray aircraft that would fly
them sixty-four hundred miles to their deployment.

The C-5 looked like some kind of odd and gigantic mytho-
logical creature. A winged shark came to mind. Its enormous
nose was hinged open all the way up to let in helicopters and
other cargo. With its nose cone pointing straight up to the sky,
and the body of the plane wide open from the front, it appeared
the cargo was being more devoured than loaded. The wings of

the plane angled downward slightly, making it look like it had
grown a little weary of all these heavy-duty cargo missions.

The handlers walked with Lucca and Bram up the metal
loading ramp and into the belly of the beast. Neither dog balked
at the loud noises of metal clanging on metal, workers shouting
to one another, and the low drone of the engine. Lucca never
seemed to get nervous, and Bram . . . Knight figured he was
probably just contemplating Kongs.

They needed to load up the dogs and get upstairs to the passenger area, so they found the wooden palettes that held their
gear—backpacks, duffel bags, five-gallon buckets of dog food, and
two portable kennel crates. The dogs sniffed the contents of the
palette, and Willingham bent down and opened the door of Lucca's crate. She walked right in, made a U-turn at the back of the
crate, and lay down facing the opening. She was already a veteran
of crate travel.

"You ready for your big trip, Lucca? Just take a nice long nap.
We'll come visit you in a while." She watched him as he spoke,
and he was pretty sure she understood.

Knight settled Bram into his crate, close to Lucca's, and with
the help of cargo workers, they made sure everything on the palettes was cinched down securely with tie-down straps. They
made their way up the metal ladder to the seating area.

Two HOURS INTO the flight, Willingham sat on the windowless
workhorse, knees jammed into a seatback pocket overflowing
with a bulky yellow flotation device, a packet of survival equipment, an empty juice box, Lucca's leather leash, and a crumpled
paper bag from lunch. He and Knight each had a full row of seats

to themselves across the aisle from each other on the transport plane.

Big as it was, they were surprised the plane had only a few passengers. Willingham liked that. It was almost as if he, Lucca, Knight, and Bram were getting their own private flight into war. Willingham and Knight hadn't taken advantage of the ability to stretch out. Instead, they sat up—never mind the knees—and talked like two excited kids on their way to their first camping trip. The old friends had not only gone through the Oketz training together, but here they were, on the same plane, going to war at the same time. Even though they'd known for a few months that they'd be deploying together, they still felt lucky.

They soared thirty-five thousand feet over the earth on a high of jokes, BS'ing, bomb detection, sports, ballbusting, family stories, BS'ing about friends, and more plain BS'ing. And dogs.

"Time to check on Bram and Mama Lucca?" Willingham asked Knight when the flurry of conversation eventually died down.

"Let's go see our daooogs!" Knight said, reaching for Bram's leash.

The crew chief escorted them to the metal ladder leading down to the cavernous cargo area. The dogs sat up in their crates when they saw who was coming their way.

Bram's welcoming barks echoed off the plane's rounded walls. Both dogs wagged enthusiastically when they were sprung from their kennels. Lucca stretched as if she had all the time in the world. It was a ten-hour flight, so her timing was fine.

"Mama Lucca! How's the flight?" Willingham leaned down to rub her ears and the sides of her head. She drew in a deep breath and let it out in a contented puff, her eyes slightly closed.

"Hey, Lucca, you want to take a walk?" He leashed up and

joined Knight and Bram, who were already partway down the length of the plane's belly. The usual business associated with dog walks had to wait. The dogs had relieved themselves just before boarding, and military dogs, who tend to be frequent fly-ers, seem to know the routine.

"This plane's a beast!" boomed Knight. Bram seconded with a single bark. Lucca didn't join the conversation.

After a few minutes, they gave their dogs just enough water but not too much, settled them back into their kennel crates, and promised to visit every couple of hours, which they did.

"You know what today is?" Willingham asked Knight as they walked with their dogs to the kennel building at Camp Slayer, part of the sprawling Victory Base Complex of military installa-tions surrounding the Baghdad International Airport. They'd had a couple of hours to settle into their rooms with their dogs—who would be their roommates—and were anxious to see the kennels. They wouldn't be leaving Lucca and Bram in the ken-nels, though. That was just where they were going so they could talk dog.

"What's today?" Knight repeated the question. "Uh, the day we arrived in Baghdad?"

"Yup, but it's also Lucca's and my anniversary." Lucca snapped her head toward him when she heard her name. "Exactly one year ago they assigned us to each other. Can you believe that? To the day!"

"Well, happy anniversary, and here's to many more." Knight raised an imaginary glass. He would have to wait another week or so for his and Bram's anniversary, and he wasn't sure he'd feel like celebrating. The dog still had some kinks to work out.

When they'd left the States, it still felt like spring, but on this Baghdad morning in late April, the thermometer was well on its way to a high of one hundred degrees. As they walked down the narrow paved road, joking with each other about who had more of a radiant glow, they were surprised at how built-up the place was, especially in the distance. They could see buildings they thought were palaces or mansions, with one that rested on the edge of a man-made lake and looked like the top of an exotic bottle of perfume. It was within sight of the low concrete structure housing the kennel, which was located in a fairly isolated section of Camp Slayer. The kennel faced a large field of dry weeds with dirt roads going off into nowhere and was flanked by a thick palm grove on one side and a concrete canal lined with reeds on the other. Perfect for a little reality-based scent training.

They were greeted by Army Private First Class Kory Wiens, whose big smile pushed at his dimples. He wore his dark brown hair shaved close on the sides, longer and thick on top. Willingham noticed a few drops of water on his hair. Wiens told them he was spraying down the kennels. Felt like being useful and not just sitting around on his off hours.

He showed them around the dogs' quarters. Lucca and Bram sniffed briskly until they got the olfactory lowdown. Dogs barked at them. Bram barked at the dogs. Lucca walked through without interjecting.

"Anything you guys need, just let me know," Wiens said.

"We'd love a tour of the whole area," Knight said.

"You got it. Let's start with the chow hall." They headed out into the bright afternoon until Wiens stopped and held up his index finger.

"Wait, I've got someone for you to meet first, if you don't mind," Wiens said, and grinned. "My son. Just a minute, OK?"

Willingham and Knight knew that a guy this young—what, nineteen, twenty tops?—couldn't have a son. Well he could, but not here, in the middle of a war-torn country. Probably not, anyway. It was all new to them.

He returned a couple of minutes later. "Here he is! This is my son, Cooper!"

Willingham looked down and saw a yellow Labrador retriever—a fairly standard-issue military breed for handlers whose dogs don't have to put the hurt on someone. Since Cooper was also a specialized search dog, there was nothing in his job description about biting the bad guy. He had long, lean features and a tail that wagged briskly when he discovered Lucca and Bram. Wiens called him over and faux wrestled his dog for a few seconds, ending with a vigorous fur rub up and down Cooper's back. Willingham couldn't tell who was smiling more broadly, dog or handler.

"Beautiful Lab," Knight said.

"Thanks. Best dog in the world," Wiens said. He glanced at Lucca and Bram and chuckled. "Well, *to me*, anyway."

Lucca stepped up to Cooper and sniffed her new acquaintance in the highly personal way all dogs do. He sniffed her right back. They circled around in a slow canine do-si-do, noses extended under tails. Bram didn't introduce himself. He watched for a few seconds and lost interest. Knight knew he was only thinking of one thing, and it wasn't new friends.

Suddenly Lucca whirled around to face Cooper and lowered

her front half, tail wagging like mad high in the air, inviting him to play.

"Yeah, Lucca!" Willingham laughed. "You like deployment, don't you?"

CHOW HALL WAS one of the few places the dogs weren't allowed at Slayer. They could go into most buildings, including resplendent old Saddam Hussein palaces, some of which were now being used as offices for coalition forces. So whenever the handlers ate, the dogs chilled in their rooms. Sometimes the marines brought them a bite of leftovers as a consolation prize, but they didn't want to upset their stomachs, which were used to a kibble-only diet, so they kept the cheat food to a minimum.

Besides the kennel and the gym, chow hall became a favorite hangout. It was relatively small—just enough room for a couple of dozen or so tables—so it had sort of a clubhouse feeling. TVs were mounted on the walls, and if the news wasn't on, chances were that at least one of the TVs was airing *Baywatch*.

A few days after arriving at Slayer, Willingham joined Knight and some new friends at chow hall for Soul Food Sunday, a down-home feast featuring fried chicken, mac and cheese, and watermelon. He thought of bringing Lucca a little piece of crunchy chicken but decided against it. When he returned to his room, he found Lucca sitting and staring at him. She was surrounded by little rubbery bits of flip-flop. "Just 'cuz you don't get fried chicken doesn't mean you have to do *this*, Mama Lucca," he joked as he surveyed the mess.

Her expression looked like a mixture of elation and concern. It was all in her brows and her eyes. One second she gazed in expectant happiness over this fun activity she'd been doing. The next, after seeing Willingham wasn't thrilled, her brows drew together and danced over her eyes as she looked left and right— almost a caricature of guilt, he thought. Then she saw his face relax, and it was back to "Check out this fun toy I found while you were gone!" mode.

Later that night, he discovered something else about Lucca that surprised him. Lucca, his sweet little girl, snored. At first he didn't know where the noise was coming from. He had no human roommate. But when he realized the deep, resonant sound was emanating from Lucca, Willingham reflected that you never really know someone until you have traveled or lived with her.

ARMY LIEUTENANT DANIELLE ROCHE stood riveted as she watched Lucca and Willingham work together. She was impressed. They reminded her of something. . . . It was as if Lucca was a beautiful kite and Willingham was flying her with an invisible string. Roche, the Ninety-Fourth Engineer Detachment commander, who oversaw about twenty-six dog handlers from the army, air force, and marines, had never seen a dog and handler so perfectly synchronized.

Willingham used subtle arm signals to send Lucca farther down the dirt road to an area he wanted her to search. Lucca turned her head to look at him every so often to make sure she got the instructions right. As their distance increased, Willingham spoke to Lucca through his radio so quietly that Roche— standing only a few feet away from him—could barely hear him. The radio, in a pocket of his dog's harness, breathed his words close to Lucca's ear. "Left." "Right." "Forward." Lucca followed every direction perfectly, her movements fluid, confident. She caught the wind, and on it she found the scent she was looking for, drifted toward it, and lay down next to it.

"That is beyond impressive," said Roche, as Willingham reeled Lucca back to him with only a quiet word. "Come!" Lucca landed by his side, wagging, reveling in his praise. Roche made a mental note that it would be handy if army SSD handlers could use radios with their specialized search dogs. She had seen them resorting to shouting when the dogs were far away. Not a great tactic when you're trying to lie low with bad guys around.

Roche reached down to pet Lucca and noticed she wasn't wearing the traditional leather military dog collar. Instead, she wore a red-and-white nylon University of Alabama Crimson Tide collar. It matched the University of Alabama flag that Willingham—Tuscaloosa born and raised—had hung in his room as soon as they'd arrived.

Well, Roll Tide, Staff Sergeant.

Lucca's harness wasn't quite standard-issue either. One side bore her name and the ID number that matched the tattoo in her left ear: K458. Normal enough. The other side simply said BAD-ASS. All caps, black on white, attached with Velcro to the black harness.

You go, girl!

Roche was in charge around here and was the only woman in the dog detachment. She liked having another strong female around—even if she *was* a dog. Roche, twenty-four, had enlisted in the army reserves right out of high school after seeing her sister thrive in the marine corps. She attended one semester of college, then went to basic training and advanced individual training. She found she loved the army so much that she needed

more than her one weekend a month and two weeks per year of
training. So she switched colleges and went to one that offered
ROTC. Roche contracted, graduated, and was commissioned as
a 21Z engineer officer; attended Engineer Officer Basic Course
at Fort Leonard Wood, Missouri; and was assigned to Second
Infantry Division in Dongducheon, South Korea.

In Korea she was the support platoon leader of the Second
Engineers, Second Infantry Division at Camp Castle, then the
support platoon leader at Camp Hovey. In this role she was responsible for the "bullets, beans, and gas"—basically, the ammu-
nition, the chow halls/MREs, and the fuel for all the vehicles.
After Korea, she went back to Fort Leonard Wood and was a
company XO (executive officer) of a basic training company. She
loved when the drill sergeants let her do PT along with them. She
was athletic and liked smoking the soldiers.

While she was the XO, she applied for the dog detachment
commander position and got it. She attended a monthlong K-9
training school in England and led the Ninety-Fourth for a year
before they deployed. Office work wasn't her favorite part of the job,
so any chance she got—every day, preferably—she trained with her
guys and their dogs and got to know their strengths and weak-
nesses. Before deploying, she also went on several training missions
and deployment exercises with the teams, including one to Alaska.

In Baghdad, despite all the work involved in coordinating which
dog teams would go where, keeping up with supplies for dogs and
handlers, and dealing with endless paperwork, she kept up her PT
alongside the handlers. She especially enjoyed going on long runs
with them. She could outrun most of them, but never Wiens.

Willingham and Knight were her first marines, and their

arrival had taken her by surprise. She had needed more handlers and was assigned the marines with pretty much no heads-up. No one bothered to tell her when they were arriving or even their names. And here they were, a couple of top dog guys appearing seemingly out of the blue—like *M*A*S*H*'s pros from Dover, only with dogs instead of golf clubs.

When Willingham and Knight showed up at the dog handler housing area at Camp Slayer in the early morning of April 23, Roche was getting ready to head out for a run. She wore a standard-issue Army Physical Fitness Uniform—gray T-shirt with black shorts. She hadn't yet slipped into her running shoes. Willingham noticed she was wearing faded pink flip-flops, and her toenails were coated with pink nail polish—a lone woman, clinging to the last vestiges of femininity from back home, in a sea of male dog handlers. Behind the always-closed door of her room in the house she shared with several handlers, a poster of a unicorn running to a rainbow in a pink sky was taped next to her windows—windows that faced a camp wall that saw earth-shaking mortars. The windows were almost entirely covered with sandbags for protection. Pink sheets and a few stuffed animals graced her single bed. So did her M4 assault rifle.

Roche had brought several of her own army dog teams over with her. She had recruited them as privates back at Fort Leonard Wood. They were all assigned to the Thirty-Fifth Engineer Battalion and had come highly recommended by their drill sergeants as top-notch soldiers, with excellent scores in their army physical fitness tests and showing promising leadership skills. After much careful vetting, Roche chose the soldiers she thought would make excellent dog handlers. She sent them to specialized search dog school at Lackland Air Force Base, where they spent months learning the canine trade.

Wiens was among her top picks. She could sense something special about this kid right away. He was passionate about life, positive about everything, mature beyond his years, and never without a smile. In their interview, when she asked if he had any work experience, he spoke with pride about his job as a junior shift manager at Burger King near his hometown of Independence, Oregon. He drew himself up like someone who'd won an award. That he could be so proud of something others might sweep away as a trivial experience left an impression on Roche. He was in.

At Camp Slayer, Wiens and some of the other newer handlers, mostly air force, spent as much time as they could learning from Willingham and Knight, who had become unofficial coaches and mentors. When they were stateside, the marines had been instructing young handlers in the art of dog handling for years, and they both loved their work. Why not help out here, where the stakes were going to be so high so soon for so many of these handlers?

Lucca didn't like being left in the room when Willingham was out with the other dogs like that. The first time, she gave him *the look*. Head tilted, dark eyebrows drawn together as if very worried or sad, eyes extra big, her sitting body shrunken to three-quarters its normal size. He wondered how she made herself look so small at times like this.

He shut the door and felt the guilt he figured she had intended for him. On the way to the training area, he realized there was really no reason she couldn't come out with him, and maybe she could even be of some help. Next time, as he was getting his gear ready for working with the handlers, Lucca became the tragic figure again. Willingham gave her the good news. "Lucca, you're going to come with me this time."

Lucca sprang up, magically becoming her own size again. She shook her whole body, ridding herself of any remnants of the pity costume that could still be clinging to her. Willingham buckled her harness, and as they left his room, she jogged out like a proud dressage horse entering the ring.

When Willingham wanted to show the handlers a tricky concept, he'd call on his canine assistant to help him do a demo. To his relief, there were no stumbles like the one at the dry creek bed demo at Yuma.

Her demo over, Lucca lay down and rested, looking with little interest at the goings-on, and then falling asleep. But when it was Cooper's turn, she always seemed to be awake. She focused on her friend, her eyes following him, ears pivoting in his direction. When he was done, she went back to her repose.

After training, if there was time, Willingham and Wiens took off their dogs' harnesses. "Woot! Go play, dogs!" Willingham told them. Lucca and Cooper ran and chased each other, giddy and fully engaged in the moment. Willingham loved that about dogs. They lived now. They didn't worry about the future.

Invariably, Lucca would slam into Cooper at just the right time, or pounce on him a split second before he was about to do the same to her. Their handlers laughed and cheered their dogs on. "Yeah, *Maaaa*-mas!" Willingham yelled to Lucca when she "won."

In time, Willingham and Wiens decided that their dogs had become an item—their courtship sealed with body slams rather than kisses. To celebrate, Wiens held out his hands, Cooper jumped onto his hind legs, and they waltzed around the room.

Cooper's eyes closed just slightly, and his mouth pulled back into a large grin. Willingham noticed that his smile looked like Wiens's, just without the dimples. Lucca stood next to Willingham, watching, wagging, and clearly enjoying the show.

Cooper, aka Coopaloop, soon had another designation around the kennels: "Lucca's boyfriend." But Lucca wasn't referred to as Cooper's girlfriend very much. Probably had something to do with her brawn.

"Everyone thinks she's a dude. Don't worry about it," Willingham would explain after anyone called her a *he*—almost a daily occurrence. "It's just because she's big, and she can kick ass."

WILLINGHAM AND KNIGHT had their own training to do. Their test was coming up—a rigorous in-theater validation—and they had to pass it if they wanted to take their dogs outside the wire.

Willingham was excited. He told Knight at dinner in the chow hall, "Lucca is gonna get out there and find some bombs!"

"Al-Qaeda better watch out for her," Knight said, chuckling. "Bram, too. At least Lucca won't eat the bad guys."

Bram wasn't supposed to bite bad guys, or anyone. The job description for SSDs says nothing about bite work. But it was in Bram's makeup to bite to protect. Or to bite just because. Knight couldn't eliminate that instinct, although he had it under control, at least by day. Nighttime was another story. Knight had to hang a sign on his doorknob before he turned out the light—a DO NOT DISTURB sign, on steroids. It warned that anyone who came in would be risking their lives because Bram was a mean bastard who would try to murder them—this only partly in jest. The dog had teeth—those that he hadn't worn to the gum line while chewing his kennel ceiling in Israel were good and sharp—and he wanted to use them.

At least once, as Knight was falling asleep, he saw the door crack a little. A soldier seeing if he was awake. "NOOOooo-oooooooooooo!" Knight shouted as he jumped out of bed and slammed the door shut just before Bram could burst out and put some serious hurt on the hapless kid.

Wiens usually joined Willingham and Knight at their table at the chow hall. Willingham had never seen anyone eat so much as Wiens yet be in such great shape. He watched with a mixture of disbelief and amusement as Wiens tanked up with burgers, fries, chicken fingers, salad, and the dessert of the day.

Wiens had been in-country a few months longer than the marines and had already passed the test and had gone on a few missions from Camp Slayer while waiting to be assigned elsewhere. Willingham and Knight picked his brain about things he had seen.

"Kory, you got some photos from that mission today?" Willingham asked. He knew that once he and Lucca passed their validation, they could go outside the wire anytime. He wanted to get the lay of the land where local missions were taking place.

"Absolutely! My camera's in my room. I'll get it after dinner and give you the grand tour." Willingham noticed that Wiens had mastered the art of talking clearly while eating.

"You the man, *Ko-ree*!"

On the way out of the chow hall, Wiens stuffed miniature bottles of Rip It energy drinks into the roomy pockets of his cargo pants. He couldn't get enough of the caffeinated, vitamin-infused stuff. *Accounts for some of his energy,* Willingham supposed.

As the two-day validation test drew near, Willingham and

Knight spent hours every morning working their dogs on skills that would be vital to their missions. Wiens accompanied them on a couple of occasions. Lucca and Cooper no longer wasted time with traditional dog greetings when they saw each other. They just went straight into chase mode as soon as Lucca's harness came off.

The marines trained their dogs on local odors—explosives scents they hadn't necessarily encountered back home. They worked in scenarios that mimicked situations they might encounter downrange: roadway searches, building searches, vehicle searches. All skills these marines had practiced for years.

Lucca aced the first day of validation, but the toughest part of the test was yet to come. The second day started a little later, and the thermometer quickly rose to 110 degrees. To Willingham, geared up from head to toe—flak and Kevlar, weapons, heavy pack, boots—it felt like 140 degrees easy. He didn't want to think about what it felt like for Lucca, in her ever-present fur coat. She was panting pretty hard, her tongue draped long from her open mouth. It wasn't ideal for scent work. Who goes around smelling things with their mouths wide open? They had been going for a couple of hours now, and he hoped it would be over soon.

On a real-life mission, he just wouldn't let Lucca work in this kind of heat. He would tell the platoon leader that the dog had to rest when temps got too hot. He would continue working alone, helping out however he could to keep his guys safe, and Lucca would get to chill in a mildly air-conditioned Humvee, or at least some shade.

But this was validation day, and he had to keep going. He stopped frequently to give Lucca water and let her rest in whatever shade he could find. Lucca's youth was on her side, but her energy was fading as the sun blazed overhead. She walked more slowly than usual, and Willingham could see her focus wasn't as sharp as it normally was.

He decided to make his dog a deal. He found some shade under a chunky palm tree no more than about ten feet tall. Its bottom fronds were straw dry, shaggy, and the color of shredded wheat. They cascaded almost to the ground along the thick trunk, which made the tree look like it sported an unkempt beard. But the top green fronds provided a little umbrella from the sun. Willingham took a bottle of water from his pack and poured it into the portable rubber bowl he kept in a pouch on his waist. Lucca drank up and lay in the shade, panting quietly. She watched as Willingham cleared away a couple of sharp rocks and a mound of palm bark that had peeled away from the cross-hatched trunk, and then he sat down next to her on the flinty ground. He took off his gloves and was struck by how sweaty they were.

"Lucca," he said, stroking the top of her head and feeling the heat of the day on the dark fur, "if you finish out for me strong, I'll carry you all the way back to the kennels. I promise."

Lucca stared at him as he talked to her. These were new words, and Willingham could see her trying to figure out if there was something new she should understand. When he had laid out the deal, her tail thumped once, creating a little cloud of dust that hung in the sweltering air. He took the tail sign as a yes.

They got up and continued down the dirt road. About a hundred feet ahead and a little to the left, Willingham saw something that didn't seem quite right. He walked a little closer, drew in a deep breath, exhaled, and took a few seconds to survey the area. There were the usual rocks and rubble that dotted the route, but in this one spot, they looked like they'd been pushed around, piled up here and there, as if to hide something. It wasn't a natural placement, but it wasn't screaming out *danger*. Only a trained eye could see that something might be suspicious. He sent Lucca forward.

About fifteen feet away from one of the piles, she became a dog renewed. Her ears stood erect, and she trotted back and forth, back and forth, narrowing in on something that was leading her—as if beckoning with invisible fingers—to the source. She threw a quick look to Willingham and lay down.

"Good girl, Lucca!" he whooped as he jogged over to her. It was his high voice—the one all handlers use to praise their dogs. "Woot! Lucca Bearrr!"

He had no doubt she had found what she was supposed to, but he was happy to get the confirmation and congrats from the kennel master and Roche. Willingham bounced Lucca's Kong on the packed earth. She grabbed it on the uptake. As she chomped it in his shadow, Willingham praised her up some more.

It was a full paycheck, and Lucca would have been perfectly happy to leave it at that. But Willingham didn't forget the promise he'd made.

After they both drank enough water and Lucca spent some quality time with the Kong, he walked her up to a small berm and had her stand on it and stay. As she stood elevated about eighteen inches off the ground, Willingham bent down very low and stuck his head under her belly. Roche wondered what was next. She'd never seen anything like this before.

Slowly, Willingham stood up, putting one hand around Lucca's front legs, the other around her back legs. As he unfurled, he looked like he was wearing a giant fur stole. She relaxed, tongue lolling out of her mouth. Willingham was grateful his dog was so good at being carried. This would come in handy if they had to traverse canals or walls.

As he began the mile-and-a-half walk back, he knew exactly what she was saying to him.

Thank you, man. I'm tired.

WILLINGHAM NOTICED VAGUE creases in the army uniform as he buttoned the sleeves at his wrists. It was the first time anyone had worn it, but it didn't scream *new*. Combat uniforms never look new unless you iron the hell out of them, and that's just not something you do in the middle of a war zone. But it would be a long time before the uniform had that broken-in feeling he liked. He couldn't call it "my uniform" just yet. He wondered if he'd ever be comfortable doing that. He glanced at himself in the small mirror on the back of his door.

"Lucca, you recognize me in an army uniform? I don't!"

Dog handlers have a price on their heads. Someone offs a dog team, and that's a lot more IEDs that won't be discovered, at least until it's too late. If handlers wear different uniforms from everyone else, they become even bigger targets. Willingham and Knight were the first marines to be embedded with soldiers there, and it was decided at Slayer that they were going to wear the uniform that would draw the least attention. Some folks back in D.C. chimed in that they didn't like the idea, but they weren't the ones walking point.

He grabbed his pack and Lucca's leash, and they walked outside and jumped into a waiting Humvee that drove them to the landing zone at Slayer. Their first outside-the-wire mission, and right on the heels of the test. Four American soldiers had been captured by al-Qaeda insurgents who had attacked an outpost south of Baghdad—an attack that killed four U.S. soldiers and one Iraqi soldier. Willingham and Lucca's job would be to look for explosives while the army platoon they were supporting sought the missing soldiers: Specialist Alex Ramon Jimenez, Private First Class Joseph John Anzack, Private Byron Wayne Fouty, and Sergeant Anthony Jason Schober.

The Black Hawk was waiting at the landing zone. Willingham, Lucca, and two other handlers—one with a tracking dog and one with a cadaver dog—ran through the rotor wash and onto the bird. The canines had it covered from every angle: one dog to keep them safe from IEDs, another to track down abducted soldiers (or the insurgents, if that's where the scent tracks led), and the third in case they got there too late. Willingham hoped the cadaver dog's talents would not be put to use.

He tried not to look too fired up. After all these years working with dogs, more than a year getting battle ready with Lucca, and now some bad guys to find and some Americans to save, it was hard not to feel the rush. Willingham glanced down at Lucca, who was lying on the floor, chilling with her head on her paws. He smiled at her repose. Clearly his excitement hadn't dumped down the leash to her.

They landed in an area that looked like everything else he'd seen so far. To the untrained eye, not much there. But there could be danger, or clues, anywhere—roadsides, lines of brush, the banks of the Tigris, compounds, fields.

The dog teams hooked up with a couple of platoons and got briefed on the mission. They spread out, looking for good guys, bad guys, hurt guys, dead guys, IEDs, any sign of what had happened, any clue about where these Americans could be. Willingham and Lucca led the way, Lucca off leash, out front, checking in with Willingham, not far behind, to make sure she was going where she needed to go, and Willingham directing her to areas they needed to traverse, always watching for signs that something wasn't quite right.

Lucca was on: swift, alert, aware, confident. Willingham felt a deep sense of pride as he watched her on her first real day on the job. "Great soldier you have there," a young soldier told him while they stopped for a break and another briefing. Willingham thanked him and decided not to correct him and tell him they were actually marines. Hell, he was wearing ACUs; how was the kid to know? He just went with it.

Willingham and Lucca worked a couple more hours, but there was no action. With no IEDs to find, no paycheck, Lucca could have easily lost interest. Without the reinforcement of finding something and getting a reward, her attention could be drawn to other things—a passing jewel beetle, a stray dog, the lingering scent of chow-hall bacon on a soldier's hand. Focus was everything. So every so often, Willingham pulled out one of various small pieces of det cord he had packed along for just this reason. Willingham couldn't smell it, but Lucca sure could. He hid one somewhere when she wasn't looking, and when she found it, she got the full reward—Kong, big-time praise, lots of fur rubs. She never lost her focus.

The day ended with no finds—no good guys, bad guys, hurt guys, dead guys, IEDs, no sign of what had happened, no clue about where these Americans could be. On the helicopter back to Slayer, Willingham thought of the families of the missing soldiers and what they must be going through in the raw dark space of not knowing if their husbands, fathers, and sons were dead, suffering, or, somehow, safe.

He thought of his pregnant wife and felt vaguely unsettled that she was alone. Jill would be OK, he reassured himself. Their house was in a safe neighborhood. She was smart, a nurse, she could take care of other people and herself. Besides, he'd left her with two weapons. One that comes with a trigger, the other that comes with teeth—a white shepherd named Alpine, trained by him to make sure nothing bad happened while he was gone.

When the Black Hawk returned to Camp Slayer, the first thing he did was change into his marine uniform. Then he headed to the phones to call Jill.

REENLISTMENT IN THE marines tends to be a unique affair, especially early in a marine's career. Willingham's first reenlistment had taken place with two of his dog-handler pals in a creek at Camp Lejeune, in a ceremony serenaded by barking dogs. These three weren't going to settle for a traditional ho-hum ceremony outside their workplace. They asked their kennel master if they could reenlist in Wallace Creek, where they'd practiced their cross-creek aggression skills. Willingham loved the amphibious nature of the idea—half in the water, half out, not unlike the marine assault amphibious vehicles he had always thought were so badass.

The kennel master asked the captain, who thought it was a fitting location. On a perfect October day, they all headed to the creek, along with their wives and about ten other marines. The guests stood close by, on the banks of the creek. The handlers waded—boots and all—into the water until it was midcalf. The water lapped up to the chests of the three dogs, who at first calmly enjoyed the experience. A first sergeant, facing them and also in the water, read the orders.

"Be it known that Sergeant Chris E. Willingham, Sergeant Matthew J. Pearson, and Corporal Aaron M. Nuckles have been accepted for reenlistment in the United States Marine Corps. Your reenlistment reflects uncommon devotion and loyalty to your country and to the Corps. It is this special kind of commitment that makes the Corps unique and respected throughout the world. The Corps is proud to have you in its ranks."

As the captain waded closer and had them raise their right hands to swear them in, one of the dog trainers from the kennel went up behind him to take photos of the men taking their oath. When Castor, a Dutch shepherd, saw the guy bending down and staring at them while aiming something at them, it must have triggered a memory of cross-creek aggression. He began barking, loudly and quickly. Minnow, a Malinois, joined him.

Willingham had another dog back then—a German shepherd named Tekky. While the duet barked away, she looked around and calmly surveyed the situation. She barked once and seemed to decide that was more than enough. Willingham felt she was the best dog he ever met. At least until Lucca.

His next reenlistment took place at the Marine Corps Ball. He wore dress blues and cut a handsome figure. The music stopped, his K-9 friends gathered round, and he swore to a few more faithful years defending Uncle Sam.

And now it was time for another reenlistment. He needed to do it before heading out to whatever unit he and Lucca would be assigned to. Knight—who had nailed the validation test as predicted with Bram—was up for his reenlistment, too. They had known they were due when they were stateside, but when you get a chance to reenlist in a combat theater, that's hard to pass up.

"What better a place to reconfirm your oath to defend the constitution than in a war zone?" Willingham said to Knight.

"Agreed."

Besides a hearty dose of marine patriotism, it didn't hurt that reenlisting in a combat zone meant the reenlistment bonus was tax-free.

At Slayer, they could have just completed the paperwork, walked into Roche's office, agreed to some stuff she read to them, signed on the dotted line, and it would be a done deal within a few minutes. But once they saw the abundance of potential settings for their reenlistment, that option seemed far too banal.

"We're marines; we don't do things the way everyone else does!" Knight and Willingham told Roche, almost in unison, when they explained their request. She wasn't surprised. Nothing these guys did surprised her. She was going to miss them when they got their assignments.

It's not unusual for officers and enlisted to develop friendships on deployment. Military customs and courtesies are a bit more relaxed, especially on smaller forward operating bases (FOBs) and outposts. When Roche arrived in Iraq, she was assigned to work under the Multi-National Corps–Iraq (MNC-I) C7 Explosive Hazards Coordination Cell. It was run like they were in garrison, with all the *yes, sirs; yes, ma'ams;* salutes; and military professionalisms she'd experienced during her entire military career.

But when she visited the smaller FOBs and outposts, where troops were outside the wire much of the time, there was a different level of respect between the enlisted ranks and officers. She thought of it as a "brotherhood bond." They could talk to one another like peers and joke around. The orders were still being given by the officers, but most realized that the senior enlisted guys had more experience than they did. The result was a mutual respect, with officers listening and learning and then heeding the advice of senior enlisted in executing decisions.

It went even beyond this with Willingham and Knight. Besides the awe she had for their level of knowledge and the way they did their jobs, they were a blast to hang out with. When the three of them were together, as long as they weren't working, someone was inevitably laughing. So it was only natural that she agreed to reenlist them at a location of their choosing that was not an office.

But where?

Camp Slayer had plenty of unique backdrops, all built around a man-made lake. There was the Perfume Palace—the one they could see from the kennel area. The story that circulated among troops and probably grew embellished over time was that during social events, Saddam Hussein would go up to a vantage point from which he could scan the guests. He would pick the most desirable woman, have her brought up to him, and have his way with her. When he was done, she would be killed and thrown into a moat. When the moat was dredged, contractors discovered dozens of victims. Or so the tale went.

They'd pass on this locale. Too gruesome, if the story was true.

They considered the Victory Over America Palace, which was never completed. An American bomb had blasted a hole in its ceiling. "Saddam Hussein gives a palace a name like that, and what did he expect?" Knight observed. "Fool!"

It was an attractive palace, and they liked the irony of the name. They put it on their short list.

The adjacent Flintstone Village—so named by the Americans, at least—looked like something straight out of the cartoon town of Bedrock. Hussein had probably built it for his grandchildren and other children of his family and friends. There were something like ten bedrooms and bathrooms, all now in disrepair, graffiti covering most surfaces.

The Hanna-Barbera backdrop didn't seem quite badass enough for reenlistment.

In the end, they decided to take their reenlistment outside Slayer, to Baghdad's Green Zone. It had been the administrative center of the Ba'ath Party until the Americans took control in 2003. Now it was one of the safest areas around, surrounded by high, protective blast walls, heavily guarded by coalition troops, and with only a few points of entry. Not that insurgents didn't try to cause harm, and sometimes succeeded in doing so. But it was about as safe as you could get in this war zone.

The ride to the Green Zone wasn't without risks, since they'd be traveling through the streets of Baghdad not controlled by coalition forces. They decided to leave their dogs at Slayer. Willingham, Knight, and Roche boarded an armored bus, a Rhino-RUNNER. These sand-colored buses were among the toughest on the planet, but they weren't perfect. Everyone boarded in flak and Kevlar.

Roche was a little nervous during the twenty-five-minute ride. Despite the road being walled by tall protective barriers, you never knew what could happen. She turned to talk to Willingham and Knight to help take the edge off the ride, but they were sleeping. She couldn't believe it.

She thought about the nap-of-the-earth Black Hawk rides

she had been on in high-threat environments while accompanying some of her handlers to their assigned FOBs and outposts. During a nap-of-the-earth, the pilot flies as close to the terrain as possible, so passengers feel every dip, every change in elevation, while seeing the land very close up—alarmingly so at times. It's good for avoiding enemy detection and attack, but not always great on the stomach and nerves.

Compared to a nap-of-the-earth, the trip on the Rhino was a pleasure ride. Still, Roche wasn't surprised when her favorite Christian songs came into her head. After a few rounds of "Our God Is an Awesome God—He Reigns!" and "Thy Word Is a Lamp unto My Feet," they arrived safely in the Green Zone.

They toured some of the sites for a couple of hours, then headed to the Victory Arch, also known as the Crossed Swords monument. Two giant bronze fists each clasped a 140-foot sword. The tips of the swords crossed each other over a wide parade ground. The concept was Saddam Hussein's, and the hands and forearms of the statues were said to be modeled after his own.

The marines concurred: no better place to reenlist in the U.S. Marine Corps for four more years.

Willingham first listened then pronounced the formal commitment smoothly and respectfully. He was in again for another four years. Then it was Knight's turn. Willingham read the certificate of reenlistment, which at this point in his career he was so familiar with that he almost had it memorized: "Be it known that Staff Sergeant Kristopher R. Knight has been accepted for reenlistment in the United States Marine Corps. Your reenlistment reflects uncommon devotion and loyalty to your country and to the Corps. It is this special kind of commitment that makes the Corps unique and respected throughout the world. The Corps is proud to have you in its ranks."

Knight buckled. There was something about his friend reading such a formal certificate that struck him as funny. He did feel uncommonly devoted to his country and the corps, but it was hard to keep a straight face when his old Texas Hold'em pal was reading it seriously. Then came the oath, read by Roche in short chunks Knight was supposed to repeat while raising his right hand.

"I, Kristopher R. Knight, do solemnly swear that I will support and defend the Constitution of the United States against all enemies, foreign and domestic; that I will bear true faith and allegiance to the same and that I will obey the orders of the President of the United States and the orders of the officers appointed over me, according to the regulations and the Uniform Code of Military Justice. So help me God."

No marine would say Staff Sergeant Knight got a case of the giggles, but it did take him three tries to get through the oath.

By EARLY JUNE, Roche was fielding requests for handlers from several units. A big military action was about to get under way, but there wasn't much detail. Just enough to know that her dog teams could be seeing some heavy action soon.

Knight and Bram headed in a Humvee to Camp Striker, not far away, still on Victory Base Complex. Wiens and Cooper took a helo down to FOB Kalsu, in Iskandariya, twenty miles south of Baghdad. Willingham awaited his assignment.

Good-byes were short, on the order of friends parting after a Super Bowl party. They didn't have to wax poetic. They knew.

"See you soon, man."

"Be safe."

"Go get 'em."

"Damned straight."

Willingham headed out last. Another hot June day. As the Black Hawk took off, Lucca lay down at Willingham's feet and rested her head on his boots. Within a couple of minutes, she was asleep.

FOB Falcon was just a few miles away, but the pilot took a long route, not the most direct. Predictable routes made the birds easier targets. After several minutes of flying, the pilot gave a heads-up that he would be doing some maneuvers so they'd be harder to hit as they approached FOB Falcon. Nap-of-the-earth time. Willingham put a hand on Lucca's harness.

The helicopter banked sharply to the right, then to the left, curved around, banked again. The crazy movement woke up Lucca. She looked at Willingham. *What the hell, man?*

"Lucca, we're fine," he said, enjoying a small adrenaline rush. "You're safe."

PART TWO

The Heat Is On

4

Hey, a Dog! *BOOM!*

WILLINGHAM FLIPPED OPEN the frayed door flap of the general-purpose tent.

"Ladies first."

Lucca entered and immediately went to work. She didn't *have* to sniff every corner, every seam, the plywood floor. She just couldn't help it. Finding no bombs, she lay down and watched Willingham unpack, as she had five weeks earlier at Camp Slayer. He unrolled his sleeping bag on one of four folding steel cots. On another cot he laid out his uniforms—army and marine, flak vest, Kevlar, and a small photo album with pictures of Jill, his parents, grandparents. Mouthwash, deodorant, razors, shaving cream, water bottles, baby wipes went on top of a broken air-conditioning unit in the corner.

He took two steel bowls from one of his bags and poured water in one. The ping of kibble as he scooped it into the other bowl caught Lucca's attention. She stood up, stretched, and chowed down.

This was their first FOB experience together, and Willingham was excited about finally getting close to the real action. FOB Falcon wasn't big; maybe one and a half miles around if he walked the inside perimeter of the twelve-foot-tall, steel-reinforced concrete protective T-walls. Falcon housed a few white two-story concrete buildings, but most of the soldiers here slept in tents, which were arranged in neat rows separated by gravel paths. It was Tim Burton–esque in its oddly perfect layout. There was hardly any vegetation, and what little there was had gone mostly brown and crispy. A few hardy trees had managed to hold on to their green despite the conditions. They stood out to Willingham, who admired their fortitude.

It was far more Spartan than Slayer had been, but Willingham didn't mind. He wasn't here for the aesthetics.

Well, not entirely.

He surveyed the tent. It was general-purpose medium, thirty-two by sixteen feet, which felt like way too much space for one marine and his dog, even with all the equipment they had brought along. He figured he'd be getting some company soon, so he didn't spread out too much.

It was slightly dark inside because of the semi-opaque olive-green tent. It needed something to liven it up, he thought. He reached under a cot and unzipped a duffel. At the bottom of the T-shirts, underwear, and socks, he felt what he was looking for. He took out his two flags—U.S. Marine Corps and University of Alabama—and hung them along the walls next to his cot. He stepped back and took in his handiwork. The red of the two flags brought some life into the gray and green interior.

"That's better! Roll Tide! Home sweet home, Lucca."

He looked around again. It was a little more colorful, but it still seemed empty. He was the lone marine in a sea of soldiers, the only dog guy on this entire FOB, and Lucca was the only dog. It could be a long five months if no one else showed up.

Not that they'd be spending all that much time here. FOB Falcon would just be a place they'd come back to for a little rest. "This is where you'll come to relax between missions," someone had told him. A big op was brewing, and they were going to be heading out within days. He knew nothing more about it, but there was something he needed to start doing right away if he and Lucca were going to get out there and help save soldiers from IEDs. He had to brief some key people on the capabilities and limitations of dogs and what they bring to the fight.

He was aware that most people in the military didn't realize the work that dog teams do. In fact, many didn't even know there were dogs in the military. Maybe they'd seen a slide of a dog team during a PowerPoint presentation back in basic training, but it was usually quickly forgotten. Earlier, on the way to their tent, he could see the surprise on the faces of several soldiers. "A dog?! Cool!" was the typical reaction, with a request to pet Lucca.

He had his work cut out for him. He decided he'd start by talking to some higher-ups. He didn't want to oversell or undersell what Lucca could do. *Proven, not perfect*—a phrase he drilled into his students at Lackland. He always told his students not to be cocky about what they could do. Confidence is one thing. But you have to be realistic. IEDs are a nasty business that can evade even the best team. Dogs are a huge added asset, but they're not infallible.

"Ready to let 'em know what we're made of?"

Lucca walked to his side and sat, panting a little from the heat of the tent. He leashed her up and they walked out into the bright, hot afternoon. As they walked away, he turned around to give the tent a quick look from the outside so he'd know where to return later, since the GP tents all looked alike. He didn't notice that over the door, stenciled with red paint that had blended into the fading green tent, was the number thirteen. It would be a few more weeks before he became aware of it. . . .

WILLINGHAM WOKE UP the next day before his body was ready to. A familiar sound, something from his time at Camp Slayer, only louder.

Boom!

Thunder? WTF?

He rubbed his eyes, trying to come out of a dream and back to wherever he was.

Boom!

Mortar. Of course.

The voice on the loudspeaker would have told him so a second later.

"Incoming! Incoming! Incoming!"

He bolted up in his cot, ready to run with Lucca to the nearest bunker—the one they'd showed him yesterday with comments like, "You'll definitely need to know where *this* is." Only minutes before that part of the tour of the Falcon grounds, he had been told the price of admission to the chow hall: Everyone who entered had to fill a two-gallon sandbag that would be used to fortify the building, which had been rocketed more than once. Grabbing a shovel and digging into the pile of sand near the entrance seemed like a small price to pay for added safety.

The sirens on FOB Falcon were wailing now. You never knew how many mortars would come in once they started. Strange as it seemed, sometimes it was just one. Sometimes it would be a barrage lasting several minutes, multiple times a day. Willingham was just about convinced it was time to beat a hasty path to the bunker, but Lucca did not share his sense of urgency. She remained lying on a blanket next to his cot and lifted her head only when she saw him move toward her food bowl. Willingham hoped her calm foretold the end of the mortaring for the morning. He slid his feet into his running shoes without bothering to lace them, just in case.

Streeeeek, BOOM!

The ground shook with this one. Lucca didn't startle. She just looked at Willingham to see what was up. He knew from experience in Baghdad that mortars make that little whining sound just before impact if they're close. Farther away it's usually just the explosion.

He grabbed Lucca's leash. "Come on, girl, let's take a walk!"

They hustled over to the bunker and squeezed in with the soldiers who were already there. It was tight but felt secure. A room with thick concrete walls, more like a small hallway, no door to shut, but a wall of sandbags just outside the entrance.

"Hey, a dog!"

"Check it out! A dog!"

Boom!

"Damn!"

"What's his name?"

"This here's Lucca; she's a specialized search dog; she finds IEDs off leash. We just got here yesterday from Slayer."

"I miss my dog. OK if I pet her?"

"Sure you can pet her. She loves people."

Before Willingham could get the words out, the soldier was stroking Lucca's head, bending down, and talking to her.

"I got a dog back home. Oscar," another soldier said. "He's s'posed to be a shepherd mix."

"Great dogs," Willingham said. "Lucca is half shepherd herself."

"How old is he? He don't bite, do he?" the lanky soldier next to him inquired.

Another soldier toward the back lit a cigarette. Crowded, smoky, friendly. It reminded Willingham of this one bar back in Tel Aviv.

"You going down on the big op?"

"I believe so. I'm going to a briefing later to find out more."

"She finds bombs? I hope she comes with our platoon!"

"That'd be great, man."

As everyone talked, Lucca sat there, looking for all the world like she was simply meeting people at a small party—maybe one of the poker games in someone's garage back home—and enjoying their attentions and the closeness of the space. The men appeared equally at ease. Lucca seemed to have that effect on everyone. Willingham looked at her and smiled, proud that she tended to bring calmness everywhere she went.

About fifteen minutes after the last mortar hit, the all clear was given. The men filed out slowly, with Lucca leading the way. Last in, first out.

"Nice meeting you, Lucca! You, too, dog guy!"

"See you 'round, OK?"

Willingham and Lucca walked back to the tent to start their day again.

"Good morning, Iraq!" Willingham said to no one in particular, but Lucca looked up at him anyway.

A PETRI DISH for al-Qaeda to grow.

As Willingham turned in that night, he thought about the briefing he had just attended and how Lieutenant Colonel Ken Adgie, commander of the First Battalion, Thirtieth Infantry Regiment (1/30th) of the Third Infantry Division, had described the Arab Jabour region. Any day now, Willingham and Lucca and hundreds of others would be heading straight into that petri dish—part of the so-called Triangle of Death.

Arab Jabour, southeast of Baghdad, was known as one of the most dangerous areas in Iraq. There was no government structure, no police, and it had been too long since coalition forces had made their presence known. Most al-Qaeda members there appeared to be not so much hard-line Islamists as simply local thugs. They worked for al-Qaeda because of the money, not because of the ideology. For more than a year, they'd been using "ultraviolence" to bring locals under their control through fear. To further control behavior, they severely limited essential resources such as water, food, and electricity.

The conditions provided a perfect setting for al-Qaeda to proliferate. It grew, with members enforcing Islamic fundamentalist law, lining roads with IEDs, and transporting IEDs into Baghdad for lethal use there.

The situation in Arab Jabour was desperate for the Iraqis caught in the grips of a full-throated civil war. Preyed on by al-Qaeda terrorists and Shi'a militiamen alike, ordinary Iraqis struggled to survive amid the daily horrors of car bombs, rocket and mortar attacks, and sectarian cleansing. Statistics gathered later in a CENTCOM update would reveal that during the week of Adgie's briefing, there were nearly sixteen hundred violent incidents in Iraq. In the month of June alone, roughly two thousand Iraqi civilians would be killed due to ethnosectarian violence.

But there was a plan—part of the huge Iraq War troop surge announced in January by president George W. Bush to salvage an increasingly unpopular and to date largely unsuccessful war. Adgie and his team described it to the twenty or so key personnel—including Willingham and Lucca, the only marines assigned to ground forces there—who were gathered in a large tent. In attendance were company commanders, first sergeants, and section leaders, as well as enablers supporting the operation, such as explosive ordinance disposal (EOD) technicians, snipers, and engineers. Willingham, as the expert on military dogs, fit into the enablers category.

In the middle of the space, on the plywood floor, was a terrain model of the area of operation, showing roads, the river, villages. Those giving the brief referred to it frequently during their explanation. Those listening sat perched in chairs around it.

Willingham looked at the briefing paper he'd been given when he and Lucca entered the guarded area. Normally these documents are one page long. This one was ten pages. Typed across the top were the words *Operation Marne Torch.*

It would be an enormous operation involving coalition forces, including elements of the Third Infantry Division, bolstered by Iraqi Army soldiers. Their numbers could climb to three thousand. They would soon begin methodically and painstakingly clearing roads and buildings from north to south. U.S. forces would get out of the FOBs and move closer to the locals, where they'd provide security and gather intelligence on the enemy. The goal: to stop the flow of "accelerants of violence" into Baghdad, defeat sectarian violence, and secure the local population. It would be a hard-striking, fast-moving operation, from both the ground and the air.

Troops would maintain a presence, not abandoning a location once they'd cleared it of bombs and bad guys. A core piece of the operation was getting to know the local population, what the people wanted, what they needed—and what they knew. Sticking around and providing protection had obvious benefits for locals but also was advantageous for the operation's goals. It was great for gathering intel on al-Qaeda. A secure area, where people are shielded from violent revenge—including beheadings, an al-Qaeda favorite—meant they might be more inclined to open up about operatives in their villages, and other information only locals would know. And it would make it more difficult for insurgents to reenter and begin their game anew.

Headquarters for Marne Torch was to be in what had once been a weekend retreat home for Saddam Hussein's sons, brothers Uday and Qusay, who had been killed in July 2003 by U.S. forces. Uday was notoriously cruel, known for his torture, murder, rape, and fraud. Younger brother Qusay had been accused of ordering the deaths of thousands of political prisoners. Their onetime getaway— a sprawling, one-story house overlooking the Tigris River— featured a swimming pool and a horse stable. Coalition forces would soon convert the whole vacation destination into Patrol Base Murray.

For the ground teams, the operation would involve a slow, arduous, door-to-door search. No one could predict just how long

Marne Torch would last. There are plenty of unknown factors when disrupting deeply rooted insurgent operations, taking away the weapons caches that are the tools of their trade, and doing it along IED-laden roads.

The meeting broke up, and everyone turned in their ten-page briefs. On their way out of the tent, Willingham looked down at his dog. She walked with an easy, confident stride.

"Yup, Lucca," he told her. "We got this covered."

A FEW DAYS later, June 16, was moving day. Hundreds of soldiers from the 1/30th gathered around Adgie as he stood on a Humvee and gave a motivational mission speech. The lieutenant colonel told the men that they'd be out there making split-second decisions and that their leaders had their backs. Willingham, age twenty-seven, liked how Adgie seemed to understand the stress of combat for these younger soldiers. The average age of the soldiers on their first deployment looked to him to be about twenty, if that. This was a large operation in a dangerous area, and Adgie didn't hide the fact that they were expecting casualties.

In his speech he acknowledged that these young men were well trained and that many of them were going to face combat for the first time. Going through compounds, coping with IED threats, dealing with an enemy that doesn't dress like the enemy, possibly losing a friend in battle—it's a lot of pressure on anyone, much less a twenty-year-old. Adgie assured them that those in leadership positions understood the challenges to the troops and were there to support them.

Willingham had packed his weapons, essential gear, enough dog food for a couple of weeks, and a sleeping bag. He left most of their belongings in the tent, since they'd be coming back to FOB Falcon fairly frequently to send after-action reports to Roche and to rest up a bit. He wondered what kind of place they were headed into that would make this mortar-prone FOB seem like a relaxing retreat.

Dozens of vehicles were readying to head out of the compound as a convoy. The parade south would be made up of tanks—Bradley fighting vehicles and M1 Abrams—as well as a variety of vehicles vital for route clearance, including RG31 mine-protected armored personnel carriers, a couple of big six-wheeled Buffalos, and other mine-clearance vehicles. The Humvees in the rugged lineup looked diminutive in comparison.

The soldiers were wrapping up their precombat checks, making sure they had everything they needed and that it was in good working order. Some were already climbing into their assigned vehicles—heavy-duty tanks, usually. It was only about fifteen miles to the future Patrol Base Murray, and the route had been cleared of IEDs, but this wasn't going to be a fast ride. Probably at least an hour to their destination, with everyone in tow.

Streeeeek, BOOM! BOOM!

Soldiers jumped; some hit the ground. A couple of mortar rounds landed inside the compound wall, in an open area about fifty yards from where Willingham and Lucca were loading into the Humvee. No one hurt, but close call. Smoke spread and Lucca calmly sniffed the familiar scent. Even Willingham could smell the explosive and its aftermath—a mix of gunpowder, burned plastic, and charred weeds—but he figured Lucca had analyzed it down to the molecule.

"Well, that's a fine send-off!" the Hummer driver said to his passengers as they jumped in. "No need for coffee this morning!"

And they set off down the dusty road to the outskirts of the Triangle of Death.

UDAY AND QUSAY HUSSEIN's former riverside getaway property was larger than Willingham had expected. It looked to be about 450 yards long by 150 yards wide and extended to the banks of the Tigris River. If he used his imagination, he could see that it had once been a decent place, but during the four years since the brothers' deaths, the sun and the heat had taken their toll, making it a faded, ghost-town version of its former self.

Despite its proximity to the river, there was almost no vegetation. The fronds on the dozen or so palm trees next to one of the outbuildings were now dry and a dead shade of gray. It looked to Willingham like they'd tried to stay alive for a while after the caretakers left but had just about lost the battle against the brutal heat. Even weeds didn't seem to stand a chance, and the few that had emerged from the ground were long dead. Everything—the horse stables, the large main house, the smaller buildings, and all the roadways—was covered in powdery sand that reminded him of moondust.

Willingham and Lucca linked up with a squad whose job was to sweep the area for explosives. They started in the horse stables. They searched the two rooms attached to the stables, then the stables themselves. It was a concrete open-air stable building, and Willingham thought it didn't seem like it would protect horses from the harsh heat. Then he realized being nice to horses was probably not a top priority for the Hussein brothers.

They searched the drained pool and then the house. Marble floors, thick sandy dust on every surface, empty rooms. Lucca nosed her way through, snuffling up dust here and there. Willingham wondered if the scent of the Hussein brothers still lingered, if their skin cells—humans shed about 50 million a minute—were still detectable, if Lucca was taking a private tour of the microscopic body flakes called scurf.

Can she smell evil?

WILLINGHAM AWOKE BEFORE dawn the next day on the roof of a compound a klick or so down the road. Most of the soldiers from the platoon crammed into rooms and hallways inside. The only guys on the roof with him were pulling security. At least up here there was plenty of real estate for him and Lucca, and it didn't reek of bad Iraqi plumbing and soldier sweat.

No time had been wasted. They had already started pushing south, clearing roadsides and compounds as engineers and workers set about transforming the Hussein estate into the shored-up, walled-off Patrol Base Murray. Compound rooftops were likely to be Willingham's bedroom for at least the next few days. He didn't mind. The moon had set hours ago, and the sky was brilliant with stars. He enjoyed waking up under the gauzy stripe of the Milky Way.

They had a long day of clearing ahead, and he was hoping the platoon leader would ask them to go first into situations where a dog's nose could be useful—to walk and point on the way through potentially dangerous areas. This is what he and Lucca were here for, after all, to keep these guys safe. But the platoon leader didn't put them in any forward positions.

Willingham didn't like it, but he understood. Most of these men had probably never worked with a dog team. Besides, those guys were soldiers; he and Lucca were marines. Trusting their lives to a stranger and his dog from another service wasn't a decision to be made lightly. He knew he had to be patient, to show them what they could do, and wait for their chance.

The previous day during a break, he had put on a demo of Lucca's capabilities, as he had done several times at FOB Falcon. He hid a couple of explosives scents and let her find them off leash with the quietest of commands.

"She's like remote control," one of the soldiers observed.

"That's what dogs like her do. You all do everything you normally do. I'm just going to be an added asset to you," Willingham told them. "I'm here to support you. I got the ability to walk on point, so we have the chance to detect an IED before we get to it. We can help search for caches. Lucca is a force multiplier. She can search a lot bigger area than soldiers can, in a faster time. She's trained to search roadways and buildings, vehicles and open areas. I've also got her trained up on some local odors, you know, explosives odors.

"She's a great dog," he finished. Then he remembered to add his rehearsed line, "But like all dogs, she's proven, not perfect."

That first day, there had been no caches, no IEDs, nothing to add to Lucca's CV. But Willingham figured that in a place called the Triangle of Death, something was bound to show up sooner or later.

At 0600 the platoon linked up with another and continued south on "Route Gnat," the main road from Arab Jabour to Baghdad, paved in places, but around here mostly compact dirt and rocks. They searched four or five compounds and the surrounding areas. When it started getting too hot—it was supposed to get up to 120 degrees—they firmed up in an abandoned compound until evening. Willingham stayed inside with Lucca for a couple of hours so she could rest and cool off from the morning's search. Only the soldiers who were pulling security on the roof were outside.

Willingham chatted with soldiers in the house while Lucca lay on her side and enjoyed a steady stream of belly and side rubs from her admirers. It was too stifling to eat lunch, but Willingham forced himself to down the peanut butter and crackers from his MRE. He drank some water—warm and not refreshing—and offered Lucca more water in her portable bowl. He took her outside for a minute because she gave him the look that said it wouldn't be a bad idea to take care of business now.

Back inside, she followed him up two short flights of stairs to the concrete compound's flat roof. Willingham asked the five soldiers if they could use help pulling security. It wasn't anything dog handlers were expected to do, but he wanted to be useful, to pull his own weight.

They were happy to have another set of eyes, and he set up a sector of fire that wasn't as well covered by the others. They all faced different directions, keeping watch for trouble, weapons ready.

Lucca stretched downward-dog fashion, circled once, and settled herself in the shade of the three-foot wall that encircled the roof, lying on a mat Willingham had found in the compound. She put her head on her paws but didn't sleep. For the next hour, she ticked her eyes from one soldier to the other, but mostly looked at the marine standing right next to her.

A few hundred yards off to the right of his sector, Willingham could see the Tigris—wide, winding through an area of thick palm groves and grasses of the Tigris River valley. He thought about the times he and his dad and some friends would float down the North River in canoes and flat-bottomed boats for hours and hours, just float through miles of western Alabama. After a while, they'd set up camp in just the right clearing, grill burgers and gulp cold drinks, take some .22s and shoot targets and go fishing.

Willingham sensed the wall of rushing heat a split second before he heard—and felt—the explosion. He swung around and saw a ball of flames receding and a section of cinder-block wall twenty feet away in rubble. Another blast, farther away, sent a tree and nearby foliage into flames. The work of rocket-propelled grenades, RPGs.

Immediately the compound began taking fire from PKM machine guns and AK-47s. Willingham adjusted his position so he had some protection from behind a high post, and fired his M4. The soldiers did the same, including one with an M249 machine gun. Radios exploded with communications from the platoon leader and the other soldiers.

As Willingham fired, he noticed that Lucca had jumped up and was wagging her tail, excited, as if they were playing a game. He realized what was going on. It *was* a game, at least to Lucca. They'd done so much gunfire training together before deployment, with constant praise and rewards for being calm, that it was just more fun in her view. Out of habit, up on the scorching roof during a firefight that was anything but a game, he began praising her as he returned fire.

Pop. Pop. Pop.

"Good . . ."

Pop. Pop.

"Girllll!"

Pop. Pop. Pop . . .

When it was over, he gave her a Kong and she went back to her blanket to enjoy her reward as if nothing had happened.

BREAKFAST MREs WERE slightly more appetizing to Willingham than lunch or dinner MREs. It was just too hot later in the day to enjoy eating food that came out of pouches and was supposed to be heated in the flameless heater enclosed in the package. He chose from his stash a meal ready to eat containing a cheese and vegetable omelet with hot sauce on the side, hash browns with bacon, toaster pastry crackers, apple butter, and a cinnamon scone.

He ate as much as he could, not bothering to heat anything. Lucca's eyebrows shifted as she glanced at the food. It was hard to be subtle with dark eyebrows like hers. She didn't beg. She peeked, discreetly. Willingham thought she looked like someone trying to see what was on the plate of a fellow customer at another table in a restaurant. He wanted to try to keep her diet as close to normal as he could, so he refrained from giving her his leftovers. She never pushed the issue, and he was glad, because after he saw how she'd handled the firefight the day before, he might have been tempted to give in.

Time to gear up. Before putting on his flak jacket, he pulled the chest panel's protective plate out of its pouch a few inches and looked at the photo he had taped at the top with electrical tape. His favorite photo of Jill. She was smiling—beaming, actually—with her face turned three-quarters to the camera, her hands on her hips, and a red rose tucked into the deep V-neck of her form-fitting olive-green shirt. When he was in Israel, she'd gone to a restaurant back home with some friends, and they decided to take a photo to send her husband halfway across the world. He'd kept it with him since.

Willingham took Lucca for a quick walk in the area they had already swept, and then met up with the soldiers gathering at Route Gnat.

"Hey, Lucca!" a soldier called. Lucca turned her head toward him and gave a wag of recognition, in what Willingham thought was kind of an "Oh yeah, hi, sorry, I don't remember your name, but you look familiar" way.

"Hey, dog guy, have a good one!" he called to Willingham, who didn't mind if others didn't know his name. He enjoyed being dog guy.

He and Lucca were ready to go. With her BADASS harness on, she knew it was work time. She stayed by his side, glancing up at Willingham, looking down the road and back up at Willingham. He smiled at her eagerness. It was as if the firefight the previous day was an appetizer, and she was hungry for whatever came next.

"Soon, Lucca, hang on."

She lay down alongside the road, nose pointed south, while they waited for their spotter, who would keep his eyes out for bad guys and his rifle ready to fire. You don't walk down roads like this without someone with a weapon watching your back.

Willingham reached into a small pouch on the side of his pack and pulled out a set of dog tags—the one his father had given him, from his time in Vietnam. He rubbed them between his thumb and forefinger, feeling the raised letters on the warm metal as he thought about this man who had been through such hell but never showed it. Never talked about it, either. He tucked the tags back in the pouch.

The spotter arrived, they discussed the plan, and the workday began. "Forward," Willingham told Lucca in a gentle voice, not demanding or commanding, but like he was asking a child to do something. Lucca walked down the left side of the road, sniffing intently for all those scents she knew he wanted her to find. When she got about fifty yards away, he called her back. They did the same on the right. She didn't detect anything. A large route-clearance vehicle rolled slowly ahead for fifty yards and waited for them to sweep the next strip. The vehicle looked like a combination tank and tractor and was equipped with ground-penetrating radar for detection of buried explosives. Mine detectors like this had a good reputation, but Willingham would stake his money on Lucca's nose any day.

Fifty yards at a time down Route Gnat, machine followed dog. With Lucca doing her job on the sides and the vehicle clearing the center of the road, it was safe for the rest of the vehicles to follow. As they pushed south, the Bradley fighting vehicles, which were lined up in a long convoy, began spreading out and setting up blocking positions. It wouldn't do any good to spend all that time clearing a road if you weren't going to protect it afterward. The armored Bradleys, with their cannons, missile launchers, and machine guns, provided the muscle to prevent insurgents from backfilling the cleared areas.

After a couple of hours of this, no one—dog team or route-clearance vehicles—had found any explosives. Lucca was panting, slowing down. Willingham returned to the Humvee with her and asked the driver if she could rest on the empty seat.

"Hop in, Lucca! We've got air-conditioning!" the driver said. It wasn't strong air-conditioning, but it would give her some relief.

Willingham walked back up Route Gnat to see how he could help without his dog. He wanted the platoon leaders to know that he was dedicated, that he'd do what it took to contribute to the mission, even when Lucca couldn't work. He wanted them to see he was serious about their safety and that he should take her up front on missions.

ROADS HAD TO be swept for bombs, but so did every structure along the road, and the roads leading to those structures. Not only were the troops looking for IEDs and insurgents; they were seeking information and building a database. Most people seemed to welcome their presence, letting them into their homes, talking behind closed doors in a way they could not do on the streets.

Interpreters explained the importance of an all-inclusive database. Willingham was surprised that few people balked at having their photos taken or supplying iris scans and fingerprints to Biometric Automated Toolset (BAT) and Handheld Interagency Identity Detection Equipment (HIIDE). In other areas of the surge, BATs and HIIDEs had already been proving effective at matching fingerprints on IEDs to people in the database.

Most searches in the early days of the operation, before there was much intel, were "soft knocks." Soldiers surrounded a compound, effectively cordoning it off, knocked, and used an interpreter to explain that they were going to search the compound. At first, Willingham would take whatever position he and Lucca could get to search the compound—from open areas and courtyards to inner rooms. They weren't first in. Sometimes they were last.

Within a few searches he got the platoon leader to understand that it was better for his dog to go through a building as soon as it was cleared of people—before other soldiers went through and disturbed odors of possible hidden explosives. He and Lucca began going in first, once the residents were no longer inside. After finishing the search, the two would go outside while the soldiers did a hand search. He knew most people there would not be comfortable with a dog in their home—even if it *was* Lucca.

So far Lucca had found only a few weapons, nothing to raise concern. People were allowed to have certain firearms. Willingham was making progress with the platoon leader, but he wasn't where he wanted to be yet—walking point down a stretch of Route Gnat to the next set of compounds.

But during a morning search on the fourth day, Willingham heard the words he had been waiting to hear. "You and Lucca can walk point."

"You won't regret it," Willingham said.

To Lucca, it was just a walk down a road on a warm afternoon, sniffing for scents that made Willingham happy. He wondered if she thought it was strange that he would become so excited when she responded to certain odors. He was glad she didn't know the stakes. If she got distracted, or if the explosives were buried too cleverly, it could prove fatal—to her, to him, to anyone near, including local children.

They'd been working toward this since they met, and he felt a calm exhilaration walking out front with Lucca. The morning of walking point had gone without incident. That was fine with him. He didn't need Lucca to find IEDs to know his dog was great. Just so long as she didn't miss one.

The soldiers reconvened later in the day, when the sun was less taxing and everyone had rested. They needed to clear a portion of a smaller dirt road off Route Gnat on their way to check some compounds. In sections of the road, tall concrete compound walls jutted in close on both sides, so there was no way to get out. People going through would have to funnel closer in. It was still a wide enough road, but Willingham knew chokepoints like this could be deadly.

When they approached the first two chokepoints, he went farther ahead than usual with Lucca so she would have time to investigate before the others got there. No sense in the others being delayed as she searched. The system had worked well so far. They were making good progress.

He saw another chokepoint coming up.

"Lucca."

She looked at him.

With his open right palm facing to the left, he sliced through the air while looking at the left side of the road.

"Forward," he told her. He wanted her to be on the left, since the wind was blowing from the right. That way she could catch scents from the whole width of road. Knowing how to use the wind to the dog's advantage is an everyday component of dog handling.

She walked up ahead, nose down, intent on her job. She got to the place where compound walls infringed on the roadside, and her pace picked up. Back and forth, back and forth, tail wagging. Each time she turned, she took fewer steps as she seemed to narrow in on a point of interest. She stopped, her tail went up slightly, and she looked at Willingham. He could see she was about to sit to indicate she had found something, but Willingham had seen enough. He didn't need her to go through the whole response.

"Come!"

She trotted back, and he praised her. No Kong here, too dangerous. She didn't seem to care. By this time the platoon leader had caught up. Willingham briefed him. EOD was summoned, and everyone moved away to a safe distance. The technicians assessed the situation. Since there was a lot of debris on the road—a thick layer of dusty dirt, pebbles, bits of dry vegetation—the techs couldn't see any sign of an IED. They decided to use propelled water from special bottles to clear the debris and see if there was anything obvious underneath.

Almost as soon as the water hit the ground, there was a huge blast. Willingham could feel it rumble inside his chest.

The explosion left a crater in the middle of the road, twelve feet across by five feet deep.

If Willingham had let Lucca sit at what proved to be a highly unstable IED, it could have been over for her, maybe for him, too. If she had been a typical leashed bomb dog, or if Lucca weren't so good at her job, that could have been the end of the road for at least the two of them.

"Luuuucca! Mama Lucca! Look what you found!" Willingham rubbed the sides of her face, the top of her head, stroked her back.

It was getting dark, so they started back to a compound they'd secured for the night. The platoon leader walked up to them.

"Hey, great work. From now on, you two are out front."

5

Triangle of Death

LUCCA KNEW. SHE just knew. Something down this gravel walkway, something she had to find. She was leashed now, because Willingham always leashed up when there were lots of people around.

She pulled Willingham forward.

"Whoa, ma'am, what's up?"

Her nose tracked along the ground as they crunched down the path. He could hear the rapid inhalations, sometimes stacked on top of one another with one quick exhale to clear the nose and start again. Ears up, tail straight out with an occasional quick wag, she trotted ahead in the heat. A dog on a mission.

She turned a corner, never looking up, just following her nose. She arrived at the entrance to their tent, pawing to get in, tail wagging like an out-of-control metronome.

She looked up at Willingham and burst in, with Willingham right behind.

"Kory! Cooper!"

Two barks from Cooper, happy greetings between handlers, and tent number thirteen instantly filled with the sounds of old friendships renewed. It had been only about three weeks since they saw each other at Slayer, before Wiens and Cooper flew down to FOB Kalsu, and less than a week since Willingham had set out from this place for Marne Torch. It felt like much longer.

Lucca and Cooper play-danced around the tent, nails clicking on the plywood floor as they chased each other around the cots, banging into supplies, sending food bowls skidding. Cooper barked a single bark again and lifted a paw onto the side of Lucca's neck. She pulled away and butted him with her flank, sending him flying forward. He came back at her. Lucca spun out of his way and Cooper skidded to a stop and returned for more.

Willingham and Wiens laughed at the antics. They were eager to catch up but happy to watch their dogs, reunited and having a ball. Wiens told him he'd been sent here for a couple of weeks or so and then would return to FOB Kalsu. Willingham filled him in on Marne Torch, the missions so far, what they were finding.

"You got way more going on up this way," Wiens said.

Willingham had come back to FOB Falcon to send after-action reports to Roche in Baghdad. He was looking forward to a couple of days here. After a week pretty much devoid of personal hygiene, he needed a trip to the shower trailer. And food. Food at the chow hall—still with the mandatory admission of a filled sandbag—was going to taste like gourmet cuisine after a week of eating out of pouches. The folding steel cot would be a welcome luxury, too.

Now he understood why the FOB was a good place to come back to, mortars and all.

For the next two days, they talked and ate. Wiens hadn't lost his appetite in the heat. They also waited out a mortar attack in a bunker. Willingham noticed that everything was more fun when Wiens was around—even avoiding mortar.

At night, he watched, amused, as Wiens stretched out on top of his sleeping bag on his cot and called Cooper to come to bed. Wiens scooched all the way to the side, and Cooper hopped on and settled right into all the spots that weren't filled with his handler.

Lucca looked at the two on the cot and at Willingham. It wasn't a look of longing to be close. If anything, she was thinking the same thing he was: *I love you, but don't even think about getting that close to me in this heat.*

In the early mornings and again in the evenings, when it wasn't too hot, they trained the dogs on explosives odors unique to the Triangle of Death. Willingham had obtained the materials from an EOD technician who understood that it was important for dogs to be fluent in the local scent language. He and Wiens paired the scent of explosives with a Kong. The dogs sniffed the strange new smell, reacted, and got rewarded with a Kong and praise. Positive association—the core of military dog training— creates eager learners. Voilà! Before long, the dogs had added a few more explosives to their olfactory repertoire.

HE WISHED HE could be in two places at once. Jill was his first crush, at age eight, the only girl on the Badgers community baseball team. She was from the less rural area of Tuscaloosa. One

day he came to a game with his sleeves rolled up a little higher
than usual, hoping she would notice the Statue of Liberty tattoo
he had bought and applied to his upper arm, just for her. He
thought it was a most patriotic design and was very proud. Jill
smiled politely when he finally pointed it out to her. They met
again when they were sixteen, at a youth group in the church
Willingham's family had begun attending. The two started dat-
ing in 1996. He was well into his career in the marines when they
married on March 23, 2002. She had become more than a crush,
more than cute. He had come to admire her—to adore her.

Still did, more than ever.

He also loved his job. He hadn't been planning on staying in
the marines very long. He wanted to be a narcotics officer, like
his dad, out there saving lives and having big adventures while
putting bad guys behind bars. But when he found out that military police (MPs) could become military dog handlers, he was
hooked. He'd grown up with dogs on the farm, and he couldn't
imagine a better fit for what he loved doing.

"Best job in the world," he told anyone who asked. "I absolutely love it." There was only one thing better in the military dog
world than training dogs and teaching students: deploying with
a dog—really doing it firsthand—keeping troops from blowing
up. And here he was.

But it was hard not to miss Jill, who was now about six months
along in her pregnancy.

Willingham used the DSN line at FOB Falcon to talk to Jill.
He tried not to phone her while she was on her nursing shift
since it was hard for her to get away. During their conversations,
he'd give her the big picture of what was going on in their part

of Iraq and how Lucca was doing. He always tried to keep it positive, regardless of the danger.

Jill updated him on the latest home news—a barbecue across the street at their good friends', the Rotenberrys', how she and their future baby girl were thriving with only three months to go before the due date, her pregnancy cravings for Chipotle salad bowls with a side of guacamole and chips. Like her husband, she tried to keep the conversation upbeat and light. No sense burdening him with day-to-day civilian problems he could do nothing about.

"I love you, babe."

"I love you, too, babe. Take good care of you and our little girl, 'K?"

"Of course. Be safe out there."

He finished writing the after-action reports he'd been working on during his short time at Falcon and sent them to Roche via a Secret Internet Protocol Router Network (SIPRNet) on what was referred to as the "secret computer." Before heading to the tent to get ready for the ride back to Patrol Base Murray, he called Roche to check in and to tell her how happy he was that Wiens was there.

"Those two make anywhere they go a better place," he told her.

"Very true. You take good care of those boys, OK?"

WIENS STASHED HIS gear next to Willingham's on the concrete slab of the open stables at Patrol Base Murray. There were dozens of cots now, and it seemed more crowded with soldiers than it had before. Willingham wondered how the dogs were going to be able to sprawl out at night and not trip anyone who needed to get up in the dark.

They claimed a couple of cots and sat down. They got their dogs in some shade behind them, and Lucca and Cooper lay in it, side by side, until the shade shrank into a thin line and disappeared.

"Let's find these dogs a better place," Willingham said.

Shade was a rare commodity at midday. But Lucca and Cooper scouted out the potential for some pretty quickly, between a couple of Humvees parked next to each other. There weren't a lot of Hummers being used in this operation, and Willingham figured they'd probably stay parked there for a while. He and Wiens grabbed their gear and their cots and set up a little home there, stretching some cammy netting from one vehicle to the other for shade. A couple of small woven rugs Willingham had found outside an abandoned compound served as the dog beds. The dogs took advantage of them as soon as they'd had some water.

There was plenty of time before evening ops. While the dogs rested, the soldier and the marine talked about dogs, football, and family.

Willingham wasn't surprised to learn that Wiens had been working since he was twelve, getting up every day at 2 A.M. with his father and brothers to deliver newspapers. It explained his work ethic. His father, Kevin, had raised his three sons by himself, working full-time as a concrete truck driver and holding down whatever extra gigs he could get in the Independence, Oregon, area to keep his boys fed and clothed. They lived in a few different mobile homes over the years—the last one a double-wide where no one had to sleep in the living room.

Wiens had always loved dogs, but they couldn't afford to keep one. Plus there was all that moving they were doing. He hoped he'd get a dog when he got a real career going one day, and maybe he could help his dad out, too. He was going to be a civilian cop, just like his older brother, Kevin Jr., wanted to be. His brother had joined the army right after high school and became an MP. He was serving somewhere in Iraq right now. When Wiens joined, he ended up in the world of combat engineers instead. When he heard he'd been recommended to become a specialized search dog handler—something non-MPs didn't get to do—he couldn't believe his luck.

"Someone up there likes me," he told his dad.

The tie to his grandfather struck Wiens at that moment. He knew he was named after his grandfather but had forgotten that his grandfather was a dog handler in the Korean War. It felt as though fate had reached through the generations and settled him into a career that he not only loved, but that ran in his blood.

There was another dog Wiens had almost brought to Iraq, a big German shepherd. He sent his dad photos of both the shepherd and Cooper. His dad was rooting for the shepherd because he looked like he'd take care of his son. But that dog didn't certify in time for deployment, so Cooper became his partner. Wiens had secretly been pulling for him ever since he met him.

"I loved him right from the start," Wiens told Willingham. "There's no son like him!"

"Ha, speak of the devil!" Willingham said.

Wiens turned around and saw Cooper, refreshed from his nap, standing behind him carrying a deflated football and wagging his tail expectantly. It was Cooper's favorite non-Kong toy from the arsenal of toys Wiens had brought to Iraq for him.

The sun was giving way to late afternoon, and it wasn't quite as oven hot as it had been when Cooper went to sleep. His dog tried to push past the cot to take his football out for a run, but he couldn't get by. Wiens adjusted the cot and ran off with Cooper to the open area right next to their little outpost within an outpost. Cooper dropped the flabby football in front of Wiens, and Wiens, the dutiful dad, threw it out for a pass. It didn't go far, and when Cooper caught it, Wiens whooped it up.

"Cooooopalooooooop!"

Lucca perked up from her nap, ears doing their radar pivot action to find out where the sound had come from.

"Lucca, you wanna play some football with your boyfriend?" Willingham asked. She ran to the field and plowed into Cooper.

"Tackle football! That's my girlll!" Willingham shouted.

Cooper abandoned the ball and for the next few minutes, he and Lucca chased and skidded and played. Wiens and Willingham cheered, proud dads at a football game. The moondust at Murray was so fine that it poofed up in big clouds as the dogs galloped over it. Before the dogs got too tired—they had an evening of work ahead—Willingham and Wiens called them back. Two chalky white apparitions came running, shook at almost the same time, and became Lucca and Cooper again.

Wiens tapped his chest. Cooper jumped up and rested his paws near his handler's shoulders. They danced together to their own music as Lucca looked and wagged.

"You cut quite the rug there, Kory!"

The afternoon flew by. Willingham and Wiens would be supporting different route-clearing platoons that evening, so they enjoyed the downtime together. They hoped they'd meet up again soon down Route Gnat, or back at Murray. Before heading off on separate missions, they bumped fists and wished each other luck.

"Be safe out there, brother," Willingham told him. Then he looked at Cooper. "Watch after him, Coopaloop."

THE "BIRD DOG" led the way. The man's entire head and face, except for his eyes and a little slit over his mouth, were wrapped in white turban material. The rest of him was covered in army cammies. No one could tell who he was, and that was the point. He was local, and he was helping the Americans. If an al-Qaeda member recognized him, he could be as good as dead. His family, too.

After Operation Marne Torch got under way, there had been a surge of al-Qaeda violence against anyone caught cooperating with the Americans. Days after the Americans arrived, al-Qaeda operatives sent a clear message to the local community. They stopped a bus carrying workers for the coalition, drove it to the Tigris River, shot to death twenty-three workers, including women—all pleading for their lives—and dumped the bodies in the river.

"The enemy is very talented out here," Adgie told *The Washington Post* about a week into Marne Torch. "It's going to be a long summer."

Willingham wasn't sure exactly how bird dogs got their name. He imagined that, like their canine counterparts, they pointed out things that weren't obvious to others—IEDs and al-Qaeda members, mostly. In theory, bird dogs are aware of who is planting what, and where, and can spot situations that aren't normal.

The routine with this bird dog was that he would look down

the road, move ahead, and then move back. If he didn't see anything out of the ordinary, Willingham would send Lucca down in their usual manner to sniff out explosives on the sides of the road, and then the Buffalo mine-protected clearance vehicle would roll through, scanning for bombs on the road itself.

Willingham and Lucca had just joined back up with the route-clearance team after spending the morning searching compounds with another platoon. Lucca had searched about forty meters down the road and was coming back. The bird dog had gone off to some side path to have a look or a smoke. This put him behind Willingham.

Suddenly the bird dog let out a frightened shriek, followed by several more in rapid succession. Willingham spun around and saw wires from a partly buried cylindrical IED. He'd later learn that the bird dog had come in from the side path—one Lucca had not yet checked—kicking the ground as he walked. His foot caught the IED just right. Willingham stopped Lucca where she was and looked in disbelief at what was going on behind him.

Closest to him was the IED. A few feet back from the IED, the bird dog had gone from screams to petrified-sounding Arabic, maybe prayers. And twenty yards beyond him was the hulking Buffalo mine-protected vehicle. Behind it, the rest of the patrol.

He and Lucca were now separated from his entire team by an IED. Ahead lay who knows what kind of danger. And he stood there with no cover. A sniper could take him out easy. Or the IED could go off. He called Lucca back to him along the side of the road she'd already inspected. He needed to have her ready at his side for whatever action he'd take next. As she trotted back to him, he walked toward her and assessed the situation. It took only seconds, and he knew what he had to do.

On the left side of the dirt road was thick vegetation, which would make a good place for a sniper to hide and aim at a clearing about twenty yards down the road. About forty yards to the left of the road, the Tigris River flowed by, and Willingham could see ample areas where snipers could take cover on the other side of it. A mound of sand here, a clump of weeds there—it was textbook sniper strategy. On the right side of the road, a palm grove, also perfect for snipers.

Just past where the vegetation cleared stood a small mud shed with three walls; its front wall was nonexistent, so it opened to the north, facing his supporting unit. It would be good cover for him and Lucca. The choice was to head there or go back toward the IED, which could have a companion. He opted for the shed. Lucca had already searched this strip the first time around, so Willingham was more concerned with snipers than IEDs.

"Come on, Lucca," he said, and poised his rifle along his chest as his eyes swept his surroundings. She walked swiftly at his side, and within ten seconds they came to the shed. "Lucca, seek." He had her do a quick search along the open north side, and they entered. He stood close to a sidewall. "Lie down, Lucca; take a rest." She obliged, panting, at his feet.

They were now protected on three sides, and he was able to see his army guys at work. He watched the EOD techs as they approached the IED and checked it out. In about seven minutes, his team rolled up to the shed.

He got the postmortem. After careful examination, the techs had determined that when the bird dog kicked the IED, the wires connected. By some fateful sleight of hand, the battery was faulty. "You guys would have been a pink mist if the battery was good," one of the techs told him, shaking his head.

★★★★★

"WE'VE GOT SOME intel about al-Qaeda down here. Tell Lucca to be on her toes," the platoon sergeant told Willingham.

"Absolutely."

"Mama Lucca," he said to her quietly, "you're always on your toes, aren't you? He doesn't know you well enough to know that yet."

Willingham was heartened to see how quickly intel was coming in. They'd been making their way down Route Gnat for more than a week, and residents were opening up to them as they realized that their chance—possibly their only chance—to rid themselves of life under al-Qaeda had arrived.

After the first big find, Lucca had some small discoveries—a weapons cache here, some det cord there. "Nothing earthshaking lately, eh?" one young soldier said to Willingham over MRE dinners one night. "Ha-ha-ha!"

Word about Lucca had spread, and Willingham was fielding requests every day to walk point for one squad or another from the Alpha and Bravo companies. They often asked for her by name. Instead of "We need a dog, and there's a dog," it was, "We need to get Lucca on this mission." He and Lucca were keeping soldiers out of harm's way. Willingham felt good that they were getting them back to their girlfriends, wives, parents, and children in one piece.

Up ahead about a hundred meters, on the left side of the road, Willingham saw a small, crumbling shack. Its roof was made of long twigs that had seen better days. A rusty bathtub sat to its side, and beside it were two cars. They looked in decent shape and seemed out of place next to the dilapidated shack. It reminded him of people back home who lived in humble conditions but drove flashy cars they couldn't afford. Since the Triangle of Death wasn't populated with car dealerships offering low-cost financing, they caught his attention. The platoon sergeant caught up with Willingham and confirmed his suspicion.

"Hey, the bird dog tells us the men who own those cars are probably al-Qaeda," the platoon sergeant told him. "Can you send Lucca in?"

"Sure thing. Lucca, forward."

She trotted ahead, and he followed a little closer than usual, so he could direct her if need be. There were two cars—a green model with some obvious mileage and a silver BMW. The green car was closest, and when Lucca got near, her tail set to wagging as if the car were a giant Kong. She needed no direction from Willingham. She had practiced vehicle inspections so much that she was on autopilot. She sniffed the front bumper, then walked quickly to the driver's side and sniffed the seam of the door, then the back door, and back and forth between the doors a couple more times. Her tail wagged harder now as she stared at the back door. She glanced at Willingham, and he read the message in her look.

We got something here. Send in EOD.

He called her back, praised her up, and gave her a Kong. She lay down in the shade and enjoyed her reward. Willingham told his security guy that Lucca had responded—something he figured was pretty obvious, but he had to make sure; not everyone spoke Lucca language. His spotter radioed the platoon leader. EOD was there quickly. The techs saw a white sack on the rear floor of the car. After making sure the door wasn't booby-trapped, they opened it and checked the contents. It was full of IED components. The BMW contained a similar payload.

The techs carefully removed the rice sacks and placed them

next to each other. They weren't going to move them any farther. They didn't know how unstable the stuff was, and it wasn't worth losing body parts, or more.

By now, everyone had retreated to a position of safety at least forty meters away. The soldiers sat in their vehicles—Bradleys, mostly—and waited. Willingham and Lucca were sitting in the Humvee that had become their mode of transportation. Bradleys were too hot for this dog. Lucca stretched out on a bench seat and fell asleep in air-conditioned bliss.

A loud *boom*, a big cloud of smoke, and it was done. Lucca opened her eyes and fell right back to sleep.

The stuff that was going to become bombs or turn the cars into vehicle-borne IEDs that could have killed dozens of innocent people rained down in fine ashes.

Willingham laughed. "Look what you did, Lucca!" he said.

EOD gave the all clear. Willingham and the soldiers left their vehicles. He headed down to look closely at the damage. There wasn't much left of the sacks, but the cars hadn't been harmed.

"Hey, K-9, you want to destroy a vehicle?" the platoon leader asked him.

"Hell yeah!"

The squad leader handed him an incendiary grenade and told him what to do. Willingham shot out the back window of the green car. The squad leader did the same to the BMW. Willingham pulled the pin, walked up, and tossed in the grenade, and within seconds, there was a spattering hiss or two, and black smoke poured out of the cars. Part of him wanted to stay and watch, but it wasn't an option. A gas tank or who knows what else could blow up. He and the squad leader walked quickly away, up the road, toward the waiting vehicles. But before they were out of sight, he turned around and could see orange-white flames mixing with the black smoke. The intense heat of the grenades was consuming everything it touched.

"Oh damn, look at those things go!" Willingham shouted.

Soldiers wooted and cheered again from their vehicles. It had been quite a day of pyrotechnics. He got into the Humvee where Lucca was waiting, and they drove on to the afternoon's next objective.

They came back the next day to check out the damage. Tires were gone. Windows had disappeared. It was impossible for him to see if they'd melted, shattered, or both. The exteriors were charred beyond recognition, with the formerly green (now ash gray) car suffering significant structural melting.

"No insurgents gonna be driving *these* cars anymore," he said. "Good job, girl."

He wondered for a moment how many lives Lucca had saved. Could be dozens. Could be just one. It didn't matter. They were putting it to the enemy.

You have to think like a terrorist to outsmart one. It was something Willingham had been telling his students for years. And out here, after a couple of weeks in 120-degree heat, carrying eighty pounds of gear, it was becoming easier to plumb the thought processes of the bad guy.

The mission was simple: Find caches while clearing south on Gnat. Local word had it that someone with al-Qaeda was stashing weapons somewhere, no idea where. That afternoon Willingham was in the platoon that took the left side of the road. Another

platoon took the right. He didn't think there would be much to
find out on their side, with real estate limited by the Tigris,
which was only about a hundred feet away. But he kept his eyes
out for anything unusual—disrupted ground cover, stacks of
branches, whatever didn't fit. He couldn't send Lucca out to cover
the whole area. She'd be exhausted in no time. He had to use her
senses wisely. So he ramped up his.

A klick or so down Route Gnat, in an empty field area dotted
with litter, he spotted a tree with something white hanging off a
branch. It could have been just a piece of trash. Or maybe something else. Willingham explained his suspicions to a soldier later
that day.

"Imagine," Willingham said, "an al-Qaeda guy says to his
friend, 'Hey, Bob, I buried a cache. If you go by Joe's house you'll
see a white sack tied in a tree by the Tigris River. Go halfway
between the tree and the river, and dig.'"

The rag or old rice sack or whatever was hanging from the
branch could be an insurgent's version of a treasure hunt. The
tree was about a hundred feet away, only a few feet from the Tigris. Willingham broke off and walked to it with Lucca. It wasn't
a field where IEDs would typically be planted—there would be
no reason to waste a good IED in a place troops would never
walk. But he was glad Lucca was there to make sure.

When they got close, he let Lucca have free range. She
walked to the tree, sniffed, went over a small bank down to the
river, then moved back to another area near the tree. She searched
for a couple of minutes, then turned toward Willingham, tail
wagging. He hadn't called her, but she walked right to his side,
sat down, and looked up. If he hadn't known better, he would
have thought his dog was just happy to see him and wanted to be

petted. But this wasn't Lucca's style out here. So he got out his e-tool shovel and dug into the area almost right under his feet. It was protocol to call in EOD, but he was 99 percent sure there wouldn't be an IED. A few inches down, he came to something hard. He cleared away the dirt with his gloved hand. Black metal, and some sort of trigger mechanism.

"Score one for Lucca! Gooooood girl; that's my Lucca Bear!" He radioed for assistance and tossed her a Kong.

A half hour later, five DShK Soviet heavy machine guns lay in the middle of Route Gnat, bent, flattened, the lives snuffed out of them, courtesy of a Bradley. Willingham looked at the machine guns and smiled. Bob would be in for some disappointment when he came a-calling for these weapons.

THE FIELD WAS so dry and dead looking that Willingham couldn't imagine anything had ever been able to grow in it. There were no irrigation canals nearby, and the soil looked like it had formed into rocklike clumps. There wasn't a sign of life as he and Lucca swept the field for weapons caches. A few minutes into the search, he thought he saw something moving out of the corner of his eye. He looked toward it, and in the distance, he saw three low figures moving. They got closer.

He could now see what was approaching: dogs. Two from the left, one head-on. They were all medium-size, tan, a little on the thin side, with a hungry look. They walked slowly, cautiously, stopping to sniff the air, to assess the situation. Clearly strays— alive only by intelligence and guile. This was no place to be a stray. But other than the occasional dog tied up in a courtyard to protect a compound, local dogs could be counted on to be strays.

Willingham thought it wasn't quite the right word. "Stray" implies that you've strayed from something or someone. These dogs had nothing to stray from. It was a rough life, usually a short life. The dogs were tough, or at least smart, or they would already be dead. He felt bad for them.

He figured Lucca, who was quite a bit larger than any of them, could hold her own if one of the strays tried anything. But she might not be a match for all three of them. More than that, he was concerned that they could pass on a disease or a parasite. Besides rabies, Willingham couldn't remember the exact names of the transmissible diseases or what they did. But rabies was more than enough. He knew from veterinary briefings that rabies was far from rare in dogs in these rural areas. In the year 2007, there would be twenty-two cases of human rabies from dog bites in Iraq. Willingham realized dogs were in more danger than humans when it came to getting bitten by a dog, and he figured the incidence of rabies in dogs was probably a good deal higher.

You don't have to get bitten to be in danger. Rabies is spread in saliva. An act as innocent as a lick from a rabid animal could transmit the deadly disease. Even though Lucca was vaccinated, the vaccines aren't 100 percent effective. A vet would have to revaccinate her and monitor her for clinical signs. Willingham wanted to keep Lucca safe.

The dogs were within seventy feet now. Willingham yelled for them to go away and thrust his body forward for effect. The dogs stopped for a moment and proceeded more cautiously, their gaits a little slower, heads a little lower. Back at Lackland, he had been warned to be prepared to shoot some dogs. His reaction was simply, "I'm a dog handler. I ain't going to shoot no dogs!" But now that he was out here, he realized some dogs were otherwise uncontrollable threats. He had to do whatever it took to protect Lucca.

Still, even now, he didn't want to have to kill any of these dogs. Thus the load of rocks he'd tucked away in a large cargo pocket on his right leg. He hoped they'd take the hint. He figured that if he aimed well, he could drive the dogs away and that would be that. He reached in and took aim. He didn't want to hit the dogs, just come close.

"Go away, dogs!" He threw half a dozen, one after the other. The dogs got the message. They turned and trotted away. They didn't look scared. More like they decided it just wasn't worth it. This guy was just too annoying.

As they retreated into the distance, one, a male, slowed and looked over his shoulder at Lucca, then joined the others. Lucca, who had been standing next to Willingham the whole time, watched until he disappeared.

"Do you like that guy, Mama Lucca? He's no good for you."

She studied him as he spoke. She seemed to take interest in new words directed at her, as if she was trying to learn the language.

"You miss your boyfriend? We'll see Cooper soon—don't worry."

Her ears pivoted almost imperceptibly. That was a name embedded in her vocabulary.

THE NEXT MORNING, Lucca seemed especially anxious to get to work. She walked faster than usual, with a little more spring than was normal for her in this heat. They approached Route Gnat and she slowed. Willingham could see her looking at something in the distance. He followed her gaze. A dog. A yellow dog, drinking water from a bottle being held by a soldier.

"Korrrrryyyyyy! Coopaloop!"

Lucca ran over to them—it was a cleared area—and the two handlers exchanged man hugs and the two dogs did their do-si-do, tails wagging.

"Your boyfriend's back, Lucca!"

The dogs played in their usual puppy fashion as Willingham and Wiens caught up in quick exchanges. They didn't have much time. The platoons they were supporting were getting under way. Wiens and Cooper were going to be sweeping one side of Route Gnat, Willingham and Lucca the other. High fives, "See you down the road," and they were off.

They passed each other a few times during the missions. There was no time for conversation, but they jammed a fist to the air whenever they crossed paths.

"K-9!"

"All the way!"

"Better believe it!"

Willingham liked the soldiers he was supporting. They had fun together and had formed friendships. But when you're K-9, there's nothing like being with another dog team on a mission. Dog teams don't often get to go on missions with each other. They head off with strangers. Some will become friends over time, but not much holds a candle to being with someone who speaks dog. The K-9 experience was so integral to Willingham that even after he graduated from Wayland Baptist University in 2005 with a bachelor's degree in management, he didn't try to become an officer. That would have meant leaving any kind of hands-on K-9 work, and he couldn't imagine that. It was the same for Knight, who graduated alongside him with a bachelor's in education.

Handlers in some areas can go weeks without seeing other handlers. It can be lonely for those who are better with dogs than with people and find it hard to make new friends. That wasn't the case for Willingham or Wiens, but just running into each other was a bright spot.

Lucca seemed equally pleased to see Cooper. She wagged at him across the road when they passed. But she was wearing her harness, so she didn't linger.

"WILLINGHAM, COULD YOU come over here and sweep?"

He looked up. An eight-foot-deep, eight-foot-wide canal separated him from the platoon sergeant who asked for his help. The canal had about two feet of murky water in it. Nothing he wanted to touch if he didn't have to.

He'd been sweeping for caches on one side of the canal and wouldn't be surprised if there were some weapons stashed on the other side. But how to get from Point A to Point B? It would be a good klick away to the next crossing point. Too far. He was getting used to canals but wasn't a fan. They were everywhere, transporting water to more arid areas. He and Lucca had crossed dozens. They walked across drier ones that weren't too big. They leapt over smaller ones. Twice, at night, he miscalculated the distance and fell short. Lucca looked at him from dry land and wagged.

"Don't laugh, Lucca. You could be next!" he said as he stood up, pant legs dripping, hands covered in mud.

But this was the daddy of all the canals he'd seen so far. His only chance of making this work was to walk on a ten-inch-wide corrugated metal pipe that crossed the canal. Its top was just an inch or so lower than the top of the canal. He was pretty sure-footed, but he knew Lucca couldn't walk on it herself. There was only one way to do it. He hoped that Lucca would be as gracious about being carried now as she had been in the past. A wiggle or squirm at the wrong time would send them plunging eight feet.

"Mama Lucca, you want to go for a little ride?"

She was panting, not too hard, but even the panting could throw him off if he wasn't careful. He reached down and scooped her into his arms. As soon as he had her balanced in the crooks of his bent elbows, she relaxed. She reminded him of a sack of potatoes. A seventy-five-pound sack of potatoes.

"Good girl, Lucca. Hold steady," he said.

He carefully sidestepped onto the pipe with his right boot and brought his left boot close to it.

Several soldiers on both sides had gathered to watch.

"C'mon, Marine!"

He inched out his right foot, then left, right, left. He felt the curve of the pipe move under his boot, and he swayed a little as he got his footing back.

He continued the slow sideways march. Right . . . left . . . right . . . left. . . . Lucca was so still he couldn't even feel her panting. Right . . . left. . . . Right foot touched land, then left. He exhaled. He set Lucca down gently on terra firma, and she shook as she would after a bath. The soldiers on that side came over and petted her head, and praised her.

"That's one calm dog you got there," the platoon sergeant said. "You two ready to get to work?"

"Always."

He had been working more than was called for—beyond helping out when Lucca needed to rest. He was starting to take chances that he knew she shouldn't have been taking. Something in him had shifted at some point. He didn't know when. It could have been the KIAs he'd heard about, where guys had gotten blown up so badly that nothing recognizable was left to send home. Or just seeing the destruction one IED can cause and knowing that he and Lucca could do something about it.

While sweeping an area on the banks of the Tigris a few days earlier, Willingham discovered some sinkholes, formed by the erosion and collapse of the upper layer of ground along the river, most likely during rainy season. The ground was a mixture of dirt and sand, and he could see how it would be easy for excess rain drainage to cause changes in this soft environment. A couple of the holes were large enough that a person could crawl in, and seemed pretty deep. When he looked into them with a flashlight, they appeared to go straight down at least ten feet, and then curve off in another direction. They reminded him of gopher tunnels, but a lot bigger.

Only Lucca and his security guy were near. He sent Lucca forward. She sniffed around, and one hole drew her attention. She looked at it for a couple of seconds and wagged, although not in the usual enthusiastic "It's right here!" manner. The wag had more of a slow, "I think I detect something but it's not that strong" lilt to it. Finding nothing obvious around the hole, and seeing nothing when he shined his flashlight in, Willingham decided to check it out himself.

He knew it was crazy to go into the hole. He would have told his students never to do anything like this. But, as with the area where they'd found the weapons near the tree, this wasn't a place where IEDs were prevalent. Digging gingerly around the dirt as he had done at the tree was one thing—bad enough. Going headfirst into a deep hole was another. Stupid, he knew. But . . . there might be weapons down there that would later be used to kill good people, and good dogs.

He got on his knees and made his way down the hole. The gritty sand and rock lining the sides allowed him to dig in with his gloves and boots. He slowly, methodically crawled his way down, bracing himself against the sides so he wouldn't lose control and slip down. A few feet in, the sides of the hole became wetter, muddy, with less sand in the mix, making his grip more tenuous. He could feel the dampness as it soaked into his gloves. He had to be extra careful.

After about twelve feet of descent, the hole leveled off for a foot or two and ended. He was struck by the strong earthy smell. It reminded him of old dirt-floor basements back home. He pulled his flashlight from where he had tucked it into a hip pocket and looked around. The level area would have been a perfect hiding place for weapons, as long as they were wrapped in plastic. All he could think was that someone had already come and taken away the cache.

He slowly backed his way up the hole. A lot tougher than going down. He emerged, muddy and wet.

Lucca stayed sitting next to the hole, just watching him. He got the impression she did not approve.

"WHO OWNS THE house?" the interpreter asked the young Iraqi man standing outside a shack about the size of a trailer. Near him was a faded sign with a television on it. "TV repair," Willingham heard someone say.

"My cousin. I'm just staying here, doing some work."

Willingham and Lucca had been searching another compound and had arrived here after a squad had set up security and searched the place. There was nothing to do except wait until the squad had wrapped things up.

Willingham was not fond of being idle.

"Can my dog and I check it out?" he asked the platoon sergeant.

"No, we have it covered. We've searched. It's clean."

"I don't mind," Willingham said. "We'll just do a quick sweep."

"OK."

They entered the one-room structure. It was tiny, worn-out looking. This wouldn't take long. Lucca went to work. Down the left side was a bed, then a sort of workbench against the wall. The bench was covered with a blue tablecloth that draped onto the floor. Lucca sniffed past the bed, walked right up to the bench, stuck her nose under the tablecloth, and sat.

"Good girl, Lucca! Nice work!" He paid her with a Kong.

He went back outside to talk to the sergeant. "Lucca had a response in there, back on the left side under the bench with the tablecloth."

A couple of soldiers came back in with them, lifted up the tablecloth, and found a cardboard box against the wall. They pulled it out and saw that it was packed full of IED-making materials. Cell phone pieces, wires, cords. Lots of them. This wasn't stuff you repair TVs or cell phones with.

They went back outside with the soldiers. The man was still standing there with them. He looked at Lucca, then at the soldiers. He started to glisten. Actually, to sweat. Willingham wondered if word among insurgents was that even worse than seeing a military dog enter your house was seeing a military dog sit in your house.

"Sir, who owns the house?" the interpreter asked again.

"I don't know whose house it is. I have no idea what they do in there. I'm just sleeping there."

"Please hold out your hand."

A soldier wiped a swab across his palm to check for explosives residue. Willingham wasn't close enough to see the result on the swab kit, but since they restrained the man with Flex-Cuffs and surrounded him with soldiers, it was clear. Once again, Lucca had nailed the enemy.

BOOM! BOOM!

Not again. Willingham rolled over in his cot.

"Incoming, incoming, incoming!"

He opened his eyes and looked over at Wiens, who was just stirring in his cot several feet away. He could see him clearly in the light of the nearly full moon of oh dark-thirty. They were both back at FOB Falcon at the same time, overlapping there for a day, enjoying the relative comforts of "home." Cooper stood up as the sirens wailed. He was used to the routine. Big booms, go to crowded bunker, smell sweaty soldiers, get lots of attention. Lucca lifted her head, looked around, and went back to sleep.

"What d'ya think? We go to the bunkers or we stay?" Wiens asked, sleep still clogging his voice.

"I'm worn out, man. I don't wanna move. How 'bout you?"

"Same."

"Screw the alarm. We sleep!"

They woke up at dawn.

"Well, we still got all our arms and legs," Willingham said. "Glad we stayed."

"Me, too."

Their return to Patrol Base Murray brought no respite. Murray had recently become a target for mortars and rockets. Sometimes bombs would hit one after another for hours. The rise of these insurgent attacks had happened quickly. So far there had been no injuries from the blasts, but they knew that if something wasn't done . . . it was like playing Russian roulette—only with larger-caliber ammo.

One morning, Willingham and Wiens were called to attend a meeting at the former Hussein house that was now HQ for the outpost. The purpose of the meeting was to figure out what to do about the indirect fire the outpost had been receiving. The handlers realized they must have made something of a name for themselves to be called into a meeting like this. Some officers and a few platoon leaders had gathered in a room with a large map of the Patrol Base Murray area on the wall. After a little discussion, the handlers were asked if they had any ideas based on their specialty.

"There's no way that an insurgent's going to walk or drive up with mortar, carry it to where he needs to launch it, leave, and do it again later," Willingham told them. "It's got to be buried out there somewhere." And Willingham knew who could find it.

Together, based on the trajectories of previous mortars, they figured out the approximate location a stash must be from the base, and they asked Willingham and Wiens to help set up the mission.

"If you used both dogs, how would you do it?" someone asked.

They came up with a plan to find the caches.

The next day at about 0400, they briefed the platoon and set out on foot. They quickly found themselves in forests of grass that grew up past their heads. It was a surprising contrast to the dry, lifeless landscape of Patrol Base Murray, just a few minutes away. The platoon passed a line of what looked in the dark like deciduous trees of some sort and came to a clearing of scrub and low grass. They stopped there and waited until dawn. It was only half a klick from the northern edge of Patrol Base Murray, but it felt worlds removed. Willingham and Wiens took off their packs and sat next to each other on a long slab of concrete to wait for sunrise. The dogs lay down at their feet.

The quiet struck Willingham. There was no sound other than dogs barking in the distance and some low radio chatter. He and Wiens talked in hushed tones about the mission, BS'd a little, and just sat, taking in the scene. It was a bright night, and they could see the Tigris—flanked by healthy-looking medium-size palm trees—snaking by a hundred feet away. As darkness faded into light, a voice singing on a loudspeaker burst into the tranquility. It was the call to morning prayer, Fajr, from a nearby village. Willingham recognized only the word *Allah*. But this Muslim prayer song, combined with the view of the Tigris at dawn, the palm trees, the amazing dogs and handler beside him, and the fact that he and Wiens had proven themselves and were asked to lead this mission—it all settled into him. It was a memory in the making. "At that moment, it was all of Iraq in one scene," he would later recount.

Sunrise. Time to move out. He put on his pack, called Lucca, fist-bumped Wiens.

"Good luck, man."

They each took two squads. Dogs off leash in front, then

handlers, then soldiers with metal detectors, then guys pulling security—everyone vigilant, looking for visual signs of where caches could be hidden, while the dogs led with their noses. The best senses of man and dog working together.

Wiens and his squads went off to the left, Willingham's squads to the right. They moved through their sections in a serpentine pattern that let them cover the area most efficiently. It would be easy to hide something in here. Left and right they looped, into clearings and back into grasses.

No finds. Nothing.

Willingham wondered if they could have been wrong. But he couldn't fathom terrorists lugging heavy mortars through this area when stealth was everything. They pushed on.

The two groups looped left, right, always moving forward. Sometimes they met in the middle when their patterns converged. About forty-five minutes into the mission, they happened to come together at a point that was clear, with a ditch, a natural drop-off of dirt about three feet deep. The two handlers both felt something was different here. It looked easier to access. They agreed to break down this area more carefully, each taking half of it.

They stopped to water the dogs. Lucca didn't pay much attention to Cooper. She'd been with him on and off for hours, and besides, she had her harness on. Cooper approached her in play mode, but all it took to stop him was a *not now* look. He drank up dutifully and set to work with Wiens.

Ten minutes later, Willingham heard radios going off. He heard his security guy talking. Something about Wiens.

"The other dog has responded positively to something."

They walked over quickly and Wiens filled him in, showing

him what Cooper had bracketed and wagged about. It was a four-foot-tall, ten-foot-wide erosion on the side of a natural drop-off in the land. Like a cave, but short and shallow. Potentially a good hiding place for bombs. Dirt on the bottom was loose, as if it had been recently disturbed. Several soldiers set up a large perimeter, eyes focused, weapons set to protect anyone within the circle. The two soldiers with metal detectors came over and swiftly narrowed in on the same small area. Willingham imagined their headphones must have been filled with beeps, because they converged quickly at the same spot.

Two more soldiers dug in—carefully, just in case. Six inches down, they hit something hard. They swept away the dirt with their hands. A curved, darkened metal surface emerged. A mortar round. They kept digging. Several more. Enough to do some serious damage. As a soldier walked around looking for signs of other caches, his boot pushed through the ground. The guys with the metal detectors checked it out. Others dug and discovered a drum containing a cache of about eight mortars.

After that, there were no more finds.

"I think we wiped out those suckers!" the platoon sergeant said.

"They'll have to go shopping for more at the mortar store," a young soldier said, laughing.

While they hadn't unearthed a treasure trove of bombs, they'd probably found all there was. They did the math and came up with a rough estimate of how many lives they may have saved by finding the mortars. None of the figures agreed with the others, but they were all more than one. It had been a worthwhile expedition.

For the rest of the day, Lucca and Cooper were happy recipients of high fives, head rubs, and firm side pats. The soldiers told them that if they had steaks, they'd give them some. But they had only MREs.

"You and Cooper need to go up and celebrate in style," Willingham told Wiens. "Why don't you take off for Falcon for the Fourth? I'll hold down the fort with Lucca; then she and I'll head up when you come back."

Wiens couldn't say no. The idea of a big barbecue on the Fourth of July was too appealing to turn down. He'd grown up celebrating the Fourth in the small-town traditional way. It would be a little piece of home at FOB Falcon. Of course, Wiens loved the idea of steak, or anything that wasn't an MRE. A shower would be good, too. Mostly, he wanted to talk to his dad. It had been too long. He didn't want him to worry. Having two out of three sons in a war couldn't be easy. He'd reassure him, let him know how great Cooper was doing, that he had nothing to worry about.

Willingham was glad he accepted so readily. The Fourth of July didn't seem like the best holiday to spend at an outpost like Murray, which was a magnet for mortars. Their recent mission had quashed mortar attacks for the last day or so, but insurgents were sure to be making new plans. He didn't let Wiens know that this was the main reason he suggested he go up, or the kid probably wouldn't have left.

On July 4, the soldiers at Patrol Base Murray enjoyed a surprise barbecue. No MREs that afternoon. Command had sent for a couple of grills, and everyone lined up for burgers and bags of chips. Lucca's nostrils sniffed the air, her nose moving rapidly left and right as they passed one soldier after another with their burgers. Several threw her bits of meat, and she didn't miss one.

It was a fine Independence Day of life's simple pleasures: eating, relaxing, talking, and downing Rip Its. That's all anyone wanted to do, with the highs that day reaching more than 120 degrees. The men were just happy that al-Qaeda didn't contribute any fireworks.

Late in the morning of July 6, Willingham and Lucca returned from a mission and found Wiens and Cooper had arrived back from their getaway. He looked well rested and seemed especially happy.

"I talked to my dad," Wiens told Willingham. "He was in his cement truck."

"How's he doing?"

"Good! I think he really misses me. I gotta call him more often."

"Did you tell him about Coopaloop?"

"Oh yeah! I bragged, of course."

"Who wouldn't?"

"He's glad he's watching out for me."

Willingham filled him in on what he knew about the upcoming afternoon mission Wiens would be going on with Cooper. It was the usual, mostly looking for caches. There was no intel suggesting anything crazy. Willingham was glad. Wiens had only a few more days on this rotation before flying back to FOB Kalsu, where the situation wasn't nearly as volatile. Not that it was a bed of roses, but it wasn't a field of IEDs either. Much as Willingham would miss him, and Lucca might miss Cooper, he was relieved that they were going to make it out of here.

But this wasn't the time for big good-byes. He and Lucca

would be at FOB Falcon for only a couple of days and would return a day or two before Wiens was to leave on a helicopter to
FOB Kalsu.

Willingham and Lucca loaded onto the Humvee.

"Catch you later, man."

"K-9!"

"K-9!"

As they drove away, Willingham watched through the road
dust as Wiens threw the flabby football for Cooper. The two running, joyous figures faded into the distance and disappeared.

6

KIA Together

"SERGEANT!" THE BREATHLESS soldier called to Willingham as he was entering his tent at Falcon after dinner that evening and about to let Lucca out of her kennel. "The patrol Kory was on was hit by an IED. It doesn't look good."

A sense of numb panic, a sick surge, gripped Willingham.

"They're missing two right now, and there's some guys wounded. We don't know anything else."

Willingham hurried to the ops center behind the soldier. He was surprised he could move. His limbs felt like lead.

The soldiers manning the ops center filled him in.

"We got two missing. Wiens and Salazar, the security guy."

He maintained his composure, solemn, strong, tough, as they waited for more news. Nothing got in his way of being a marine on the outside. Especially as the only marine at this whole damned FOB. He was glad they couldn't see what was going on inside him.

The soldier monitoring the secure line between Patrol Base Murray and FOB Falcon kept them up-to-date as he got word on the situation.

"They've sent out a helicopter."

I should have stayed. I should have been the one out there.

Ten minutes that seemed like hours later, more news.

"They've found what was left of the dog."

Cooper, no . . .

"They've located the victims. PFC Bruce Salazar. PFC Kory Wiens. They were KIA immediately, during a mission near Muhammad Sath."

"I'm sorry, Staff Sergeant."

Willingham walked back to his tent. *Their* tent. Wiens had just been here a few hours ago.

He let Lucca out of her kennel as he looked around the tent. Wiens's belongings were everywhere. Freshly folded clothing lay across his cot. His well-worn running shoes peeked out from under his cot. Cooper's "extra" toys lay in the last spot the dog had been playing with them.

The force of the blow hit him, and he couldn't stand anymore. He sat on the plywood floor and broke down. Silent weeping, building up inside for the last hour, now still silent—he didn't want anyone to hear him.

Lucca's eyes fixed on him, and her dark brows pushed together. She walked over, lay down close to him, and put her head on his lap. She had never seen him or anyone like this before, and her ears sank low.

"Lucca, it should have been me out there. Not him. I had

only one dog team to bring home safely, and I couldn't even do that."

Lucca, the devoted marine, stayed at his side the rest of the afternoon.

EARLIER THAT DAY, at a Department of Defense news briefing, Major General Rick Lynch, commander, Multinational Division Center and Third Infantry Division, updated media on Operation Marne Torch via a teleconference from Iraq.

At the end of questioning by reporters from NBC, CNN, Reuters, and other news outlets, he thanked them for what they do to keep the public informed about the war. And then he digressed slightly.

> You know, on the 4th of July, I had the great opportunity to be involved in the re-enlistment ceremony and the citizenship ceremony for about 600 great Americans; 500-plus soldiers re-enlisted, almost 200 soldiers became American citizens, and by golly, I was so very proud to be part of that. And every day when I'm out and about wearing 60 pounds of body armor in 111-degree temperature, I re-enlist soldiers, and they raise their right hand and say, "I'll support and defend the Constitution of the United States against all enemies, foreign and domestic." And they're doing that between attacks, between memorial services, between mortar rounds coming in, so I just take such confidence in the fact that we got great Americans who have committed themselves to service to our nation, and I'd like you to have that same encouragement.

You know, it bothers me when people say the Army is on the verge of breaking. We'll never break because we've got great soldiers.

The reports on the incident laid out the event in the dispassionate manner of such documents:

Wiens was assigned to Bravo 1/30th infantry for the mission. The staff sergeant that Wiens was attached to for the mission received instructions for the dog team to search a nearby farm, which consisted of a walled compound that had suspicious holes dug around it. The squad picked up Wiens and Cooper at a nearby school and briefed them on the situation. They were to search that building. The dog had a possible find, which Wiens noted, but they all believed it was residual odor left over from something previous. The team moved to an open inner corral. He provided the dog water and a rest break. A detonation cord approximately two feet in length was discovered and identified by Wiens as a Yugoslavian det cord.

Wiens and Cooper continued their search of the compound. There were no hits from that area. Wiens dropped a training aid so the dog wouldn't get bored, and the dog played with a ball for a while. The staff sergeant told them to come back out. Wiens saw a haystack and sent Cooper to check it out, following him. That's when the IED was detonated. Wiens and Cooper were killed instantly and four others were injured. PFC Bruce Salazar, who was working security for the team, was also KIA. They were all wearing protective gear. It is believed the IED was detonated from a truck that was passing by on the road. It was either a cell phone detonation or command trigger.

They are the first military dog team known to be killed together since the beginning of the war.

THE SMELL—SICKLY sweet and chemical—hit Willingham as he entered the morgue at FOB Falcon with Lucca. It had been three days since the IED killed Wiens, Cooper, and Salazar. He had barely slept or eaten since. Sleep came for only an hour or so when it did. When he ventured out of his tent, soldiers would come up to him to pat him on the back and say they were so sorry. He wanted to keep upholding the image of a strong marine, but at the same time he wished there were other marines there, or another dog team. He might have opened up to them. Nice as everyone was being, no one asked him if he needed help, if he wanted to talk about it. He wouldn't have told them he did, because at the time he didn't realize it himself.

Lucca pulled on the leash to get out of the morgue. Unflappable in mortar attacks and firefights, she wanted to run out of this place. He didn't know if it was the pungent smell of morgue, or if maybe she detected, through all the strange morgue odors, the scent of Cooper's remains. He was zipped in a body bag on one of three nylon stretchers. Body bags containing Wiens and Salazar rested on the other two stretchers.

"It's OK, Lucca," Willingham told her in a gentle, weakened voice. "Hold on."

They were here to help send their friends home. Eleven soldiers joined them in the morgue to begin the Fallen Hero Ceremony. Everyone wore simple cammies, no gear, no weapon, no covers. Four men were assigned to each stretcher. Willingham got Wiens's. A nod of the head, and the first four lifted Salazar's stretcher and exited the morgue. Willingham's right hand gripped a metal handle in the front. He held Lucca's leash in his left. He and three soldiers lifted the stretcher and followed. Cooper's stretcher was carried out last.

This was the last time Willingham would walk with his friend. He tried not to feel anything as they made their way to the flight line—a hundred yards. Two Black Hawks were waiting. A chaplain said some words, and the soldiers were loaded on, Salazar in the first Black Hawk and Wiens and Cooper together in the second.

The men who had carried the stretchers walked back to a line of another dozen soldiers who had come out for the ceremony. They stood in formation. As the helicopters rose, Willingham stood at attention, per marine tradition. The soldiers saluted and stayed that way until the helicopters were out of sight. Lucca, calm again, just sat and took it all in.

THE SUN WAS low, and the evening comfortable. The way the birds were singing, if you closed your eyes you could be in a lush English garden having tea. Palm trees rustled in the light breeze behind the concrete T-walls. But the memorial at FOB Kalsu on July 12 for Corporal Kory D. Wiens—he had received a posthumous promotion—brought little comfort to Willingham. He listened to officers and his kennel master from Slayer talk about what a great soldier, handler, and man Wiens was, and what a perfect team he made with Cooper. But as he sat in his folding chair, one thought would not leave him.

I'm the one who got him killed. This wonderful person everyone loved, I'm responsible for his death. I'm the reason they're all here.

The firing of volleys, then "Taps" played from a recording—the ceremony brought tears almost all around.

Willingham sat by Knight—one of many handlers flown in for the memorial. They faced a little bench that held the usual heartbreaking downrange memorial arrangement—combat boots, a helmet, flags, a Purple Heart, and a photo of Wiens and Cooper. Willingham's weight loss was noticeable to Knight. He was worried about him. After the memorial, Willingham told Knight about his guilt, how he couldn't shake it and didn't think he ever deserved to get rid of it—an albatross he tied to his own neck.

"You didn't do anything wrong. You did not get him killed," Knight tried his best to reassure him. "There's nothing you can do about it. It was God's will. Every person that was that perfect always dies. Like God comes and says, 'OK, you pass, come on up!'"

Willingham looked at him and nodded.

"You know," Knight continued, looking up to the darkening sky, "I'm always gonna keep some little part of me a sinner."

OF THE THIRTY-SEVEN dogs lined up outside the Faith Evangelical Free Church in Dallas, Oregon, on July 18, not one barked, growled, or whined as they stood at their handlers' sides during the ninety-minute service in Wiens's hometown. To Danielle Roche, it seemed like the dogs—army, navy, air force, marines, and police—knew what they were here for and were paying their last respects to a fellow dog and his handler.

Roche had been back home on a short R & R break in Texas when she got the phone call. She felt as if someone had gut punched her, leaving her with no breath. She collapsed into a chair. The next days were a blur of phone calls, travel arrangements, and raw emptiness. She spoke at a memorial at Fort Leonard Wood, and now she was here, in front of this packed church, in her Class A uniform. She looked out at Wiens's father and brothers—one brother could have been his twin—and had to pause to collect herself as she finished her eulogy.

"Corporal Wiens always consistently wanted to be a better soldier and person even if the road was long and narrow. I never discovered why he was so hungry. I never discovered what he was so hungry for, or why he pushed himself so hard, but this was Corporal Wiens. He pushed himself to be the best. He wanted to be the best. If you know Corporal Wiens and think about the way he was, you'd realize that this was the way he was in all aspects of his life. . . .

"It's very reassuring to know that Wiens and Cooper are together, and continue to dance in heaven. May God bless Corporal Wiens and Cooper."

THE CREMATED REMAINS of Wiens and Cooper were buried together at Salt Creek Cemetery after a last ride with a long police entourage and the Patriot Guard Riders escorting them on motorcycles. Wiens's father was given a small box containing some of the ashes from his son and Cooper, mixed together as he requested, "because they were inseparable in life and in death," he said. He brought them home with him and placed them in a special memorial cabinet in the living room of his double-wide trailer, so he could be with them every day.

FOB FALCON HAD never felt so lonely to Willingham, even back in those first days when he was the only dog handler. Wiens's belongings had been inventoried and cleared out of the tent shortly after he died. Willingham happened to be there when the lieutenant came in to do the job. He helped out. As Willingham called out his friend's personal belongings, the lieutenant documented them on a form.

"Three T-shirts."

Check.

"Five pairs of socks."

Check.

"Seven dog toys."

He paused, took a breath.

Check.

Other than Cooper's toys, the rest of the items could have been almost anyone's, so he tried not to think about whose they were. All the photos and videos Willingham had taken were on disks, so he didn't have to face them. The belongings inventoried, they were locked up, tagged, and prepared to ship home.

And now there were two new handlers here. Good guys, but they weren't Wiens and Cooper. He had to help the handlers get up to speed. He had them train on local odors, gave them tips on the best search techniques for what lay ahead. He checked out how they worked in real scenarios.

He was lonelier than ever.

One handler froze when he ventured outside the wire with Willingham, not far from where Wiens had been killed. His dog waited for him, but the guy couldn't move. It was as if his boots were made of iron and the earth under him was a strong magnet. The only way he could proceed was if Willingham led the way to the objective, telling him to step where he was stepping. And even then, the handler was sweating.

He had passed the validation process at Baghdad, but that was a controlled situation, no real IEDs, no chance of death. The ultimate test was outside the wire. Most handlers couldn't wait to get out. Every handler was supposed to be ready. But it wasn't for everyone. Willingham was glad that FOBs also needed handlers inside the gate checking vehicles.

The other dog team was strong, ready to go. But Willingham didn't want that dog or handler going out, either. He was driven by the idea that he would not let anyone get hurt again.

Knight had told him, "It's not your fault. You did nothing wrong." He repeated the sentences in his head, but they were just words. They didn't change emotional realities. Instead of sending the strong dog team off on missions they were fully capable of handling, he tried to take many of them himself. There was always a reason. He had to get Lucca back up to speed after being idle for a while. Or there was some stuff on this mission he'd seen before and he needed to be the one to deal with it. He sent them out on a few easy missions, with trepidation, and was relieved when they came back unscathed.

After Wiens died, Willingham wanted to put it to al-Qaeda more than ever, and this section of the Triangle of Death was providing plenty of opportunity. It felt good to keep busy. Focusing on bombs prevented him from going to dark places, at least while he was out there. On missions, he was like Lucca, completely attuned to the surroundings. He was one with the mission, one with Lucca.

But then the orders came in. He was to leave FOB Falcon for a month and go to FOB Kalsu, where Wiens had been based before coming up to FOB Falcon and Patrol Base Murray. They had been counting on Wiens coming back and needed another handler. From what Wiens had told him, the action down there had been nothing compared to what was going on with Operation Marne Torch. Willingham felt like someone was taking pity on him, giving him an easy rotation. It was the opposite of what he wanted.

As he packed up his and Lucca's gear, anger welled up in him. He didn't want a break. He wanted to be where the action was, where he and Lucca could do what they needed to do. As if reading his thoughts, Lucca came and sat down next to the cot, where he was folding the Marine Corps flag into a small square so it wouldn't get wrinkled in his duffel. She stared at him, eyes calm and steady. He relaxed a little.

"OK, Lucca. Got it, ma'am. Charlie Mike—continue mission."

7

The Way Back

"ONE MINUTE OUT!" the Chinook pilot yelled to the crewman above the engine noise and *whop-whop-whop* of the twin rotors.

"One minute out!" the crewman shouted to the two soldiers closest to him. The soldiers, sitting in two rows facing each other along the sides of the bird, shouted the time alert down the line. The helicopter was flying blacked out, no lights inside or out, so the soldiers could see each other only through their night-vision goggles (NVGs), making everyone look bright green.

"Ten seconds!" the crewman yelled. No time for anyone else to yell. The closest soldier put his hand on the knee of the next, who put his hand on the knee of the next, and the chain reaction went to the end within a few seconds.

The Chinook touched down hard in the farm field. Thirty

soldiers from the 501st Airborne Infantry Regiment jolted, got their legs, and poured out into the night.

This was the first air assault mission for Willingham and Lucca. He adjusted her Doggles over her eyes, held her leather leash looped in his hand, and tried to keep her out of everyone's way while holding his M4, running down the ramp, and bolting over the uneven field through the dust and debris kicked up by the rotors. He and Lucca fanned out to their position. They had practiced this dozens of times. He'd lie down quickly on his stomach and keep his weapon at the ready, and she'd lie low right beside him.

But as he was going prone, he felt the smooth leather yank out of his hand. He realized the rotor wash must have spooked Lucca. He looked frantically around through the cloud of rapidly spiraling dirt and debris and caught sight of Lucca running away. He called to her, but the noise from the helicopter lifting off drowned him out. Within seconds all he could see was the infra-red Cyalume ChemLight he'd attached to her harness. Its white-green glow was visible only through NVGs, and he watched it get smaller until it disappeared. His eyes desperately searched the green horizon for any clue of her whereabouts.

"All right, K-9, let's go over here!" the squad leader called as some of the soldiers were forming up after the bird flew off.

Willingham couldn't just go up to him and say, "I'm the new dog handler here, but funny thing—I don't have a dog. She just ran off in the middle of Iraq on my first mission with you guys." What to do?

"OK, K-9, you up?"

He didn't want to think of what could happen to Lucca, alone in hostile territory. At least the enemy couldn't see her Chem-

Light, as long as they weren't wearing NVGs. But no way he was leaving her out there by herself. He jogged over to tell the squad leader what was going on, to admit his error, but the guy was busy talking to a couple of soldiers.

Willingham couldn't take his eyes off the spot where he had last seen Lucca. He thought he saw something move. A speck, almost a mist, then a tiny white-green glow, now moving up and down. He held his breath. Under the glow of the ChemLight on top of her harness, he made out the shape of Lucca about two hundred feet away, nose down, tracking her way back to him.

"Lucca! Come!"

She lifted her head, looked toward where she heard his voice, and dashed straight to Willingham. As he bent down to hug her and stroke her head, she wagged so hard that her entire hind end wiggled, just like when they'd first met. She was panting hard.

"I feel exactly the same, Mama Lucca," he said, and he praised her up for coming back. She briefly stopped panting, came close to his face, and seemed like she was going to plant one on his cheek. But not being a big kisser, she refrained and went back to panting.

He vowed that from then on, he would attach her leash to a carabiner on his vest before air assault missions. Chinooks for Dog Handlers 101. He'd have to pass that little tip to other handlers.

The whole incident had taken maybe two minutes. Two long, long minutes. No one else had even noticed what happened. He grabbed her leash and reported for duty.

WHEN WILLINGHAM ARRIVED at FOB Kalsu the previous day, he could see immediately that this was nothing like the "give the poor guy a break" venue he'd been dreading. The place was alive with missions coming and going.

A new operation—Marne Avalanche—was getting under way here. The area around FOB Kalsu was similar to Arab Jabour before Marne Torch: an al-Qaeda refuge laced with weapons caches, protected by IEDs, and with very little military intervention for months. And it was within the Triangle of Death.

Just the kind of territory Willingham wanted.

Instead of doing the kind of clearance ops they had done along Route Gnat, he learned that most of his and Lucca's work would involve nighttime air assaults, targeting people or places intel showed to be important to al-Qaeda. Chinooks would do fast offloads a few klicks from an objective, and then he, Lucca, and the soldiers would walk in formation, usually through farm fields, to get there.

The fields had proven safe from IEDs, since they were far off the beaten path. So Willingham and Lucca would search roadways only at points where the soldiers would cross over, and other areas along the way where there could be a danger of explosives. They'd all arrive at the objective with an element of surprise, and dirty boots. Once there, he and Lucca would search exteriors and interiors of compounds and afterward make sure there were no newly planted IEDs on the way back to the Chinook pickup area—which was never the same as the drop-off, just in case.

There would be no tent mates here. No tent, even. He and Lucca had their own containerized housing unit, CHU. Four walls, a bed, and a little desk and chair. It was little more than a shipping container made livable, with a couple of small windows. But the living area felt absolutely luxurious compared with Patrol Base Murray and was a step up from FOB Falcon.

Since missions usually lasted several hours, not days, he was at the FOB more than he'd been at Falcon. He got to talk to Jill regularly and kept in touch with Knight. Part of him wanted to talk to them about how he continued to be haunted by the loss of Wiens and Cooper, how their deaths crept into his CHU at night and kept him awake, tormenting him with the what-ifs, causing him to imagine all the ways it could have ended differently, without sending them off in body bags.

He wanted to tell someone about the enormous guilt that clung to him. But he wouldn't be convinced it wasn't his fault, and Knight and Jill would try, so why bring it up?

He wondered if Lucca missed Cooper—if the scent in the morgue told her it was over, or if she was still waiting for him to come bounding through the door with a smile on his face and a flabby football in his mouth.

ANOTHER NIGHT OP starting. He was ready. Willingham and Lucca ran toward the compound door. She swiftly sniffed its seams. Nothing. They stepped to the side, and two soldiers behind them kicked down the door and entered the compound. Several soldiers followed, rifles drawn.

From outside, Willingham heard the commotion of the "hard knock" mission. He knew it well by now, after a couple of weeks of nighttime air assault missions for high-value targets, HVTs. The men they were seeking weren't the former teenage delinquents who planted IEDs and terrorized the locals. They were more the brains behind the insurgent operations—some in charge of IED production, others funding it, some coming up with intricate plans to foil, or destroy, coalition forces.

He bent down to pet Lucca as he heard the now familiar sounds: The soldiers who knew some basic Arabic shouting instructions to the home's occupants. The pounding footsteps of military-age males being separated from the others and led to an area outside the compound. The explanation of why they were here, the request to please cooperate. The women and children inside, some crying, the soldiers telling them in their limited Arabic—but mostly simply through a much gentler tone of voice— not to be scared. The interpreters helping with communications.

As soon as the people were secured in their areas, Lucca and Willingham set to work, searching each room for explosives. In these situations, the goods could be hidden in walls or even secret rooms. Tonight they found nothing, so they went back outside as others in his team started their detailed hand search of every room, looking for intel.

On this mission, they were after a man in his twenties who was responsible for the financial side of an IED-making operation. Willingham had been told after his search that none of the men here matched the photos of the man they were seeking. That meant hours of questioning of the others and intel inspections to see if they could determine where he was. And that meant a long night of nothing to do for Lucca and Willingham, whose job was over until they headed to where the Chinook would pick up the squads at the end of the mission.

He didn't like the waiting business. Never did, but especially not since Wiens had been killed. He wanted to keep busy, to use his and Lucca's time to stop the enemy before they could hurt anyone else. It would be at least three hours before the soldiers were done with the intel gathering. He looked at Lucca, who was lying down at his feet.

"Lucca, you want to find some weapons?"

She sprang up, wagging at a mellow clip, eyes cast up to his.

It would be too dangerous to search for weapons on their own, at night, on the property of a man known to be in deep with al-Qaeda. So he put together a four-man fire team. The soldiers were also happy to have something to do. They'd have his back while he focused on watching Lucca and guiding her by voice through the dark.

They started at the back side of the property, which led to a large farm field. The fire team was spread out about ten steps behind him. Lucca, off leash now, walked in front.

"Lucca, left!" Willingham didn't have to say it loudly. The sounds from the house had died down, and the night air was heavy and quiet. Lucca turned left and searched for about twenty yards.

"Lucca, right!" She changed directions. Her nose guided her through the rough, dry field, but she would have no problem seeing at night, since dogs have strong night vision. The humans on the mission had to wear NVGs to see. They all kept pushing ahead, angling across the field. Willingham doubted they'd find anything, but it was better than sitting around with nothing to do all night.

They were about twenty yards from a large canal when Willingham saw Lucca throw a change of behavior—and not the usual. Willingham didn't know what to make of it at first. He watched as she stopped and lowered her head, staring in the direction of the canal. He could almost hear her think.

What the hell is going on here?

To an onlooker, her behavior wouldn't seem like a big deal. Just a dog stopping and checking something out. But to Willingham, it was a red flag that she was onto something other than explosives.

It was a different game now. He leashed Lucca and quietly talked to his team.

"Hey, fellas, she's seeing something out here. We gotta be careful."

They took two more steps and Lucca stopped and lowered her head again—her ears were slightly back, her tail stiff and raised. She let out a low, menacing growl. Willingham had never heard anything like this from her. She had growled a couple of times when Iraqis were taunting her, but nothing like this. She looked like she was ready to attack if she needed to.

The fire team walked up to be in line with him and Lucca, rifles poised to protect the team from whatever lay ahead. Willingham walked forward with Lucca, who was still in an attack stance. The dry soil crumbled under the soldiers' boots as they walked to where Lucca was staring. Suddenly the soldier to Willingham's left screamed out one of the Arabic phrases they had all learned in predeployment training: "*Er-fah EE-dee-yek!* Get your hands up!"

A second later, Willingham saw what the soldier had seen. There, crouched in the bottom of the muddy, nearly empty eight-foot-deep canal, was a clean-shaven man in his twenties. He was wearing a traditional long cotton garment, a *thawb*, in light blue, or maybe white—Willingham couldn't tell exactly, because it looked glowing bright green through his NVGs. His arms were now raised above his head. A soldier jumped into the canal and cuffed him with zip ties. The canal was wide, with forty-five-degree banks, so it wasn't hard for the soldier to escort the man out.

The man eyed Lucca nervously. They brought him back to

the compound, only about a hundred yards away, and turned him over to the intel experts for identification. Willingham had no idea if he was the one they were looking for. He just knew they'd found someone hiding in a canal, and people who bolt and hide in canals at night tend to have something to hide.

After some data comparison, it looked like he was the HVT they had been seeking.

"We never would have found him if it weren't for her," a squad leader told him as he patted Lucca's head.

Willingham could feel his heart quicken with this praise of his girl.

Word of Lucca's heroics quickly spread. For the rest of the night, Lucca was the recipient of many thanks and ear rubs.

"How'd she do it?" asked one of the soldiers who was on his fire team. "I didn't know she's an attack dog."

"She's not. Never even been trained on scouting, much less aggression," Willingham answered, still stunned at the evening's turn of events.

"So what happened?"

"I figure it this way. If she can find a minute amount of explosives buried in the ground, she can smell a hundred-and-fifty-pound man scared shitless a few yards in front of her."

"And she was gonna do something about it. She wasn't just saying 'Yoo-hoo! Looky at this guy here!'"

"Well, there's a reason for that," Willingham said. "It's 'cause Lucca is a real marine."

MISSIONS AT KALSU sometimes took them to strange places. One evening Willingham and Lucca found themselves in a large cemetery surrounded by single-occupant, aboveground concrete crypts. They were only about waist high, and mostly unadorned.

Lucca took an interest in an old-looking tomb with a side seam that was wide enough to let her nose get a good whiff. She wagged happily, looking at Willingham, who could have thought of a thousand places he'd rather have her respond.

"Really, Lucca?"

He rewarded her with his usual enthusiasm but hoped she hadn't just gotten happy over the smell of old corpse. His spotter notified the platoon leader, and a few soldiers came over and lifted the heavy lid off the tomb. They looked inside.

"Whoa, check it out, Staff Sergeant!" one called to him.

Willingham walked over, not knowing what to expect, and looked down into the crypt.

There was no body, just a small cache of several bags containing RPK machine-gun rounds and some AKs.

Willingham wondered what had become of the bodies and then decided not to go there. It was getting dark now.

A few days later, Willingham and Lucca were leading a squad through a chicken barn at night.

"Never thought you'd be doing this when you signed up for the marines, did you, Mama Lucca?"

He looked at her through his NVGs and could tell she was enjoying the atmosphere. Running birds, flying feathers, and the smell of chicken manure. "Doesn't get much better than this for your kind, does it, Lucca?"

The chickens were getting underfoot in an annoying way as the squad searched for weapons that were supposed to be somewhere on the property. Willingham flipped his rifle's infrared laser to its normal red mode and took off his NVGs. To his surprise, the chickens ran away from the laser. Left and right, he aimed the laser, and left and right they scattered. He used this technique to clear a chicken-free path for everyone to walk in.

"We're like Moses parting a sea of chickens," he told Lucca. But she was too busy sniffing for explosives and enjoying the crazy surroundings to acknowledge his joke.

THE MONTH AT Kalsu passed quickly, filled with air assault missions to kill or capture high-value targets, and sometimes simply to search for caches or IED factories. The platoons Willingham and Lucca supported never had to kill HVTs, but a couple of HVTs may have been intent on destroying themselves—along with many others. During raids, suicide-bombing vests were found in two insurgent leaders' homes. Willingham knew the kind of loss of life that could have led to if they hadn't been discovered.

When they arrived back at FOB Falcon, the operation tempo had slowed down considerably. There was talk of the successes of Marne Torch, and it looked like there was something to it. The areas he and Lucca were now clearing appeared less treacherous, with IED finds and insurgent encounters greatly diminished.

Whether or not it would stay this calm would remain to be seen, but for now, Willingham continued to try to keep as busy as he could, even without back-to-back missions. Being at FOB Falcon resurrected the ghosts of time spent with Wiens—how the two of them sat up and talked for hours in this tent, how he laughed at Wiens gorging himself on chow-hall food at that table, how Cooper and Lucca played tug-of-war over in those open areas. Being fully engaged in working with Lucca or other dog handlers was a way of keeping the grief and guilt from overwhelming him.

Roche heard the pain in Willingham's voice when they spoke by phone after mission reports. One afternoon she made him an offer.

"I can't promise anything, but I want to do what I can to get you back home for the birth of your daughter," she told him.

He wanted to tell her what he was feeling: *I sent Kory home in a body bag, loaded him up myself and sent him back to his family. Now I get a chance to go home early? I don't deserve this, and I can't do this.*

But he didn't say that.

"You know how much I want to be there for Jill and the baby, but I've still got a job to do here with Lucca. Thank you anyway, but don't even try."

LUCCA SNIFFED THE trunk seam of the parked car, sat down, and looked at Willingham. He saw her through his NVGs and told his spotter, who radioed the find to the platoon leader.

It was 0300, and they were wrapping up an air assault out of FOB Falcon, heading back to a landing area to meet the Chinook. The soldiers had come up empty on their search for the HVT they were seeking, and all that separated them from their cots was a half-a-klick walk and a short Chinook ride back to FOB Falcon.

A couple of locals who were working with their platoon told them that the property belonged to some men involved with al-Qaeda. Between this, Lucca's strong response, and the late hour, the platoon leader decided not to wait for EOD. The car was history no matter what.

He called in an Apache to dispatch it with a Hellfire missile.

Willingham and most of the soldiers were sitting on the ground, waiting at the helicopter landing zone, when they heard the helo. Lucca, who had fallen asleep with her head on Willingham's lap, didn't stir. Willingham couldn't see anything through the rows of palm trees blocking the view. The Apache flew slowly to its target and locked in on it with the laser guide, then paused in the air as the trigger on the air-to-surface missile was pulled.

Whoosh! Boom! BOOM!

One hundred pounds of missile slammed into the car, and the large explosion was followed immediately by a smaller secondary explosion, courtesy of the contents of the trunk.

Lucca opened her eyes, stretched, looked around, and fell back to sleep.

It wasn't the first time ordnance was dropped because of Lucca's nose, but Willingham never ceased to be amazed by the ways his dog could stick it to the enemy.

As she lay there, the BADASS on her harness seemed to glow brighter than ever from Willingham's view—no NVGs needed.

ON SEPTEMBER 20, Willingham sat in a chair at the Morale, Welfare, and Recreation facility at FOB Falcon, phone clamped tightly to his ear. On the other end, at the hospital at Lackland Air Force Base, Jill was undergoing an emergency cesarean. Willingham had been on the phone with her every hour or two throughout the day and night, encouraging her best he could from so far away as she went through labor. Eventually it was decided that the only way this baby was getting out was by C-section.

Her sister held her cell phone out toward Jill's belly as the doctor lifted their daughter, Claire, into the world. She came out screaming at 1:22 A.M. San Antonio time, 9:22 A.M. Iraq time, and Willingham whooped and high-fived everyone within reach.

That evening, as he celebrated with some soldier pals, it struck him how much his life had just changed, and yet had also stayed the same.

"I'm in a shit-hole country, I walked into the MWR like I always had, and I'm walking out a brand-new dad. But still in a shit-hole country," he told them.

He passed out cigars. Someone brought a plastic pink flamingo to the occasion. It wasn't exactly a stork, but it was the best he could do under the circumstances.

ON THE C-5 home at the end of their deployment a month later, Knight and Willingham talked across the aisle, each sitting in their own row of seats again.

"I didn't tell you about Bram's little issue on the roof of a compound yet, did I?"

"I don't think so."

"So there he is, strutting around all proud with his Kong. He's running around and he drops it and it bounces off the roof. Without hesitation, before I could say or do anything, he jumps to retrieve it."

"Your crazy dog! What happened?!"

"The roof was eighteen feet off the ground. I gotta show you pictures. That crazy bastard's lucky to be alive. He was on light duty for three weeks."

Willingham laughed.

But there were signs that all was not well with Willingham.

Knight realized he was still carrying the burden from the death of Wiens and Cooper. Eventually he brought the conversation around to this, to try to reassure him, once again, that he did nothing wrong.

"You know logically it's not your fault. He went on that mission happily. No one forced him to. He loved working."

"I know. I'll be OK."

"Yeah, you will. And you've got your little girl now."

"Claire. Claire Elizabeth."

"You're going to be one great dad. You already are. Just look at Lucca!"

Willingham knew he should be feeling over the moon. Soon he'd be with Jill again and meeting his baby. He was excited and couldn't wait to see them. At the same time he could not let go of the feeling that he did not deserve this happiness, that he couldn't celebrate life when Wiens's dad was mourning his son's death.

"Want to go check the daooooggs?" Knight asked Willingham. "I think they could use a visit."

JILL GREETED WILLINGHAM at the airport with Claire. After Jill hugged Lucca and thanked her for bringing her husband home safely, Knight took Lucca to the side with Bram so Willingham could focus on his family without worrying about a leash. Claire, one month old, was wearing a marine cammy outfit.

She was asleep, and her father held her carefully, not knowing quite what to do with her head. While he held her close, there was nothing else in the world. Her tiny body even crowded out his sadness.

He felt his family would be complete if he could take Lucca home. But she had to go back to the kennels. It was the rule, and as much as he didn't like it, he had been at this long enough to know there was no fighting it.

Spending nearly 24/7 on deployment with dogs and then having to put them back in a concrete kennel when they got home was hard on handlers. He imagined it wasn't a walk in the park for the dogs, but they seemed to adjust to almost anything. After their return, he saw Lucca as much as he could, taking her on walks, bringing her with him to specialized search dog classes. They did some detection problems, but he took it easy on her. She'd done enough detection in Iraq to last a lifetime. He liked to go hang out with her in her walk-in kennel. He brushed her, talked to her, just sat with her without having to say a word. They had been through so much together over there. He felt they could read each other just by being near each other.

On one bad morning, as he was sitting and thinking about Wiens, he felt her eyes on him. He turned his head and saw her studying him, ears forward, her little black brows raised a little, pointing slightly toward each other. He thought she looked so wise and concerned.

"Come here, Mama Lucca," he said, patting the floor next to him.

She lay down, put her head in his lap, and looked up at him. Then she sighed, closed her eyes, and within a minute, drifted off.

WILLINGHAM AWOKE IN his bed with a start and looked for Lucca. Not on the floor, not in the bed.

"Lucca! Lucca!" he called out.

Then he realized where he was. Home, in bed with Jill. He was used to Lucca being at his side all the time. But she was back at the kennels. He *had* to start remembering that. It wasn't the first time he woke up worried that Lucca wasn't there. He wondered if she woke up looking for him sometimes.

He had other disturbing dreams, nightmares. Wars, violence, people getting shot or exploded. Jill had to wake him up a few times in the early months home because he was screaming in his sleep. Once he woke himself up shouting, "No, Kory!"

Jill never questioned him, never pushed him to talk about his experiences. Once she found him sitting on a box in the garage, crying with his head in his hands, surrounded by the military gear he stored there. Jill realized something had reminded him of Wiens, but she didn't ask. She just sat with him a minute and held his hand, then let him grieve on his own.

He was grateful.

A part of him had not come home. In one year, he would be back in Iraq on his second deployment—and a part of him would remain with Jill. This could mess with anyone's head.

PART THREE

Full Circle

8

Lessons Learned

"WELL, HERE WE are in Afghanistan!" Willingham said as he looked around the small room in the Mobile Expandable Container Configuration (MECC) shelter at Camp Leatherneck.

He stowed his gear, including his M4 and two sleeping bags—one for hot and one for cold, since he'd be there from June through late December—in the wall locker underneath his rack. It was like all the other times he'd moved into new quarters during his Iraq deployments.

Only not quite.

The room was missing something vital, something he had never been without at war. Lucca.

He grabbed his flak jacket off his duffel and sat on his cot. He opened the flap inside the front panel and slowly withdrew the five-pound ceramic protection plate. His favorite photo of Jill, the one where she was beaming, with the bright red rose tucked into the V of her shirt, was still taped in the middle of it, as it had been from his first deployment three years earlier. Below her, a photo of his two children, Claire and Michael.

On top of the two photos, staring back at him with those eyes he knew so well, a photo of Lucca.

She was back at Pendleton, stuck in a kennel, while he was here, halfway around the globe, about to face the enemy without her. He looked at her photo for a few seconds and then pushed the insert back into the vest.

He tried to shake a sense of foreboding that had been with him since he learned he was going to Afghanistan. With Lucca at his side, he and hundreds of others had survived two deployments to Iraq unharmed. But now he was kennel master at Camp Pendleton, and in charge of thirty U.S. Marine Corps dog teams—I Marine Expeditionary Force (I MEF) K-9—and Lucca couldn't be here.

Willingham understood the reasons his command wouldn't let her come with him: It hadn't been done before, and it just wasn't something kennel masters do, since there are so many other responsibilities. But he had tried.

He had laid it out for the decision makers. She could do demos for all the units during his dog capabilities talks to unit leaders. She could go out on short missions to give other dogs a break. And she would be a great public relations dog for getting others used to military dogs—she wasn't the type to eat you when you went to pet her.

When he was told she couldn't come, he accepted the decision. There really was no choice. But it was a blow. He wouldn't leave his flak and Kevlar behind, and Lucca was so much more than that. Sure, officially military dogs were considered equipment, but he knew of no handlers who considered their dogs anything but fellow marines, soldiers, sailors, airmen—and more than anything, loyal friends.

"Everyone's dog is top dog to them," he said to Jill one evening, after his second deployment to Iraq with Lucca. "Every handler thinks their dog is the best. But I'm the only one telling the truth." He laughed, but he realized it wasn't completely a joke.

"Of course, we all know Lucca is the best dog in the world," Jill concurred, smiling. She meant it—this dog was smart, calm, sweet, stunning, and heroic, and had brought her husband home alive twice. But she couldn't help being amused by the irony of all these dogs being the best dogs ever at the same time. It was like the guy on the radio said. All the children are above average.

Willingham had taken out extra life insurance before his Afghanistan deployment and could not precisely say why. He wrote a five-page letter to his family and left it with a neighbor to give to Jill in the event of the worst. He read bedtime stories to his children on video, so they wouldn't forget him, and so they'd always have him with them, in case. Two deployments so far, and he had come through unscathed—at least physically. He hoped "three strikes and you're out" didn't apply, but in his way he prepared.

He had carved out a few minutes to see Lucca in the kennel the day he and his dog teams were shipping out. He loved her up and gave her a pep talk.

"You keep an eye on this place while I'm gone, and show 'em what you've got."

She alternated between staring at him and glancing out at the activity going on around her as other handlers got their dogs ready. Willingham wondered if she understood that she wouldn't be going, or if she was just waiting for him to click her harness around her chest and go off to their third deployment together.

He couldn't look behind him as he shut the kennel door and walked away.

HE HAD SPENT the last year helping prepare his thirty dog teams for this deployment. He trained with the teams, sent them to Yuma Proving Ground's intensive military dog team predeployment course, and then trained some more. The handlers were physically ready, mentally strong, and mostly in synch with their dogs. Only six had deployed before, but he was very confident in everyone's abilities, proud of all his teams.

The dogs were, for the most part, kicking ass at their jobs. The canine half of the platoon consisted of twelve specialized search dogs, twelve patrol explosives detector dogs (PEDDs), four combat tracker dogs (CTDs), and two patrol narcotics detector dogs (PNDDs).

Everyone in the platoon flew to Camp Leatherneck together, on a C-17. On the flight, the dogs stayed in their Vari Kennels between the two rows of handlers, who were facing each other along the sides of the plane. Some dogs barked occasionally, but it was a relatively quiet ride, considering there were two and a half dozen war dogs packed side by side in long rows of kennels.

Willingham was determined that this was not going to be a one-way journey for any of his handlers. He planned to accompany as many of them as he could outside the wire, to act as their spotter and give them tips if he could see ways they could improve and stay safe. These were his guys, they were family, and he wasn't going to lose another brother, wasn't going to let anyone else lose a son. Not if he could help it.

As he lay in bed that first night in his MECC room, he thought about the scrapbook his father, Elden, had put together with the assistance of his mother, Martha, during his first deployment in Iraq. Every morning they leafed through *The Tuscaloosa News* for stories about Iraq, read them, and clipped them out. They attached the articles to the pages of a scrapbook with a glue stick. Sometimes his mother got out a sheet of scrapbook paper covered with a happy design, like bright balloons or American flags, and glued an article to the decorative paper before attaching it to the scrapbook page. She thought it made the news seem a little less daunting. As a nurse, she was used to balloons and flags brightening the mood of the hospital rooms of even the sickest patients.

This daily routine helped them deal with the uncertainty of their only child being in a war zone, and it gave them something they could actively do to feel a little closer to the situation. Sometimes facing the monster is the best way to defeat it.

By the time Willingham came back safely from his deployment and visited them with Jill and the kids, the scrapbook was four inches thick. He couldn't believe they had gone to all the trouble. As he turned the pages in awe of what they had done, he saw the headline ALABAMA SOLDIER KILLED BY BOMB IN IRAQ. He wondered if it had made his parents' hearts race, and if they had skimmed the article praying not to see his name. Surely they would have been told the news before it got in the paper. Besides, he was a marine, not a soldier. But still, it was too close to home, and they must have mourned for the poor young man and his family.

★★★★★

WILLINGHAM RETURNED FROM that deployment weighed down by the guilt over Wiens. He told his father a little about what he was going through, but the elder Willingham knew that no amount of reassurance that Wiens's death wasn't his son's fault would help at this point. He'd been through something like this himself, in Vietnam. He had never told his son what happened there. All Willingham knew was that his dad had been through hell in Vietnam. Upon his return, protestors spit on him.

One evening during his visit to the Tuscaloosa farm, the two were sitting on a brown couch and matching love seat in the sun-room in the back of the house. The room overlooked the rolling property, a pond in the distance. It was one of Willingham's favorite views. No one else was around, if you didn't count the huge elk head mounted to a plaque on the one wall that wasn't glass. The elder Willingham decided it was finally time to tell his story.

"It was a long time before I could talk about what happened to me," said his dad, who had been in narcotics law enforcement most of his career. "I felt the same guilt. You question every move; you wonder how you could have prevented it. But that's a losing game—it's war, and you just don't have control."

In September 1970, nineteen-year-old Elden arrived in Southeast Asia with Charlie Company, First Battalion, First Marine Division, whose mission included defending the vast Da Nang Air Base. Elden found himself assigned to a small outpost on top of Hill 52, a bald, bulldozed slope several miles from the base. The only means of supply was by helicopter.

Hill 52 had been made into a huge hive of trenches, pits, and bunkers and was surrounded by razor wire, and beyond the wire

there were trip flares and claymore mines. The hill was cleared
of all vegetation to provide free-fire zones and to keep the perim-
eters visible. Charlie Company did the usual grunt work of war,
digging holes, repairing trenches, preparing ambushes, and going out on patrol, often at night.

In late September, the hill was put on 100 percent alert, following an intelligence tip suggesting an attack was imminent.
Everyone was required to stand watch all night.

Among the marines in Elden's squad was Private First Class
Jose Munoz Jr., or JJ, a kid from California who always seemed
to be smiling and telling jokes. Then there was the squad leader,
Lance Corporal Bryce Leroy Kendrick, also from California, an
amiable fellow and a good leader. And finally, Lance Corporal
William Mark Predovic, the point man, an Ohioan who Elden
thought would have been one heck of a football fullback. He was
stocky and muscular, like a typical fullback, and he also had the
look of someone who would be a workhorse clearing a path for
running backs.

"After dark on September 28, our squad left Hill 52," Elden
told his son. "We walked half a mile or so to our ambush site. It
was raining and miserable. The rice paddy fields were filling up
with water and every one of us was soaking wet. We carried no
ponchos, as they made too much noise. We only had the liners.
Visibility was next to nothing.

"Around midnight JJ heard people speaking Vietnamese and
saw movement in a nearby tree line. Kendrick attempted to contact the communications center on base to alert them to the situation, but the radio wasn't working. We had a prearranged
signal that if we shot off two designated flares, say a red one
followed by a green one, it meant that we had no communica-

tions and were requesting to return to the hill. In response, if someone on the hill shot off a designated flare sequence, then we could head in.

"Kendrick shot off the flares and we received the response that allowed us to return. We started back in with Predovic walking point; a marine from Tennessee was next; then Kendrick, then our radioman, then JJ, and then me and the two members of my gun team.

"As we got to the razor wire at the hill we started to receive fire. Predovic was hit by a rocket-propelled grenade. It killed him instantly. Kendrick received some type of wound to the head and was immediately incapacitated. The radioman received a severe wound to his hip area.

"The marine from Tennessee was calling for JJ to get some illumination up. I called to JJ but he didn't respond. He was on his knees with his face on the ground. I crawled up to him and discovered he was wounded. When I turned him over I saw he had a severe wound to his neck. His eyes were open, but minutes later he died as I held him."

His son sat riveted on the couch. He had no idea his father had had it this bad.

"After a short time," Elden continued, "I started firing the grenade launcher and my M16. Eventually, we decided to try to make it onto the hill. The guys from my gun team came up and we found Kendrick still alive. A marine from Texas, Rafael Gonzales, came off the hill to help us. I went back to get JJ but was having a hard time lifting him and walking in the mud. The next thing I know Gonzales was there and we were able to get JJ onto the hill.

"We continued to receive fire throughout the night. After getting on the hill I started carrying mortars to the mortar pit. During the night several NVA were spotted coming across the river on a raft. The mortar men took care of that threat. Then one marine who had been dropping the mortars in the tube did not get his hand clear in time. The fin from the mortar round ripped his hand open.

"The next morning after the wounded and dead had been taken from the hill by helicopter, the members of my squad met with the lieutenant in a bunker to do an after-action report. Inside the bunker was a PFC from New York. After the debriefing, everyone left the bunker except him. As we were leaving the bunker, the kid said something like, 'I can't take this; I'm only eighteen years old, too young to die.'

"Not long after we left the bunker, it received a direct hit from a mortar round or maybe from a recoilless rifle round. He was killed instantly."

Elden paused to collect himself. His son sat, silent and stunned. All this horror, and a man, barely older than a boy, had died in his father's arms, when his father was barely older than a boy himself. Death in a landscape of devastation had marked his life at such a vital point, and yet he had come through it. He had gone on to live a generous life.

"It's hard to explain," his father continued, "but you wonder why one person dies or something tragic happens to them and you are right next to them and come out without a scratch. JJ, Predovic, and Kendrick did not deserve to die like they did. Neither did Kory Wiens. At some time you realize there really wasn't anything you could have done.

"You'll still have your days. But you do your best and keep going."

OVER THE YEARS, Chris Willingham had met dog handlers who had served in Vietnam. While he was an instructor at Lackland, several Vietnam War dog handlers worked with his students to put together a memorial there for a Vietnam hero dog named Nemo. The German shepherd had attacked some Vietcong who were attacking his men. In the attack, Nemo got shot in the nose and the eye. Even though he was blinded by his injury, he managed to run over to his fallen handler and lie on his body, guarding him until help arrived.

Nemo was one of only about two hundred dogs who returned from Vietnam, out of about four thousand who deployed. Most of the others were euthanized in-country or given to the South Vietnamese Army, which they figured amounted to the same fate, or worse. Times change. Willingham was grateful the Defense Department had learned a lesson, had listened to the people, and that now all war dogs return from war with their handlers. He didn't think he could be in the profession if that weren't the case. War without dogs like Lucca—prized by not just their handlers but everyone in the military who met them—had become, in one generation, hard to imagine.

Vietnam War dog handlers had spoken to Willingham on many occasions about the affection they had for their military dogs. Some devoted a cabinet or wall in their home to their dogs. Other guys kept their dog's collar on a hook, at the ready, as if they would pop it on their dog when he came in wanting to go for a walk. Many of the veterans went to Vietnam dog handler meetings, where they rattle off their dogs' names and tattoo numbers as easily as their own, without hesitation. Willingham could tell the dogs were a part of these handlers, just as today's dogs were an extension of their handlers. Some of these men had reenlisted despite the nightmare conditions, just so their dogs would live longer, so that maybe something would change and the dogs could come home. And then one day they finally had to say good-bye after trying everything in their power to keep the dogs alive.

Willingham might miss Lucca, but at least it wasn't like that.

"Posha! You're looking good, boy! And who's this guy you dragged along with you?"

"Long time no see!" Marine Sergeant William (Billy) Soutra Jr. said as the two handlers hugged with a couple of hearty back slaps at Leatherneck.

"Your girlfriend ain't here, Posha. I couldn't bring Lucca this time."

Posha, a black German shepherd with larger-than-life ears that angled outward in a wonky but endearing way, sniffed the air a few times when he heard Lucca's name, then lay down at Soutra's feet. It had been a long week of supporting Marine Corps Forces Special Operations Command (MARSOC), and he wasn't his usual high-energy self.

Soutra and Willingham had served together during Willingham's second deployment to Iraq. They were based at FOB Echo, in Diwaniya—about 120 miles south of Baghdad—with two other handlers, from October 2008 to April 2009. It was a far less treacherous deployment than the first one. IEDs, firefights, and weapons caches were no longer everyday affairs. He thought it might have been because Operation Marne Torch, and the troop surge in general, had accomplished what they had set out to do, but who knew? In the fog of war no one on the ground is too sure why exactly these were easier days. Marines don't ask. Dogs don't care.

Because of the decreased ops tempo, the four handlers also had more chances to kick back at night in a makeshift office/ living room, play poker, and watch every episode of *Scrubs* while huddled around a small laptop.

They weren't the only ones enjoying more downtime than usual.

Slam!

Lucca swung her hind end into Posha's side, and she whirled around in front of him, in the puppy play stance, waiting for some response. Posha had a reputation of being a phenomenal SSD and a badass with other dogs. But never with Lucca. It seemed clear to Willingham and Soutra that Posha had a soft spot for her.

"He has good taste, that dog of yours," Willingham told Soutra.

When Lucca had first tried to play with Posha, he just stood there as if he had no idea what to do. He stuck his chest out, his ears went straight back, and he kept looking at Soutra. Willingham thought he looked like a sixteen-year-old boy going on his first date.

Dad, she's flirting! I think she likes me! What do I do?

As they spent more time together, Posha grew more accustomed to this new friendship. Willingham still thought Posha looked a bit befuddled around Lucca, but he had started playing with her. He was a little stiff in his movements, like someone who needed to get out of a business suit before he could really relax, but it was enough for Willingham to proclaim them an item.

Lucca had another dog friend named Buddy. "Just a friend," Willingham joked to a soldier who saw them sleeping next to each other one lazy afternoon on FOB Echo. "I don't want my girl to get a bad reputation."

Buddy was an army patrol explosives detector dog (PEDD) that had seen or heard too much on a previous deployment with another handler. He had stopped working nine months into that last twelve-month deployment. His current handler, Sergeant Tyler Barriere, had done his best to get Buddy ready for their own yearlong deployment but was worried about taking this dog to war. It was before the DOD officially recognized post-traumatic stress disorder in dogs, so off Buddy went to Iraq again, despite the concerns Barriere had raised.

When they got to Iraq, nothing had changed. Buddy stood frozen in fear, tail between his legs, at the sound of bombs or gunfire. Sometimes he'd back up, in a fruitless attempt to get away from the noises. Iraqis frightened him as well. He would become so distracted around them that his lack of focus made it hard for him to do his job. Barriere couldn't imagine why he'd be so scared of locals and could only conclude that during Buddy's first deployment he had encountered some Iraqis with hostile intentions.

Willingham worked with the team and helped Buddy get to the point where he could go on low-risk missions outside FOB Echo. Inside the wire at Echo, Barriere used Buddy's exquisite bite work to demonstrate this skill to future Iraqi handlers. The exposure to Iraqis in a task Buddy loved helped him move past this fear, but only during the time he was in his zone, focused completely on leaping on one of the U.S. handlers in a bite suit and ripping into him. After the joy of the bite work, it was back to his fearful glancing at the Iraqi onlookers.

"Heard anything from Barriere about Buddy deploying again?" Willingham asked Soutra after they'd talked about old times and caught up on the latest with their Afghanistan deployments.

"No, you?"

"Last I heard he was still at Fort Campbell with Barriere. That poor dog needs to get dispo'd and become somebody's couch potato. Not like your beast!"

He looked down at Posha, who was nodding off. "What are you up to that he's so tired out?"

Willingham had handpicked Soutra to deploy in support of MARSOC. Both Soutra and Posha had the strength, skills, and unflappable nature to do well with MARSOC. They also had the kind of bond Willingham knew could help them get through a challenging deployment. Like other great dog teams, it was hard to think of one without the other. Kind of like partners in a good marriage, Willingham figured.

Soutra and Posha had flown out with their elite marine unit a couple of months before Willingham and his thirty dog handlers had left Pendleton. He told Willingham about some of the action they'd already seen. Almost every mission, they took casualties. Firefights, IEDs, explosions of all kinds. Nothing they couldn't handle. Quite the opposite.

"It's just what Posha and I are meant to do together."

Two weeks later, on the night of July 12, Soutra walked over to Willingham's quarters from the MARSOC compound adjacent to Leatherneck. He was without Posha. Willingham could see something wasn't right.

"What's up, man? You OK?"

"A rough couple of days out there. Bad."

Willingham thought the worst but didn't say it.

Soutra could read his friend's expression and laid the fear to rest.

"Posha's fine. I just left him in the kennel over there because of all the dogs you got here."

"I figured he'd come through anything, that dog of yours," Willingham said. "You OK talking about what happened?"

Soutra sketched out the events of the previous two days. It started with a critical mission to capture an IED factory and a Taliban command center and to clear compounds where insurgents were known to be sleeping. Soutra, Posha, and their MAR-SOC team flew to the area in a helo for a night operation. Posha got right to work under cover of darkness and quickly located IEDs and other explosives.

The marines and Afghan commandos took over the factory, but by dawn more than fifty insurgents were attacking them with a variety of weapons, from heavy DShK machine guns to command-detonated IEDs. Their attack was relentless. It was two days of hell, with ammo and water running low and their element leader, Staff Sergeant Christopher Antonik, mortally wounded by an IED. Eventually the marines got the upper hand, but the loss of Antonik, a close friend and great warrior, was devastating.

Soutra didn't talk much about his role. But he was happy to talk about Posha.

"Posha was a hero. With everything going on nonstop for two days, he never hesitated. He was right at my side, doing everything exactly with me. He performed perfectly. He's like a part of me. Hard to explain it."

Willingham understood it, although he'd never been in such a ferocious battle with Lucca. But he didn't fully understand Soutra's role until a couple more weeks went by, and Soutra told him he was being put in for the Navy Cross—the second-highest combat award in the nation. He mentioned it as an afterthought, and he seemed almost embarrassed about the accolade.

"I was just doing what I was trained to."

Willingham read some reports and found out more about Soutra's role in the battle. He led counterattacks. He pushed into the enemy position. After an airdrop of water, ammo, and medical gear landed in a creek, he volunteered to locate another platoon that could give them some supplies. When Antonik went down, Soutra took charge and via hand signals got his men to fire in one area while he and another marine ran through enemy rounds to get to Antonik and some wounded Afghans. He applied a tourniquet to one man, preventing him from bleeding out. Then he organized a quick-reaction force to subdue the enemy so a medevac helicopter could land. He fired on the insurgents and got the wounded to safety.

The team leader said Soutra "performed flawlessly" and never hesitated in any of his actions. Willingham wasn't surprised about the description. It was almost exactly how Soutra described Posha's actions that night. Willingham knew that the best dogs and handlers became more like each other over time. Being in synch helps them survive the life-or-death situations they face every day.

Even the most outstanding dog teams can't bring everyone

home alive. He knew Soutra's torment at losing Antonik all too well. It was the collateral damage of IEDs, which don't have to touch you physically to cause indescribable pain. He realized it was a lot like what his dad had gone through in Vietnam.

You can't lose anyone, and then you do.

9

All for One and One for All

THE SECURE PHONE line at Willingham's desk rang just as he was sitting down to go through a growing pile of reports the morning of August 4. He had been out with his handlers on missions more than usual lately, pulling security for them and making sure they were as ready as possible for whatever the Taliban might have in store. But now he had to face the paperwork before falling too far behind.

He picked up the line, hoping it wasn't a request for reports he hadn't yet finished compiling. On the other end of the phone, a unit marine master sergeant identified himself, calm, grave.

"Staff Sergeant Willingham, one of your men has been severely injured."

"What happened?" The air went out of him. "Who?"

In a flash he felt the weight of Kory Wiens on the morgue stretcher, saw the body bag as he loaded it into the Black Hawk.

"I need you to confirm some information."

Willingham clicked on the "secret" computer to open the file with the list of his men who were on an intensive clearing operation in the area of Safar Bazaar, in southern Helmand Province. Within the last couple of weeks, marines had made their presence there known, and the Taliban decided to hightail it out of the once-thriving open-air marketplace. Willingham sent two combat tracking teams to catch any remaining Taliban if they pulled nonsense and then tried to run away. The term for bad guys who flee is squirters, and the dogs would have been all too happy to chase after them and prevent them from squirting away to do more harm on another day.

Willingham also assigned six bomb detector teams to begin the painstaking process of helping to sweep the extensive market area for explosives. Insurgents had hidden them everywhere at night, after they violently enforced their 7 P.M. curfew on all residents. Intel was weak there because few locals could point them to where the bombs had been planted.

Willingham had been there just days earlier, watching the backs of some of his teams as they walked through the dangerous main street of the market. He knew firsthand what they were up against.

"OK, I'm ready," Willingham said when the document opened. The list contained vital information on the marines, including their social security numbers and blood type. It was known casually as a "kill roster." It was used, in part, to compare and confirm identification information from dog tags. The U.S. Marine Corps was the only branch of the armed forces whose gas mask size was on its dog tags. But that bit of info wasn't on his roster. Just the basics.

The master sergeant read the birth date and the last four digits of the social security number, and Willingham's eyes skimmed the list. He didn't want it to be any of his marines. But he found the numbers and with his finger traced the line back to the name.

Corporal Max Donahue.

The master sergeant confirmed.

Willingham had pulled security for Donahue and his PEDD, Fenji, in the Safar area less than a week ago. Donahue had everything going for him: He had deployed before, he was smart, he was a great handler, he would do anything for anyone who needed help, and his dog was an excellent explosives detector who would do anything for him. Beyond this, Max was funny. Bad boy in that young marine way, only twenty-three.

"They were on a search with Third Battalion, First Marines, walking point. They found some IEDs but something happened, probably a command wire, at the last one."

"How is he?"

"He's lost some limbs. I don't have details. His dog is being treated, too."

Willingham got the location where Donahue had been flown.

"I'll be there on the first bird possible."

He opened a large map of Helmand Province on the computer and searched among dozens of icons for the one indicating an IED had gone off. He found one at Safar Bazaar and clicked on it to see what other information was available. Social security number, bird dispatched, transferred to FOB Dwyer, triple amputee.

He told himself Donahue would be OK. There are all kinds of advances in prosthetics that could let him lead a close-to-normal life. Besides, he was Max. That spirit would take him through anything.

It took an act of will to believe what he was telling himself.

STAFF SERGEANT AARON Nuckles stood on one side of Donahue's hospital bed, Willingham on the other. Lieutenant Shaun Locklear, the platoon commander who had raced down from Leatherneck with Willingham, had left the bedside to let them have some time alone with Donahue.

If they just looked at his face, it was as though Donahue was simply sleeping. Willingham let his eyes travel to where Donahue's legs should be, but there was nothing between the top and bottom sheets. The doctor had told them that one arm was so badly maimed that they had to amputate. Anywhere his flak had covered looked unscathed.

They talked to each other, tried to be optimistic, for Donahue's sake, but also for their own.

"We're gonna be here for you, Max. We're gonna see you through this all the way," Willingham said. "We'll take good care of Fenji 'til you're better."

They all wiped their eyes and Willingham prayed there standing by the bed.

On August 6, he got the call. Donahue had been transported to the military hospital at Landstuhl, Germany. Tests showed that the injury had left him brain-dead. There was nothing more to do. There would be no recovery.

Donahue had wanted to be an organ donor. In his final act of being there for others, his kidneys and liver went to save the lives of two men and one boy.

It occurred to Willingham that Lucca had always been there during the worst times. He went to the kennel where the handlers had been taking turns looking after Fenji. The blast had ruptured her eardrums and propelled debris into her eyes, but she was going to be OK.

"Fenji, we're gonna be here for you. Don't you worry," he told her as he opened the kennel gate and took her for a walk. "Marines take care of their own."

Nuckles had returned to Leatherneck because they were gearing up to clear sites for the upcoming elections. When Wiens died, Willingham had no one to talk with except Lucca. He didn't even tell Jill because she was pregnant, and somehow it just didn't seem right. But Nuckles was a friend, someone he could talk to if it hit him hard.

Willingham let his handlers know about what happened. "Don't post anything on Facebook," he told them. Handlers still out on ops and loved ones who didn't know yet wouldn't find out through social media. He wanted to tell the handlers himself, face to face. And he needed to give them something he didn't have when Wiens was killed. Someone there to listen.

"Don't bottle it up. It's the worst thing you can do—trust me. I'm here if you want to talk. Nuckles is, too. We can get you the chaplain or any help you need.

"Also, if you're not ready to go back out when I send you, just let me know. There is no pressure. I won't think any less of you."

Because there were so many handlers, he knew they'd help one another grieve in a healthier way than he had. He saw it at the memorial at Leatherneck. Toward the end of such ceremonies, it's customary for everyone to walk up to the memorial and pay respects before departing the area. Most will touch the

Kevlar or the dog tags and say a quick prayer before stepping away.

Once the general who attended Donahue's memorial had paid his respects, the first marine handler walked up, put his hand on the Kevlar, and broke down. At seeing their brother grieve like this, all eighteen handlers who were able to attend instantly surrounded the memorial and took a knee—no words needed. They put their hands on the shoulders of the handlers next to them and grieved together, praying silently before collectively walking back to the kennels.

After the memorial, they recounted stories of their friend—the funny ones, the heroic ones. Some marines laughed, some stared off quietly, a couple cried. Willingham saw the benefits of not being alone, of at least knowing that if his handlers needed someone to talk to, they'd have plenty of support.

Willingham was experiencing this himself. He missed Lucca's unconditional comfort. But now he had Nuckles and Locklear to lean on if he needed to talk. Billy Soutra also came to check in on him at the memorial.

"How are you, man?"

"It's tough, man," Willingham told him. "But we'll push through."

It was decided that the military working dog area of Leatherneck would be named in honor of Donahue. That *Max W. Donahue* and *military working dog* shared the same initials was a nice coincidence. The handlers worked together to build a kiosk with CAMP DONAHUE in large red letters at the top. Under it, on a concrete barrier, they created a memorial mural featuring Donahue and Fenji, with marine and military working dog logos to the sides. Corporal Alfred Brenner, who would have gone to art school if he hadn't joined the marines, drew them in pencil. He went through a whole pack of pencils.

To see his marines working together so well on something that would keep Donahue's memory alive made Willingham feel good about his tight-knit group and more confident they would get through anything that came at them.

Corporal Juan "Rod" Rodriguez was one of the last to find out about Donahue. He arrived back at Leatherneck two weeks after Donahue's death. He and Rrolfe had been on a thirty-day operation with First Recon Battalion in an isolated outpost with no phone or Internet. He heard about Donahue's death from a marine he met at an unexpected stop, but it hadn't seemed possible. When Willingham confirmed the story, the ground collapsed under him. At least it felt that way. Not only did he lose a friend and someone he looked up to; he lost his sense of immortality—something shared by many twenty-year-olds, even in the middle of a war in Afghanistan.

"The reality of this happening never crossed my mind," he eventually told Willingham. "I never thought I'd have to experience something like that. You think about it in your head, but it's just not real until it happens."

No one took Willingham up on his offer to stay inside the wire when they were assigned to a mission. Handlers no longer took it for granted that everyone was going to make it back from these missions. Willingham could see the subtle change in how they said good-bye. It was more serious. "Take care, brother," took on some gravitas.

"It's always in the back of your mind after something like that," Willingham told Rod. "You can't put Pandora back into the box."

"That's exactly it."

"You can't think about the reality too much. It'll paralyze you," Willingham said.

The genie was definitely out of the bottle, and they were going to run with it.

Two CH-53 SUPER Stallion helos hung several feet above the landing area and gently touched down at FOB Wilson in Kandahar Province. Twenty-two dog teams streamed out and onto the gravel, one after another, disappearing momentarily in the dusty rotor wash and reappearing a few seconds later, farther away.

Willingham had been tracking the birds' progress and was there to greet them at the flight line. He'd been at FOB Wilson for five days, giving capabilities and limitations briefings so the unit leaders would know how to best use the teams for a large-scale clearing op that was getting under way.

"Looking good, men! Welcome to FOB Wilson, your new home away from home! Let's get you settled in, give you the grand tour, and I'll tell you what's going down."

They set up in large tents and let their dogs rest in Vari Kennels beside their cots while they met up. Willingham spoke confidently, his authority sitting comfortably in his voice. They would be supporting five army units over the next few weeks. Two were located at FOB Wilson. They'd all be here for the first four days, conducting training, and then the handlers would be broken into five teams. Three teams would move out to other FOBs with their units. Some missions would be just a few hours, others a week or more.

"You will be supporting several major clearing operations

throughout Kandahar," he said. "I'll be bouncing between each of the units during these ops. The supporting units know you're coming and they're looking forward to working with you. As always, let me know if you need anything while you're out there."

Several days later, Willingham joined Rod and his Malinois PEDD as they walked point through farm fields and past compounds. Willingham walked behind, working as his spotter, hands poised on his rifle, and helping him watch for signs of IEDs.

Rod worked Rrolfe well. It didn't surprise Willingham, but he hadn't previously witnessed directly how Rod interacted with others on a mission. He'd only heard the excellent First Recon reports. What he saw confirmed everything they said and everything he'd seen during training. Rod was positive, confident, and humble, never complained, and had a quiet humor Willingham loved. Reminded him of Wiens, in a way.

Their patrol took them through marijuana fields. The plants were lush, and in a couple of fields, they towered taller than the men. Rrolfe sniffed his way through the pot forest as if it were just another overgrown place.

"Good thing he's not a drug dog!" one of the soldiers shouted over to him.

The platoon stopped for a short break near a protective wall at the end of an empty field. Rod took out his water bowl for Rrolfe, who drank thirstily.

"I think he wants that thing filled with food, Rod!" Willingham said. "He's probably got the munchies after all that."

Rod laughed. They were a sight. Bits of marijuana had gotten stuck in their boots and their packs. Rrolfe even had some caught in his harness.

"That ain't gonna go well if we go back to the FOB looking

like this," Willingham joked as they picked the leaves and stems away.

GENERAL DAVID PETRAEUS, dressed in army cammies and cap, walked over to the two handlers Willingham had selected to meet him while he was making the rounds at FOB Wilson on October 7. Willingham had chosen them because they were still at the FOB and for one other reason he told the handlers.

"Your dogs won't accidentally attack the general. Eating generals is not good for the career," he told them. He said it in humor, but there were a couple of more ornery dogs he would not let do a meet and greet when the commander of NATO International Security Assistance Force (ISAF) conducted a visit to Second Brigade Combat Team at FOB Wilson.

Petraeus leaned down and stroked the head of Sara, a German shepherd, who looked up at him appreciatively. Willingham gave the general a shorter-than-usual brief about the platoon of dogs and what they were doing. Petraeus was already sold on the importance of dogs. "The capability they bring to the fight cannot be replaced by man or machine," he had once said, and media all over the world quoted him. Willingham knew he was preaching to the choir, but praising his teams was fine with him anytime.

BACK HOME IN Cream Ridge, New Jersey, Megan Brenner couldn't believe what she saw when her husband, Corporal Alfred Brenner—the handler who drew the memorial to Donahue—Skyped her two nights before his last planned mission at Combat Outpost Terminator, in southern Afghanistan. Grief, a mostly black German shepherd with tan legs, was a little hard to see on her monitor, and the audio wasn't working well, but Megan could make out enough of him to tell he was being downright loving to her husband. She could see Grief coming in for head rubs, snuggling up against her husband, and then, most amazing of all, sitting on her husband's lap. Brenner had told his wife about his newfound affectionate nature a couple of months earlier, but she had to see it for herself. This was the first time they were able to Skype since his deployment nearly six months earlier, and she was floored.

The dog's tan eyebrows seemed especially expressive when Grief gazed at her husband.

"Are you sure that's Grief?" she asked.

Grief, a PEDD, had started out with a general dislike of human beings. "He hates everyone," Brenner had told his wife. He wondered if the dog's European breeders named him because he caused them grief, or if there was some other reason. Grief was stubborn in training, didn't like to be petted, didn't like treats. It was hard getting through to Grief in the beginning, and Brenner wasn't sure they were going to make it as a team. But as often happens in bumpy starts between military dogs and handlers, one day something clicked. During training the dog started listening.

"All of a sudden, he just wanted to work with me," he told Megan that day. "I think he actually is starting to like me." Still, he wasn't exactly what she would consider the ideal pet. She had grown up with dogs, hugging, cuddling, and loving them. Grief liked none of the above.

Downrange, all that changed. Being together 24/7, where one life depends on the other, creates the kind of deep bonds that handlers say nothing can compare to in civilian life. In late August, Brenner and Grief were on a mission and the nighttime temperature plummeted. He called Grief over to keep him warm, and they ended up spooning to sleep. Brenner was amazed that Grief seemed to like being held. After that, the dog often approached Brenner to sleep next to him on cots or on sleeping bags during longer missions when they'd stay out for days.

The new sleeping arrangements were especially surprising when he thought about the weeks they stayed at a hotel in New York City to work security for the United Nations General Assembly. He thought it would be a treat for Grief to stay on a real bed. The dog had slept only in hard kennels until then. He coerced Grief onto the bed, but the dog wanted nothing to do with it. Grief looked alarmed in that "I'm being punished for something and I have no idea what" way and jumped off the bed to sleep in his travel kennel. During their time in New York, the dog never accepted Brenner's invitation to share the mattress.

But now, in the deserts of Afghanistan, Brenner was sure that if Grief had another chance to share a comfortable hotel bed, he'd be all over it.

"What would you think of adopting him?" he asked his wife on that last Skype call before their mission. She couldn't hear him well, but he could hear her now.

"Oh that's awesome! He's keeping you alive. The least we can do is give him a good home."

Grief was only three years old, but he had been experiencing some minor seizures on deployment. It could be disastrous if this happened in a firefight or during a clearing operation. Brenner was thinking his dog might get dispo'd after this deployment and was happy Megan felt the same way about making him part of their family.

The mission they were about to go on would be roughly seven days long. Another handler, Lance Corporal Stephen Lahr, would head out with a platoon at the same time. Willingham had also brought Corporal Jorge "Gonzo" Gonzalez and Rod to this outpost so they could support the big clearing push. They'd follow shortly after, when other platoons headed out.

About forty-eight hours after the Skype call with his wife, Brenner and Grief were sweeping the sides of the road just outside Terminator as the route-clearance vehicle checked for bombs on the road itself. They were a klick away from the combat outpost when the route-clearance vehicle located two IEDs. Everyone got to a standoff distance and waited for EOD. Brenner and a few soldiers sat against the wall of an abandoned civilian compound, and Grief lay at his feet. The one-story house had sand-colored adobe walls with no doors and no sign of life. Brenner realized there were no civilians anywhere in this area. In his experience, that was always a bad sign.

A short time later they got the call that EOD was going to blow up the IEDs in five minutes and to get farther back. They got up to put more distance between them and the blast and—

Boom!

"What was that?!"

"What the hell? What's going on?!"

"They blew it too soon. I don't know!"

Within seconds, darkness descended around them and chunks of small rocks and debris pummeled them. Brenner immediately realized that the explosion had nothing to do with the

IEDs that the EOD team was about to blow in place. It was an IED that had been buried near the wall, undiscovered because they hadn't gone that route yet. Brenner whirled around to find Grief. His retractable leash was out thirty feet and he couldn't see him.

"Grief, come!" he called in alarm, dreading what he'd find.

He continued yelling for him and pulled the leash, but it was taut. As the debris cleared, he saw Grief and was relieved that he was standing and looked unharmed. He ran to him to pick him up and get him away, but as he was doing so he looked down and saw a gaping crater. Then he heard the screaming. Down deep in the bottom was a young soldier, yelling for help. Brenner could see him flailing his arms and legs, so he was reassured he hadn't lost any limbs. He summoned help, and as others ran over, he pulled security, guarding the area with his rifle. They got the soldier out of the crater, and he heard a sergeant order a medevac on his radio.

"Hey, can you and your dog go search for a landing zone?" he asked Brenner.

"Sure."

But something was wrong. He tried to get Grief's attention, but the dog just stared at him as if he didn't understand—or hear him. Brenner realized that the blast had made Grief deaf. Brenner hoped it would be very short-lived. He brought him on his search, but Grief didn't do his usual search activity. So instead of their normal long-leash search, where Grief would take the lead and sniff where his nose told him to go with just a little guidance, Brenner kept him on a shorter leash and directed him. He felt like he was using a handheld mine detector the way he helped him back and forth. He figured Grief would still respond to an explosive because it was almost a reflex with him. At least he hoped he would. Brenner used his eyes, too. They found nothing.

On their way back to the compound, Brenner heard another huge explosion. He ran as best he could with Grief in tow on a path he figured they'd already swept. The place was frantic once again. Another soldier had stepped on a pressure-plate IED while heading to the roof of the compound. He was killed instantly.

It was only the start of the mission, and already they had one KIA, one injured, and a deaf dog. It wasn't looking good. Rather than push ahead, they decided that since it was getting toward dark, they'd find a compound and stay the night. It was just safer, they figured, and they needed to catch their breath.

They came to another compound that looked like a small fortress, with a thick outer wall that rose fifteen feet, and a large, sturdy metal front door on the dwelling. The building and surrounding area needed to be searched for explosives before they could go in.

"Hey, my dog is done," Brenner said, looking at Grief, who was panting and staring blankly ahead. "But I'll take him around and give it my professional eye. It's only going to be me searching, not my dog."

The metal door was locked—no big surprise—so Brenner and eight U.S. and Afghan army soldiers carefully walked around the building to find another entrance. Grief was with him but wasn't sniffing anything. Just along for the ride, to be with Brenner. Brenner knew leaving Grief with someone else at this time of confusion would make a bad situation even worse for his dog. They needed to stay together.

The back door was locked as well.

"You know, it's never a good thing when you've got locked

doors like these around here," Brenner said. He had encountered compounds like this before. He was outranked here, so there was only so much he could push his opinion.

"This is a good spot to hang out for the night," one said. "Don't worry, we'll find a way in."

One handed Brenner his weapon with a "Thanks" and began trying to peel and chip away at the hard mud around the door. Another said he was going to try to find a different way in. He also handed Brenner his weapon. An officer did the same and joined the soldier who was working on the door.

Brenner stood there holding three rifles and the leash of his deaf, confused dog. If Grief hadn't just been deafened by a bomb, maybe he would have refused to hold the rifles—being a rifle rack wasn't part of his job—but he wasn't thinking straight. He wished he could have left the scene, but that's not how he operated.

The guys working on the door made an opening just big enough to look inside.

"Sir," Brenner said. "Do you see any wires? We have to be really careful."

A couple of minutes later, the door was down. Almost as soon as it fell, the soldier who'd gone looking for another entrance came bounding around the corner.

"Hey, I found a way in!" he announced. Then he saw they'd beat him to it.

Brenner turned around to give him back his rifle and took two steps. Before he could take the third step, his world went white.

At first, he didn't hear anything. He didn't think anything. He didn't see anything. It was a sensation he'd never felt before.

Then he became aware of flipping through the air. Just flying and flipping, slow motion. He felt like he flipped several times, and all of a sudden the flipping stopped and he sensed the ground under his body. He didn't feel arms or legs, but he could hear again—an extremely loud, high-pitched sound.

He started to feel people messing with his body, cutting off his boots. He knew he still had feet. They were doing things to his arms, so he realized he still had arms. He lay there getting very cold and praying. It was all he could do.

"Hey, how you doing?" he heard someone say.

"I'm freezing! Freezing!" The only warmth was from the ground around him. It was getting warmer, and it felt good. He didn't realize at the time he was lying in his pooling blood.

He felt tourniquets go on. One arm, one leg, another leg.

"Make it tighter!" he cried. He barely felt them. He realized he should probably be feeling a lot more pain than he did, but he was glad he wasn't.

"You're gonna be fine," the medic told him as he covered Brenner with blankets.

"Shut up. That's what you tell people before they die."

"No, I'm serious. You're going to send me a postcard in three weeks from the hospital."

He heard a call go out on the 9 Line for a medevac request.

"We have one wounded, one KIA."

Brenner figured the KIA was the guy who took down the door.

As they placed him on a makeshift stretcher and moved him to the medevac landing area, he became aware that he couldn't open his eyes. It wasn't alarming. His sense of hearing was now everything. He heard the medevac helicopter coming in. *Chop-chop-chop-chop* filled his head. It got louder as the helo got closer.

He took a little comfort knowing he'd be on his way soon to the hospital at Kandahar Airfield, the best military medical facility anywhere close. He realized maybe he wouldn't die after all.

Then the sounded faded. The *chop-chop-chop-chop* grew more distant. The helicopter was going away.

"Where'd they go? Am I going to die here?"

"No, they probably see something suspicious. Don't worry, you'll be on your way in no time."

"STAFF SERGEANT! STAFF Sergeant!" Willingham was working with Rod to set up training problems at an open area of COP Terminator when Gonzo ran up to him. "One of the handlers has been injured! We don't know which one. Brenner or Lahr."

"Any word on his condition?"

"He's got tourniquets on both legs and an arm."

Willingham felt his mouth get dry. Wiens . . . Donahue . . . Now . . .

He ran to the ops center for more info and to try to get on a bird to the hospital. He compared the information on his kill roster to the numbers he was given.

"It's Brenner," he told Gonzo and Rod, who had followed him.

It was all too familiar. As he ran to the landing zone to wait for the chopper, he said the simple prayer so many before him had said throughout the history of war.

"Don't let him die. Please, God, don't let him die."

THE BIRD SWEPT back in to load Brenner quickly and get out of the treacherous area before it could be shot out of the sky. Brenner thought he'd never heard anything as loud as the inside of the medevac helicopter, except maybe for the explosions, but the helo noise just kept going on and on and on. The noise of the engine and rotors and the shouts of the medics as they tried to talk to him were almost painful. He wondered if his ears were already making up for his not being able to see.

After what seemed like days, he felt the helo land and the jostling of the stretcher under him. Then he heard the opening of a metal door. And suddenly, silence. He heard the hum of fluorescent lights and the concerned whispers of people talking in some kind of medical jargon. Now the quiet hurt his ears.

A funeral home? A morgue? A library?

He faded away.

"WELL IT'S ABOUT time! Wondering when you were going to be paying us a visit!" The first words Brenner remembers hearing when he came to in his hospital room were those of a friendly sounding guy with a southern accent. There was another familiar voice he recognized, too. Willingham and Locklear.

"Cool, I got visitors already!"

Willingham couldn't have been happier to hear those words— any words—from Brenner. It had already been determined that he had a traumatic brain injury from the blast, and Willingham wasn't sure of its extent. Seeing Brenner with his sense of humor intact so quickly was more than he'd been hoping for.

He had gotten word from the doctor that with some complicated surgeries, Brenner should be able to keep his badly damaged arm. His other arm had only minor injuries. His legs were in no danger of amputation as long as infection didn't set in. His face was pocked with shrapnel and his eyes were so swollen from it that there was no way to open them. It would likely be days, the doctor had told Willingham.

"So when I get my Purple Heart, does that mean I'll get free drinks for the rest of my life?"

Willingham had to laugh. This kid didn't miss a beat. They joked around as if they were friends enjoying a couple of beers. But in a lull, Brenner thought about asking a question he didn't want to. He hoped that by not asking, he could go on a little longer in recovery mode, having fun with the guys. But finally he had to know.

"What about Grief?"

It was the question Willingham had been dreading. He knew the answer, because the helicopter he and Locklear had flown there in contained the body bag of a marine who was KIA. When they landed, the veterinarian met them and they carried the remains of Grief to the veterinary tent before going to the hospital to see Brenner.

"I'm sorry, man," Willingham said. "Grief didn't make it."

Brenner lay silently in his hospital bed. Although his eyes were swollen tightly shut, the tears still flowed.

Willingham just stood beside the bed. And it seemed to Willingham that Lucca was there, standing just behind him.

10

Home for the Holidays?

No MATTER WHERE they are in the world, no matter how austere the conditions, no matter who they have lost and the hell they have seen, marines do whatever it takes to honor the Marine Corps birthday every November 10. They have been doing this since 1921, when General John A. Lejeune, thirteenth commandant of the Marine Corps, ordered that a summary of the history, mission, and tradition of the corps be read to all marines on that day.

On November 10, 2010, eight marine dog handlers who happened to be at FOB Wilson and two intel marines gathered in the chow hall to celebrate the Marine Corps birthday. Willingham read the 235th birthday message from the current commandant. Next, a marine read the 1921 birthday message from

Lejeune—aka "the greatest of all Leathernecks." Willingham always especially liked the last paragraph.

> This high name of distinction and soldierly repute we who are marines today have received from those who preceded us in the Corps. With it we also received from them the eternal spirit which has animated our Corps from generation to generation and has been the distinguishing mark of the Marines in every age. So long as that spirit continues to flourish, Marines will be found equal to every emergency in the future as they have been in the past, and the men of our Nation will regard us as worthy successors to the long line of illustrious men who have served as "Soldiers of the Sea" since the founding of the Corps.

Images of his father and of Lucca—two of his favorite marines—came to Willingham. Although the U.S. was barely getting its military dog program off the ground when Lejeune died in 1942, Willingham decided he'd have been proud of Lucca and other great marine dogs.

He wondered what Lucca was up to in the kennels at Pendleton on the corps' birthday. Probably just another day of waiting until their return, but he hoped she would get out with a couple of the guys who were looking after her. Maybe there would be an e-mail from one of them. Once they'd built up some rapport with Lucca, they were amazed by her detection skills, at how well she worked off leash with a minimum of quiet commands. It was surprising to Willingham how much he liked hearing about Lucca's abilities, even with so many miles and months between them.

The birthday celebration continued, with the special ceremony of the cutting of the cake. A week earlier, Willingham had arranged with the chow-hall staff to have a Marine Corps cake on November 10. It was a two-layer vanilla cake with white frosting, red and blue sprinkles, and a Marine Corps seal on top. He was impressed, especially considering they were in the middle of a desert in Afghanistan.

Lance Corporal Johnathan Thorman cut the cake with his M4's fixed bayonet. He gave the first piece to Willingham, who, at thirty-one, was the oldest marine present. Willingham ate a bite and handed it back to Thorman, twenty-one, the youngest marine there. The tradition symbolizes the passage of knowledge from older, more experienced marines to the newer generation of marines.

If he could have made one birthday wish, it would have been that Donahue and Brenner could be here, enjoying cake, and looking forward to heading home with them in just a little more than a month, in time for Christmas.

By early December, all the dog teams were together again at Leatherneck, waiting to go home. Missions were completed, dozens of explosives and caches found, countless lives saved. Staff Sergeant Chuck Rotenberry and his thirty dog teams from Camp Lejeune—II MEF K-9—had arrived to take their place, and the transition was going smoothly. Willingham tried to make it as seamless as possible for Rotenberry, a good friend from way back in the marines.

In one week, if all went as planned, Willingham and his teams would be on a plane back home. But as they all knew, in the military, travel arrangements don't always go as planned, and on December 19, they were still waiting to go back. Willingham was beginning to have doubts about a Christmas homecoming.

But this was a good day to be stuck at Leatherneck. Actor Mark Wahlberg had arrived to present a screening of his new movie, *The Fighter,* inside a hangar. It had come out in theaters in the U.S. nine days earlier, so it was a hot acquisition for this far-flung, makeshift cinema. Dozens of service members waited in line for his autograph and a photograph with him. Willingham was impressed by the actor's humility and what seemed to be genuine caring and respect for every person he met. He didn't rush people along. This was clearly not a celeb photo op for him.

Wahlberg had expressed interest in seeing military dogs, and when word got to Willingham and his crew, they were more than happy to accommodate. Gonzo was particularly excited.

"Do you think I can meet him in person?" he asked Willingham.

"We'll certainly try," Willingham told him.

When the time came, Willingham gave Wahlberg a brief about what the dogs can do and how well the teams did on this deployment.

"Did you lose anybody?" Wahlberg asked.

"Yes, we lost one great marine, Corporal Max Donahue, and we had a serious injury. Corporal Alfred Brenner. It was tough, man."

"I'm so sorry for your losses," Wahlberg told him. They talked a little more and Willingham was struck by how down-to-earth he was. He seemed so attentive and likable. Willingham imagined introducing Wahlberg to Lucca.

For the dog-work demo, Willingham chose Corporal Aaron Stice and his specialized search dog, Johnny, to show Wahlberg some off-leash bomb detection. On the way to the training area, Johnny, a Malinois, trotted up to Wahlberg and greeted him in the up-close-and-personal way dogs have.

"Whoa, what's going on here?" Wahlberg said, laughing, as Stice called back his dog.

"I'm sorry about that," Willingham said.

"Hey, no problem. He's a dog!"

Crotch hound, Willingham thought.

Stice and Johnny did their bomb detection demo, and Lance Corporal Anthony Liberatore put on a bite suit and played the bad guy as Rod and Corporal Andrew Sanchez sent out a dog to apprehend him.

Willingham asked Wahlberg if he wanted to put on the bite suit.

"Thank you"—he grinned—"but that's OK."

Afterward, Wahlberg met with the handlers for about ten minutes.

As promised, Gonzo got his turn. But when it came time to say something, he froze. This brave marine—a respected NCO who had been engaged in numerous firefights, had several finds with his dog, and spent most of his time in Helmand supporting British Special Forces—just stared and smiled.

After Wahlberg left, some serious ballbusting ensued.

"Deer in headlights! This is you, dude!" and his friends made their eyes giant and starstruck.

"Hey," Gonzo told them, "I was trained in combat, not celebrities."

★★★★★

ON THE CHILLY morning of December 22, Willingham and his teams said their good-byes to Rotenberry's handlers from II MEF, and good riddance to the treacherous land that had claimed Donahue and Grief and badly injured Brenner. With their packs on their backs and their K-9 partners heeling at left, they walked in two rows to the C-17 waiting for them at the flight line at Leatherneck.

Even with the planned overnight stop in Qatar, they thought they'd make it back by Christmas Eve, easy. They let their families know to set a place for them at the table. But one night turned to two, and on the morning of Christmas Eve, they were still in Qatar.

They were able to get a plane to Germany later that morning, but instead of going direct, they had to fly to Iraq first and pick up some guys, then drop them off in Kuwait. By the time they arrived at Ramstein Air Base that night, there were no flights heading back home. Nothing was open except for a convenience store, so the handlers stocked up on candy bars and sodas and hung out in one another's rooms 'til late.

"Christmas Eve in Germany," Nuckles said to Willingham. "Not where we're supposed to be."

"I know. I can think of worse places, like the one we just left a few days ago," Willingham said.

On Christmas morning, the handlers took their dogs out to enjoy a romp in the snow to burn off some energy before the flight. Willingham watched the dogs playing in the falling snow, rolling and wriggling in it, and kicking up powder as they ran.

Their resilience, the way they were in the moment, the way the past was the past and life was all about mouthfuls of snow or whatever was going on in the present—that was worth stopping and thinking about on a holiday.

He wondered if Lucca would still remember him when he got home.

WILLINGHAM FELT BAD that his marines weren't going to make it back in time for Christmas day festivities with their families. They were looking at Christmas night, at best. He couldn't give them a turkey dinner, so he did the next best thing. Before the flight, he and Nuckles got a ride to the Burger King on base and bought sixty cheeseburgers and thirty orders of fries and gave them out on the C-17.

"Merry Christmas, everyone!"

He lost himself for a few minutes in the sound of paper wrappers crinkling, the loud talking of the marines going home, the barking of excited dogs in their kennels, the familiar—reassuring—smell of burgers and fries. It felt good. Then he saw the spot where Donahue had sat on the way to Afghanistan, when Willingham had hoped that they'd all be returning together. He had worked so hard for so long to try to make that happen. And in his mind he saw Donahue in the hospital. The memory tangled with the image of Brenner in the hospital, the weight of Grief in the body bag and of Wiens on his stretcher from the morgue.

He tried not to go there. It was Christmas. He wanted to be like the dogs and be here, now.

★★★★★

IT WAS JUST after midnight, minutes after Christmas day officially ended, when they landed at March Air Reserve Base, about sixty miles from the San Diego area and Camp Pendleton. Some Patriot Guard Riders had been intending to meet them there earlier in the day to welcome them home. The main mission of Patriot Guard Riders is attending the funerals of members of the armed forces, police, and firefighters, and providing escort, often by motorcycle—as they had at Wiens's funeral. Sometimes the volunteers rallied a group for special occasions beyond funerals. Welcoming home a busload of marine dog teams on Christmas fit that bill.

But when Willingham realized how late the flight was going to get them in, he contacted them from Germany and told them not to worry. "You've got family to be with. We'll be fine."

At the air base, the marines loaded onto the waiting bus for the ride to the kennels. "Whoa, Santa's here!" some of them called out when getting aboard.

"Yo, Santa!"

The bus driver, with a real white-gray beard and a Santa hat, played up the role, with an occasional "Ho, ho, ho. Merry Christmas!"

Before they started the final leg of their trip home, Willingham heard motorcycles and looked out the window. He was astonished to see twenty motorcycles pulling up to the bus. Most of the riders stayed with their bikes, waving, holding flags, revving engines. A few climbed aboard.

"Welcome home, fellas! Merry Christmas! We're here to escort you home safely."

The marines cheered.

"Thank you so much for doing this for us," Willingham told them.

"It's our honor. It's what we do. Thank *you* for your service to our country."

About an hour later they arrived at the Camp Pendleton kennels. The Patriot Guard Riders parked and waited while the handlers took their dogs to their old kennels and said their good-byes and thank-yous to their dogs. They'd be back the next day, or maybe the day after. They'd give their dogs a break from training but take them out and have fun with them.

Leaving each other this first night after seven months of being together so much of the time was hard. Many wished they could take their dogs home, as Willingham had twice wanted to do with Lucca after deployments. They tried not to let it get them down and told themselves that at least their dogs knew this place, and that they were safe here, and they'd see them soon.

While the others were saying good-byes, Willingham decided to check in on an old friend. He walked up to Lucca's kennel. She was already sitting there, looking at all the action of these dogs coming home after being gone so long. It was almost the way he'd left her seven months earlier.

Any doubt that she would remember him was gone as soon as she saw him. He opened the door and hurried into her kennel.

"Mama Lucca!"

She wagged so hard her whole body wriggled. She jumped up, licked his face once, and raced around the kennel, running between his legs every pass. Excited, whine-like noises came out of her, something he never heard before, but it sounded like pure canine thrill.

He wanted to hug her, but she barely stood still long enough to get an ear rub and some head strokes. Then off she went, tearing around the kennel, overjoyed that her marine was finally home. The visit had to be short, because the Patriot Guard Riders were waiting to escort the marines to their final stop—a warehouse where their families and friends awaited their own reunions.

After a couple of minutes, she settled down a little, and he managed to give her a hug. "I gotta go, Lucca, but I'll be back soon!"

This time, as he walked away, he did look back. She was standing there, watching him, and wagging. He beamed back at her. He wondered if they both had the same thought: Thank you for not forgetting me.

THE WILLINGHAM FAMILY celebrated Christmas on December 27, after Willingham had a day to rest and adjust. Claire, now three, and Michael, eighteen months, had warmed up quickly to their dad. They opened their presents in their pajamas, Jill cooked up a feast, and Willingham reveled in the happiness of being home. He felt like he had one foot in a Norman Rockwell painting. But he couldn't go all in, as much as he loved his family, as much as he tried. Part of him was still in Afghanistan, responsible for thirty dog teams and all the troops they were supporting—lives hanging in the balance, ready to be snuffed out if a dog didn't hit an odor because of the way an IED was buried, or the way the wind was blowing, or fatigue. He thought of what Donahue's family must be going through this first Christmas without him, and of the seemingly endless surgeries Brenner was enduring.

He had been racing at 120 miles per hour in a war zone, and he couldn't find the brakes to slow his mind to the cruising speed of domestic life, diapers and all. Even weeks after his return, he realized something had changed in him with this deployment. He'd never been one to anger easily, but he was snapping at small things, drinking more. Samuel Adams had once been a nodding acquaintance. Now it was a frequent companion. Harder stuff, too.

"Babe," Jill said one morning early in the New Year over coffee in the kitchen. "I don't think you can take another deployment. I don't think I can, either."

Hard as it was to admit it to himself, he knew she was right. The deployments had taken a toll on both of them. He wasn't the only one bearing the burden of war. In his absence, Jill had been working full-time as a nurse until some day-care scheduling issues came up, and taking care of their two young children almost entirely on her own. He didn't know how she managed, and neither did she. She tried to keep up with her running, training for half and full marathons when she could. It's the one activity she had that was just hers and that helped clear her head and keep her centered—something she needed as she tried not to think of what could happen to her husband in that godforsaken place.

Claire also felt the pain of her dad being gone, even though her mom always kept it light when they talked about him. When she was two and a half years old and he was in Afghanistan, Claire seemed a little down. Jill asked why she was sad. "I miss my daddy so much in my heart that it hurts," Claire told her. Jill's own heart tightened. She didn't tell her husband how badly Claire missed him. What was the point?

Jill looked for ways to help her daughter and decided to play the DVDs of her husband more often for Claire and Michael.

One of their favorites was Willingham reading *The Little Engine That Could*. They also loved the songs he sang, laughing every single time he sang, "I'm a Little Teapot." They sprouted a handle and a spout when their dad did, and when he tipped over and poured, so did they.

Willingham knew his wife was right about not deploying again. It wouldn't be easy. Besides his family, military working dogs were his life—one military working dog in particular. It was clear he would never deploy with Lucca again, even if he deployed as a kennel master. It's what happens when military dog handlers rise through the ranks. They get to a certain point of responsibility, and they don't get a dog. The clock was running out on Lucca being "his" dog. It had been a long run together— nearly four years—longer than most dogs and handlers have together. She would have to become someone else's dog no matter what he did.

He was seeing her every day at the kennels, taking her out for walks, playing with her, grooming her. It was like old times, except without the war and the intensive training. Whenever he showed up, she watched and wagged as he opened the kennel door, her little black eyebrows raised in anticipation. Once he entered, she did a happy dance until he settled her down.

Three months after his return from Afghanistan, in March 2011, he had her out on a walk in the nearby hills. They came to a flat, grassy spot near the top of a hill, and he sat down. She joined him and stretched out in the sunshine.

"Lucca," he said as he stroked her coat and felt how it was already getting slightly warm from the sun. Nothing like back in Iraq, though. "I got something to tell you. I gotta find you another handler soon."

She looked up at him, and he could see she was a little uncertain—why was he so serious? It wasn't his normal style.

He recognized the look and cut to the chase. "But I've got a plan, and I think you're gonna like it."

IN MAY, ROD was wrapping up specialized search dog school at Lackland. He'd been wanting to do SSD training since Afghanistan. He liked seeing the way the dogs worked untethered, tied to the handler with something stronger than a leash. While deployed, he'd heard Willingham would be choosing several handlers to go to SSD school in January. Rod approached Willingham to find out if he'd consider him.

"I've been hoping you'd ask. I think you'd make a great SSD handler," said Willingham.

A few weeks after their return from Afghanistan, Rod started school. And now graduation was around the corner. Due to an unforeseen glitch, there weren't enough dogs to go back to home bases with the students, and Rod was among the handlers who would be returning empty-handed. All the training could go down the drain if he couldn't get a dog.

His cell phone rang as he was making dinner a few nights before graduation.

"How do you like the course, Rod?" Willingham asked.

"It's going great. I enjoyed being a PEDD handler, but I really like SSD."

"I'm glad to hear it's going well. I'd like to talk to you about Lucca for a minute."

Rod had met Lucca for the first time a couple of years earlier, in 2009, when he was new to the unit and getting a tour of the

Camp Pendleton kennels. The handler taking him around was telling him about the personality traits and tics of each dog. This was important info, because sometimes he'd be feeding them and doing kennel care by himself at night. The handler told him which dogs were fine, which were aggressive, which were escape artists, and which were painters. Painters made cleanup especially tough because they jumped and spun in their kennels with no regard for the feces that might be on their floor before someone had a chance to clean it up. Their high-energy antics would spread the stuff all around, essentially painting the kennel walls and floor with it.

The dogs were going crazy because of the humans in their midst. Some were spinning round and round. All were barking. All, that is, except this one dog, with her normally upright ears relaxed slightly to the sides, and small, dark triangular eyebrow markings poised over her expressive eyes. Rod thought she looked extremely humble and sweet. She sat quietly and looked at the marines.

"This is Lucca. She's a good girl, and an amazing specialized search dog," the handler told him. "She'll never cause you any problems."

As they walked closer to her kennel, he took a knee, and Lucca walked toward the kennel door and leaned hard against it, which allowed him to pet her through the kennel bars. He knew right then that this was going to be one of his favorite dogs.

He had watched in awe as Willingham trained with her at Pendleton. And now here was his staff sergeant on the other end of the phone, wanting to talk to him about this amazing dog.

Willingham explained he was taking a break from deployments and submitting his marine security guard package to serve at a far-off American embassy for the next three years—two eighteen-month tours, back to back.

"Over the last couple months, I've been looking at our platoon roster and evaluating who would be a good fit for Lucca," Willingham told him. "I think you'd be a great fit. Your personality will mesh well with Lucca's, and you've done a great job in combat and the training environment."

Rod tried to maintain his composure on the phone. As surprised and excited as he was about being chosen as Lucca's next handler, he wanted to sound as professional and calm as his staff sergeant sounded.

"Thanks, Staff Sergeant. I'd love to work with Lucca. I really appreciate the opportunity."

"Good to go!" Willingham said. "I'm happy to hear that. One thing. I'm hoping to adopt Lucca when she retires. I'd like her to be part of my family. I just wanted to let you know that from the outset."

"I'll take good care of her, but she'll be your couch potato, Staff Sergeant."

"Seek, Lucca!"

Rodriguez had been building up rapport with Lucca for a week by grooming her, feeding her, taking her for walks. Now it was time to start training. She sniffed where he directed her, but in a few seconds she stopped, her nose greedily sniffing the air. She whipped around and ran to a bush, tail wagging furiously. Up popped her "find"—Willingham.

"Busted!" he shouted, laughing, and clambered out of the bush.

Willingham had wanted to watch Rodriguez train her so he

could offer tips on how to work with Lucca. But as he saw her bounding over to his hiding place, it dawned on him that he should have known better than to think he could hide from this dog—the same dog who had scouted out the al-Qaeda guy in the canal.

"That was just dumb. Of course you'd find me, Bearcat Jones!"

He'd have to find another place to play helicopter handler. For the next few weeks, whenever he got a chance, he'd watch Rodriguez and Lucca train together from a pickup truck—windows rolled up, just in case.

Even without his scent, for a while Lucca seemed to always be looking over her shoulder for Willingham, wondering where he might be hiding this time. He had pulled back his visits to Lucca after he knew she'd be making the transition to Rod. It was important for her to want to bond with someone else. Once Rod took over, Willingham backed off all the way. Willingham talked to her about it and sealed it with a hug.

"This isn't good-bye, Lucca. It's just a temporary thing. Rod's a great guy, and he'll take good care of you."

It wasn't easy, but he realized it would have been much harder if he had just returned from deployment with Lucca. His previous deployment without her had served as a buffer for him to start detaching a little. He knew she needed to look to Rod as she'd once looked to him. Their bond would be a matter of life and death when they deployed in a few months, and he couldn't let sentiment get in the way.

In November, Willingham was getting ready to leave for his new role as a detachment commander tasked with providing internal security at the American embassy in Helsinki, Finland. It would be difficult not to be in K-9, but he knew it was for the best. For the last few months, some of the tensions he'd felt after his Afghanistan deployment had eased up, as had his drinking, and he was back to his usual affable, unflappable self. His heart was still in K-9, but he needed to make this move. He was relieved that he'd be able to make it with his family at his side.

Well, not quite the whole family.

Lucca would be deploying to Afghanistan with Rod in a couple of weeks, and she wasn't scheduled to return for seven months, in summer 2012. They'd still be in the embassy security program for another two and a half years.

It would be a long, long time before they'd meet again.

Willingham drove the pickup to the training area one last time to watch Rod and Lucca. They looked like they'd been doing this together for years. She did everything he asked her to in his gentle manner. She searched left, right, and forward, and came back, all without hesitation. She worked for him enthusiastically, and he praised with equal gusto. Willingham felt like he was watching his child graduate and move on without him. He was thrilled, but he was going to miss her like hell.

"It's a shitty place you're going to, Mama Lucca," he said quietly as he watched them work from the cab of the pickup. "Keep everyone safe, and you come home safe so you can go home with me soon."

She was far, far off leash now.

PART FOUR

Back to Work

11

Special Forces

THE SMELL OF hashish wafted in through an open door of the compound. Lucca turned her head toward it and sniffed a few times. The smell meant nothing special to her, and she returned to observing what was going on inside.

About a dozen Green Berets and Afghan Local Police were sipping tea with a village elder and a few friends who were visiting his home. The elder and his chai boy walked around the room pouring the brew from a large silver vessel into small glass cups, handing them to anyone who looked interested when they inquired, "Chai?"

"*Manana*," Rod said, easily remembering the Pashto word for *thank you*, which was taught to him by his friend and brother in arms, U.S. Army Special Forces Sergeant Jake Parker, who had learned the language—considered a Category IV language because of its level of difficulty for native English speakers—as part of his Special Forces training. Rod held the glass of steaming amber liquid in his hands and took a sip. Tea was not his usual drink of choice, but its warmth and the spicy taste felt good on this January afternoon, especially after the seven klicks he and the others had walked to reach this small village in the Nahri Saraj District of Helmand Province.

Lucca sat quietly, observing the curious tea party. The four members of the Afghan Local Police wore such different uniforms from one another that it looked like someone had gone through the clearance bin at an army surplus store. One wore an official ALP khaki uniform; the others wore hand-me-downs from the Americans—anything they could get ahold of that would mark them as not Taliban. None wore any sort of protective gear.

Rod had grown as much of a beard as he could since arriving for deployment the month before, and now matched the rest of the Green Berets he and Lucca were supporting, as well as the local police working with them. He welcomed the break from daily shaving and was glad that his beard came in better than his mustache, which wasn't making its presence known nearly as well.

Parker sported a similar look, with a naturally short beard and just a shadow of a mustache. He knew of guys who couldn't grow more than fuzz on their faces, so he was grateful for what he had. It wasn't a matter of blending in with locals. It was a matter of building rapport. Around these parts, clean-faced males were looked on as less than manly—as boys, even. So any facial hair was better than nothing. It was common knowledge that you'd be taken more seriously if you sported a beard. But not too long a beard. That was generally reserved for village elders.

There was one man, however, who didn't need a beard. Jan

(pronounced *John*) Mohammed, the de facto leader of the Afghan Local Police in the district and beyond, towered over all the other Afghans and even most of the Green Berets. He was a robust six foot four, and his only facial hair was a vast black mustache that started and ended well beyond the corners of his mouth. The Green Berets dubbed it a "power 'stache."

Those who bathed near him saw that he bore scars all over his body from the bullet and shrapnel wounds he had collected during his thirty-eight or so years of living and fighting here. "He looks like Swiss cheese, he's got so many holes," one soldier who had seen the evidence firsthand told Rod.

Mohammed, known to the Americans as "J Mo," or sometimes just "Mo," drank his tea and spoke with the owner of the compound in Pashto, one of the two official languages of Afghanistan. Pashto, the native tongue of the Pashtun people, Afghanistan's main ethnic group, was widely spoken in this rural area. Dari, Afghanistan's lingua franca, could also be heard here but was used more commonly in urban environments. Mohammed had arranged for the men who were having tea, and the other dozen pulling security outside, to bed down here for the night, as they were conducting village stability operations.

A native of the area, Mohammed knew almost everyone in the nearby districts, or at least their relatives. His connections throughout Helmand Province were strong. He had proved invaluable for helping the Americans train Afghan Local Police to patrol their area, and for making inroads to remote rural communities where the Taliban liked to take their business. It was a strategy endorsed by General Petraeus, who held that the strong local policing of thousands of rural villages was essential for defeating the Taliban.

Since Parker was the only one on the Special Forces team who spoke Pashto, he spent a lot of time with Mohammed. The team had hired native Afghan interpreters who helped with heavy language lifting, but Parker was the go-to man when Mohammed wanted to speak on his own to the Americans.

The two worked together on several matters, including some relatively mundane ones, such as payroll for the dozens of Afghan Local Police who worked with them. Parker voluntarily took on creating a payroll system for these men, who had no bank accounts and who were part of an ever-changing base of workers with very little structure. Here today, gone tomorrow, but here's this guy's friend to take his place. If Mohammed vetted the new guy, he was OK.

What would have been an HR specialist's nightmare back home was only a temporary headache for a Green Beret like Parker. If he could get through some of the world's most challenging training—including a Special Forces SERE (Survival, Evasion, Resistance, and Escape) course about, among other things, how to handle being held in the worst ways by bad guys, as well as the grueling two-week Robin Sage warfare exercise, which served as a sort of Green Beret final exam—he could handle payday in a remote combat outpost. Besides, Mohammed was there the first couple of times to introduce the men until Parker got to know them himself. He got it under control quickly, and payday became an excellent way to interact with the men.

As part of earning their monthly cash, the local police, sometimes with Mohammed but usually without, would join the Green Beret team and hump from the combat outpost for up to a week at a time, walking from village to village. They wouldn't go the most direct route, because Taliban could easily plant IEDs on the roads, and they weren't set up to do route clearance. Instead, they walked through farm fields and other areas far from the beaten path. When possible, they avoided even the smallest roads and trails.

On patrols, the Green Berets, with the help of the local police, established relationships with local elders, finding out how they could help the villages, and getting information from them about suspected insurgents. They developed strategic checkpoints that would house several police and keep the Taliban at bay when fighting season started. They cleared suspicious buildings and surrounding areas of IEDs and caches. They were prepared to root out Taliban, too, if they came across any.

Lucca once again had a big role to play, helping lead the way through the rural areas and being an essential part of clearing compounds of deadly explosives. There was plenty of work to do, and most days, many miles to walk.

She was enjoying something of a job-share arrangement with a specialized search dog named Darko. The high-energy Belgian Malinois had a Kong obsession Lucca had probably seen only once before, with Bram. His handler, Marine Corporal Daniel Cornier, said he was the only dog he'd ever met who could chew apart an "indestructible" Kong in less than thirty minutes. The dogs were highly regarded by the Green Berets, many of whom had worked with other dogs—dogs who didn't have anywhere near the noses or drive these dogs did. "We had a couple dogs once that couldn't smell a stick of C-4 right in front of their noses," one soldier told Rod.

As lauded as Lucca and Darko were, they were as opposite as they could be in personalities and search methods. Lucca was methodical, taking her time on searches. Anyone who watched her said they could almost see her thinking. When she wasn't work-ing, she loved hanging out with the team. She made friends with whoever had time to pet her or snuggle her. Parker was one of her favorites. He rubbed her just right around the ears and talked to her in an enthusiastic and kind manner.

Lucca was a huge morale booster around the combat outpost. Despite the relatively nonviolent months leading up to fighting season, being a Green Beret in Taliban country was still an in-tense job. And while Special Forces are among the toughest of the tough, that didn't stop them from missing home. As she had in Iraq, Lucca brought a piece of home with her. Soldiers petted her, talked to her, told her their troubles. "She's really calming," Parker told Rod while petting her one day. "You can't say that for a mine sweeper."

They couldn't say that for Darko, either. One cold night on a mission, Parker—who was used to seeing Lucca lie right next to Rod on overnight missions—tried to lie next to Darko. Darko snapped at him. End of cuddle time.

Darko had such high energy on missions that if you didn't know better, you'd swear he had a stash of Rip Its hidden under his bed. Some military dogs tremble in anticipation of being able to do bite work. This dog trembled and whined in anticipation of being able to do searches. His investigations were completed in the blink of an eye. *Forward, left, right, come,* done. Fast, but dis-ciplined and careful. He had never missed. Neither had Lucca.

Parker had great admiration for both dogs and felt much more secure knowing Lucca and Darko were helping them ma-neuver safely through areas known for IEDs. They seemed to embody most of the core attributes of the Special Forces, includ-ing adaptability, perseverance, a team player mentality, courage, capability, and professionalism. The other two attributes, integrity and personal responsibility, could possibly belong to Lucca. Darko he wasn't quite so sure about. "You never know what he's thinking," he joked to Cornier. "He's in a world of his own."

On missions, either Lucca or Darko would walk point while the other dog walked toward the back on leash without searching. When the point dog needed a break, the dog teams switched places. On other occasions, the dogs would split up, going with different elements for part of the day. When they headed off to go separate ways, Lucca would sometimes watch Darko for a few beats. But Darko never looked back.

Darko didn't often interact with Lucca. If he had a Kong, that was his world. If he didn't have a Kong, his world was all about getting one. He had little time for the frivolities of dog life.

It was the cold, rainy season in Afghanistan, a time when Taliban activity tended to be at a low. The Green Berets and local police were working hard now, before fighting season, to prevent insurgents from even being able to set foot in the area, much less set up operations or plant a bumper crop of IEDs. Their jobs in these months tended to be more diplomat than warrior—not the kind of exciting work some Green Berets signed up for, but all part of the unconventional warfare that helped them earn the moniker "the quiet professionals." These Special Forces soldiers were well aware that an ounce of prevention now could save a bunch of guys later. Not that that made the long slogs without action any more appealing.

For Lucca and Darko, enthusiasm for the job never waned. Noses to the ground, they sniffed one klick after the next. Even Mohammed, while reluctant to pet the dogs, more than once told their handlers, with a nod and a smile, "*Shah spay*"—good dog.

Lucca looked up at Mohammed when he spoke. To Rod, it appeared as if somehow she knew what he was saying. Or maybe she smelled his authority. But whatever the reason, when he spoke, she paid close attention.

PROVERBS ARE FAR more popular in Afghanistan than they are in the United States. They come up regularly in conversation, pepper everyday speech, turn the mundane into the poetic.

The proverb that seemed most fitting for Parker on this deployment was a simple one. "The first day you meet, you are friends. The next day you meet, you are brothers."

The first time he met Rod and Cornier was on a very cold winter evening when the handlers were manning the small guard-post area on base. It was located outside, and shifts were long. Parker was with two friends, Navy EOD1 Sean P. Carson and Lieutenant Christopher Mosko, also a navy EOD specialist, who happened to be out at the same time as Parker, so they joined him.

Parker was a Bravo, the team's weapons sergeant. Teams usually have two soldiers with this military occupational specialty, but on this deployment, Parker was the only one. As the weapons sergeant, he was in charge of the security at the camp, so he went to see the new guys. When the three approached Rod and Cornier, it was clear that despite being fairly bundled up, they were very cold. So Parker, Mosko, and Carson collected some wood and came back and built them a fire. They stayed with them and talked. They felt like they'd known one another for years. Friendships were natural and fast and quickly became solid. Brothers.

Parker never expected two marine dog handlers and two navy

EOD specialists to be among his closest friends on deployment, but then again, it didn't really surprise him. Special Forces soldiers in Afghanistan were used to working with men from other branches of the military when they needed expertise beyond what was available to them within SF. It was all about the mission, not about the uniform. And formalities are out the window. Everyone was on a first-name basis, and to a great extent, even rank didn't come into play when it came to friendships.

That meant it was easy for Parker when he decided everyone on the team needed to learn some Pashto. He'd already given some very basic English lessons to the local police stationed at the outpost. He didn't need to do this. They could get by just fine without English. It was more about building that all-important rapport. The dozen or so men who showed up seemed to enjoy it, and Parker had fun spending time with them.

He wanted the Americans to learn some Pashto for the same reason—creating trust and understanding with locals. So at a weekly meeting, he passed out worksheets he made up. He listed several key words and phrases, in transliteration. Things like:

> *Stah num tsa dhe—What is your name?*
> *Ta sanga yee—How are you?*
> *Da khoday pa amaan—Good-bye.*

Simple stuff, but it could make a difference. If the Afghans trusted them and wanted to work hard with them, everyone was safer. There could be more intel. There would be less chance of green-on-blue surprises. As an article in the *National Review* said, "The old joke that you cannot buy an Afghan, you can only rent him has much truth to it: Afghan troops are very loyal until they are not." Learning some of their language could go a little way toward gaining the coveted loyalty.

Parker reminded the Americans whenever he saw them that they needed to study their words. In a couple of weeks, he gave a pop quiz. Those who didn't do well had to write and rewrite the phrases during the next week until they memorized them.

When he was assigned Pashto as his language back in the Special Forces Qualification Course (aka the Q Course), he wasn't thrilled. Most of his friends were learning Spanish or other Category I languages. He and his four Pashto classmates were still struggling through the Pashto alphabet while the guys in Spanish were learning basic sentences. Their course lasted weeks longer than the Spanish course did. They went to class five hours a day, five days a week, for six months. And there was a lot of studying after hours. But in the end, he was glad he'd been chosen to learn the language. It brought him closer to the Afghans, and he hoped in turn, that would bring the Afghans closer to the Americans.

Lucca was already doing a pretty good job of that herself.

ROD REACHED AROUND Lucca and unbuckled her harness. He had received a new harness for this deployment. Instead of one side reading BADASS, he had customized it with a smaller name tape with the word LEGEND.

"When it comes to the military dog world, she's a legend," he told Willingham when he showed him the patch.

Rod and Lucca were back at their Special Operations outpost

in Nahri Saraj, just settling in at an outdoor table for dinner after a three-day patrol. Within a minute of her harness coming off, a young member of the Afghan Local Police approached her.

"Looooka?"

Rod nodded and smiled. "Yes, Lucca."

"Loooooka!" He cautiously stroked her head, and when he saw that she seemed to like it, he grinned and petted her in earnest.

Parker walked over to Rod and Lucca.

"Ready for some real food?" he asked.

"Absolutely." Rod didn't mind MREs as much as some guys, but he was hungry for a decent meal.

They walked in the direction of the kitchen, avoiding the flooded and muddy areas along the way. Inside, a small Afghan man named Rauf was dishing out a local chicken-and-rice specialty he had cooked.

"*Spay sarray!*" he greeted Rod. When Rauf first started calling him this, Parker translated. "He said, 'dog man,'" a name Rod was used to, only in its more casual American form, "dog guy."

"*Salim!*" Rauf greeted Parker with his Pashto name. Rauf ladled fragrant-smelling chicken with red sauce on top of a mound of rice that was dotted with raisins. One of the perks that came with being in Special Forces here was hiring local cooks when possible. It helped village relations, brought a little money to the locals, and boosted morale around the outposts. A from-scratch hot meal was a luxury few at such remote outposts took for granted, even if it wasn't the kind of food they were used to back home.

At the outpost, Rod, Cornier, Lucca, and Darko shared a

small room. The handlers slept in bunk beds. The dogs slept on an exercise mat their handlers had taken from the makeshift gym there. Darko liked his space, so they cut the mat in half so the dogs would have more room. They topped the mats with green wool blankets.

One evening, Rod and Cornier left the dogs in the room by themselves for a couple of hours when they went to eat and watch TV in the common area. It was something they'd done several times, and the dogs were usually sleeping when they returned. But when they came back this time, the dogs were awake, sitting and looking blankly at them, surrounded by mauled MRE containers, torn-up bags of Jolly Ranchers and Starburst fruit chews, and slobbery wrappers that had once contained granola bars and potato chips. It looked like a party gone bad.

"What?!" Rod and Cornier shouted at the same time.

"I can't believe it!"

"Rod! Look what Lucca did!"

"Not my Lucca! That's Darko's work!"

Lucca's dark brows darted diagonally over her eyes as she glanced from Darko to the mess to Rod and back. Her ears wilted alongside her head. Darko appeared to get physically smaller.

Mosko and Carson came out to check out the commotion. They burst out laughing when they saw the mess of care-package contents and MREs. Rod and Cornier started laughing, too.

On seeing the reaction, Lucca's eyebrows relaxed and her ears perked up. Darko inflated back to his normal size. Their tails wagged, and Rod thought they looked not only relieved that they weren't in trouble, but pleased with the merry and impromptu gathering in their room.

The handlers cleaned up and stayed up late to make sure the

dogs were OK, giving them a couple of extra walks. They vowed never to leave food anywhere within reach again.

When they finally went to bed, Lucca snored heartily. Despite his fatigue, Rod had to chuckle.

"So much for my perfect princess," he said before drifting off.

THE RAIN CAME down in plump drops that rolled off Lucca's thick fur. She was walking point down a narrow dirt trail between farm fields. As she kept her nose to the ground, droplets ran off it in little rivulets.

"She's like the postman," one of the Green Berets walking next to Rod said. "Neither rain nor sleet nor dark of night . . ."

Lucca approached a ten-by-ten mud-wall structure at the edge of a field. One of the sides had crumbled from age and the elements, revealing a mound of old hay stacked inside.

"Forward, Lucca." Lucca knew exactly what he wanted. She trotted over to the structure and sniffed to the right, along the open front. Her wet nose then inspected the bottom perimeter of the three walls. Finding nothing to report, she trotted back to Rod.

"She's a great dog," the Green Beret said when she continued walking point.

"She's amazing," Rod said.

Rod knew how special her talents were. Most dogs need to be directed to search the exteriors of buildings and vehicles, often with handlers using sweeping hand motions wherever they want the dog to search. Lucca didn't need any guidance with these tasks. It was her job, and even though it had been more than a couple of years since the end of her last deployment, she hadn't lost her touch. She knew what was expected.

Each time he asked her to search a car or structure exterior, she gave him a split-second glance of confirmation, as if telling him, *Don't worry. I got that.*

Right . . . left . . . around . . . checking any door seams, every perimeter . . . done.

The Green Berets, Afghan Local Police, Rod, and Lucca continued for a couple of klicks. Along the way, the rain stopped, and Lucca shook the excess off her coat. They came to a small road that dead-ended into a walled courtyard. There was no house structure, and the ground appeared to have been ripped up in places. It was already drying. Around here, with the earth so dry most of the year, it takes a lot more than a downpour to keep the ground wet.

"I don't like it," Rod told Parker. "Looks shady to me."

After having Lucca check around the outside of the wall, he sent her inside the walled area to search without blow-by-blow instructions from him, trusting her nose to lead her where she needed to go, and following closely so she wouldn't get so far ahead that he couldn't spot red flags. If she found nothing, he would direct her in a more systematic search.

She walked in, continued for about fifteen feet, stopped, and looked up at Rod with a little tail wag.

"Lucca, come!"

She ran toward him, and he praised her up for a few seconds before telling the guys behind him what they'd already come to know. Lucca had another potential find. They set up a security perimeter so no insurgents could surprise them. The Green Berets faced outward with their M-4s, and the Afghan Local Police did the same with their AKs.

A Special Forces engineer checked out what Lucca had responded on. It was buried loosely under some dirt, and he didn't want to move it. He set up some C-4 close to it and ran a fuse back to a safe distance.

A fiery flash, a boom, and the IED was history.

Compliments all around.

"Nice work, Lucca!"

"Loooooka!"

She looked up from where she was lying and wagged a couple of times. But she had a Kong to chew and got right back to business.

"HAYSTACKS ARE NICE at home, not so nice in Afghanistan," Rod told Lucca as they approached the first of three haystacks along the mission route. Whenever they came to areas where intel indicated Taliban activity, every haystack was suspect. The five-foot-high mounds of hay or straw were popular hiding places for weapons caches. They were easy to access, and if the weapons were found, no one could take the rap for them—unlike those found within the walls of someone's compound.

The caches posed no immediate threat. The greater danger was when insurgents—knowing haystacks were subject to inspection by their enemies—concealed IEDs in or near them. Most haystacks were just haystacks. You couldn't tell the good ones from the bad ones without a dog.

"Seek, Lucca," Rod told her when they got close to the haystack. She needed no more guidance. She went in, nose down, and circled around the haystack. She sniffed upward in a few spots and was done in thirty seconds.

The second haystack also turned up nothing.

A little farther away, Lucca walked up to the third haystack, went partway around, came back a little, then back and forth a couple more times, as if narrowing in on a cone of scent. Rod knew what was coming next.

Lucca stopped and stared at him.

"Come!" She trotted over to him, wagging. "Gooood girllll!"

"Lucca responded over here on this haystack," he called out to one of the Green Berets behind him. The engineer walked over as Rod was giving Lucca a belly-rub paycheck. Rod stood up and indicated where Lucca had responded.

Everyone cleared out. The engineer tossed an incendiary grenade to the bottom of the hay. Even though the hay was still damp from the recent rains, once the grenade activated, it burned quickly, heaving up light gray smoke. For a moment, Rod wondered if it was a false alarm.

An explosion put an end to that question.

Parker walked over and fist-bumped Rod. "Lucca does it again!" He reached down and scratched her behind the ears.

"I hate those things," Parker told Rod. "IEDs are like snakes. You keep messing with them and you're gonna get bit."

12

Rock-Paper-Scissors

THE ALARM ON Rod's 32 GB iPod Touch went off at 0430. He shut it off, turned on a reading light, and looked down at Lucca from his raised cot. She glanced up at him, yawned, and shut her eyes again.

"No snooze alarm today, Mama Lucca. Time to rise and shine. Got a long day ahead."

He climbed down from his bed, crouched beside Lucca, and stroked her head.

"Come on, sleepyhead. Wanna eat?"

At the sound of the word *eat*, she opened her eyes and propped herself up on her elbow.

Her tail thumped her mat a couple of times as she watched Rod pour two scoops of Science Diet into her portable bowl. She moseyed over and dug into breakfast.

"I don't know how you can be hungry at this hour, Lucca."

He was happy she had a good early morning appetite. Whenever they went on missions, he had her eat two hours before the patrol to help prevent bloat, a life-threatening digestive emergency most common in large-breed dogs with deep chests—like most military working dog breeds. Fortunately, the gastropexy surgeries all dogs larger than thirty-five pounds undergo prevents the deadly part of bloat. Still, handlers take no chances.

Rod let Lucca out for her morning constitutional at the adjacent dog area and knocked on Cornier's door. Cornier and Darko had gotten their own room when the navy EOD techs moved to another base. The two handlers had each other's backs when it came to making sure they weren't oversleeping on mission days.

"You up, bro?"

The door opened, he heard a "Hey" from the room, and Darko walked out.

Rod said, "Hey," and went back inside his room. There was no rush to get ready. They weren't meeting the others until just after sunrise, at 0630.

He hit the portable latrine, brushed his teeth, came back, changed into his cammies, and checked his pack to make sure he had all the essentials. Today's patrol was supposed to last all day, into evening. He could get by with one MRE and a couple of scoops of kibble for Lucca, but he always packed more food and water than necessary. You never knew where you'd really end up at the end of the day around here.

Lucca strolled back in and walked straight over to a small desk with two boxes of treats. One was from Rod's mom, the other from the mother of a Green Beret who wanted to thank Lucca and Darko for helping keep her son safe. Rod took a couple of treats from each box, put them in a plastic bag, and stuck them in a side pocket of his pack. Lucca walked over, sniffed the pack, and wagged expectantly.

"Those are for later, Lucca. We'll save them for snack time."

Rod found her brush and called her over to his chair. He usually groomed her after missions, and outside, but it was still dark, and there wasn't much else to do. Lucca stood with her eyes half-closed in pure pleasure. Her neck dropped slightly. Her tail went limp. When he stopped brushing she gave him *the look*, as he called it, and he continued.

Eventually he walked over to the kitchen to get breakfast. Other guys were already there, prepping their morning meals. They toasted Pop-Tarts, ate fruit, microwaved scrambled eggs, poured heaping bowls of cereal. It was every man for himself. Rauf, the local cook, made only dinner.

Rod ate a chocolate chip Clif Bar and drank a bottle of water. It was all he could stomach at this hour. He grabbed a few energy bars for later. Back at his room he let Lucca out one more time. When she returned, he geared up and clicked on her harness, and they walked to meet the others outside the command room.

A few Green Berets had already gathered for "pregame." It was starting to get light. As more gathered, they did radio checks to make sure all radios were in working order. The sound of static and amplified voices punctuated the quiet morning. Everyone made sure they had enough of what would take them through the mission; water, food, working batteries. Someone noticed that the Afghan Local Police guys weren't there yet.

"Hey, Parker, go get your kids!"

Not that it was his job, but of anyone there, he had become pretty tight with the Afghans. Knowing the same language helped, but there was something beyond that. They seemed to have come to trust him, and he enjoyed their company. Parker jogged off to find the Afghans who were supposed to join them. They were late, but that wasn't unusual. Parker often had to act as their alarm clock.

"Hey, come on, up, up!" he told them in Pashto as he entered their living quarters, on the outer edge of the compound. "I told you yesterday, remember? Man, you guys like to get your beauty sleep." They rallied and were soon outside with the Americans for pregame. Parker hoped they were prepared.

"You guys got any water?" Parker asked them.

"No."

He went in and pulled out enough water bottles for six guys.

"You got food, right?"

"No."

He went back to the kitchen and grabbed whatever portable foods he could find. Energy bars and their favorite—strawberry Pop-Tarts.

As he helped get them ready, Lucca was making her usual rounds. She had become the star of pregame—a mascot of sorts. While Darko generally sat by Cornier, leashed, and not in the mood for socializing, Lucca seemed to make a point of spending a little time with each Green Beret. Sometimes the local police even beckoned her over for some pats.

Lucca walked over to Cornier and Darko. Darko took a quick glance and continued staring off somewhere in the distance. Or nowhere at all. Just not at Lucca, or Rod, who followed.

The team received the mission brief. It was to be a patrol like most of their others—getting the lay of the land, scoping out places for future checkpoints, establishing relationships with residents, and, if need be, dealing with trouble along the way. There was some intel about possible IEDs a few klicks away, and they'd regroup before that.

"You want to do infil or exfil, Rod?" Cornier asked. They usually decided between them who would start walking point on the way out, and who would take over on the way back. Cornier likened it to rock-paper-scissors. Random, luck of the draw. So far Darko had been in the right place at the right time more often than Lucca when it came to IEDs. He had found several more than Lucca had. He was paper; she was rock. He knew if she'd been on the path Darko had been on, she'd have been scissors to his paper.

Either way, between them, they had it covered.

"Doesn't matter," Rod said. "I guess we'll take infil."

The platoon set out. Several Afghan Local Police led the way, then Lucca, followed by Rod, then the Green Berets, and bringing up the rear, Darko and Cornier. Rod watched Lucca as she walked with the rising sun behind her. She was a dark silhouette against the orange sky. He wished he had his camera handy to capture the image forever.

SEVERAL HOURS INTO the patrol, they came across two boys, ten and twelve years old, tending a poppy field near a compound. The poppies were about a month or so away from harvest, by the looks of it. The buds were still on the stems but hadn't yet blossomed into the pink and white petals that float over the land in spring. The petals still needed to grow, then fall away to reveal a green pod that would eventually become the size of a small egg.

As it ripened, it would produce opium. Farmers got more money for growing opium than other crops, but their profit was scant. The big money would be made several rungs up the ladder.

The boys were doing what farm boys do all around the world—whatever the farmer, who may have been their father, told them to do to keep the crops thriving. The Americans who saw them walking down the rows and looking at the plants had no idea what they were doing.

Parker approached the boys and greeted them in Pashto. After a brief exchange of formalities, one boy asked if Parker had anything they could have. They had clearly heard about the NATO troops carrying little gifts. Parker unzipped a side pouch on his backpack and withdrew two new ballpoint pens. "*Qalam!*" the boys exclaimed, smiling in delight. Parker knew a lot of soldiers who gave out candy in these situations, but twelve-year-old boys in these parts aren't the same as twelve-year-old boys back home. Candy might be OK for little kids, but if you're twelve around here, you're not a kid. He respected that and gave them something they might be able to use—even though they probably didn't know how to read or write. Still, maybe the pens would come in handy.

Parker and one of the Afghan police spoke with the boys for a couple of minutes in Pashto. It was a friendly conversation, Rod could hear, but he understood only one word in their conversation: *Taliban*.

The platoon moved on for a few minutes and stopped for an update. The boys had told them that Taliban insurgents might have planted some explosives in fields in the area. They had no idea where. Probably not too close to here, since the Taliban wasn't out to kill locals, especially children.

If the Green Berets didn't have intel already saying there could be IEDs around here, they might not have put much stock in the boys' warning. They knew all too well that anything anyone told them out there was to be taken with a grain of salt. But when you add a local tip to trusted intel, it can be the start of a dangerous equation. Intel + Tip = Problem. They proceeded cautiously, Afghan Local Police first to scope their native land with their expert eyes, then Lucca, to inspect it with her expert nose.

THE IED THAT took Lucca out of the fight on the afternoon of March 23 was likely one of two types.

It may have been an IED with a small main charge. Such IEDs, sometimes known as "toe poppers," intend to hurt, to take off one or two legs, but not kill—usually. Just destroy the morale of the unit and ensure that a soldier, seaman, airman, or marine will never walk this soil again.

Or it could have been a larger pressure-plate IED that had "low-ordered," or deteriorated, due to many reasons, including moisture, a blasting cap with inadequate power, or age-related factors. If it had been in good working order, there would not have been much left of Lucca. A high-order explosive can detonate at speeds of nine thousand to twenty-seven thousand feet per second, and according to the Centers for Disease Control, "produce a defining supersonic over-pressurization shock wave." If the victim is not instantly killed, injuries can be numerous and life threatening and can include blast lung, concussion, eye rupture, and open brain injuries, in addition to traumatic amputation of entire limbs.

Within ten minutes of the blast, the medevac helicopter was

whisking Lucca and Rod to Camp Leatherneck, twenty minutes away. Rod's heart was racing, but he tried to maintain calm, for Lucca's sake. She had enough problems. She didn't need to sniff fear and anxiety in her handler. One of the medics brought out a bag that read MWD KIT, and Rod instantly knew she was in good hands. Anyone who carried a special emergency kit for dogs was obviously well prepared for anything that came their way on four legs. Or three legs and a mangled fourth.

The helicopter was so loud that everyone had to shout to be heard.

"Are there any other wounds you know about?" a medic asked Rod above the helicopter noise after he had examined Lucca. Rod pointed to the burns the medic had already explored.

"Any shrapnel or gunshots?"

Rod shook his head.

"Is she on any medications?"

"No, just the morphine the Delta gave her," he said. He thought about the poppies they'd walked through that day, and how the plants would soon be producing opium, and how morphine was the most abundant opiate in the opium. He found himself feeling grateful to the local plants, even though they weren't the legally grown ones that are used for medicine. Somewhere, a poppy field that looked a lot like the ones they walked through had made the morphine that was now helping Lucca not feel the searing pain.

The men Rod and Lucca left behind regrouped. Cornier brought Darko up to the front element, and they continued through the field and on to the next. Parker, who was relieved that his good friend Rod was OK, tried not to let himself think about how much he would miss Lucca—how much they'd all miss their mascot.

THREE MEMBERS OF a veterinary team met the Black Hawk when it landed at the Leatherneck flight line. They helped Rod carry Lucca in her makeshift stretcher—a blanket—to the back of the pickup truck. One veterinarian rode with Lucca, comforting her as he checked her vitals and did a quick initial evaluation of her condition.

They arrived at the veterinary tent and lifted Lucca onto a stainless steel table. She was panting but not heavily. The morphine the medic had given her seemed to be working. She lay still, her eyes half-open, staring at nothing. Rod stroked her head.

"You're going to be OK, Mama Lucca," he told her, trying to sound convincing—he realized more for his sake than hers. Her eyes turned slowly to look at him and drifted back to their empty stare.

The veterinarians carefully cut off the bandages and assessed Lucca's wounds—the muscles, tendons, and sharp bone edges of what was left of her lower left leg, the burns and lacerations on her chest, the blisters forming around her lips. They performed blood work and urinalysis, an abdominal ultrasound to look for internal bleeding, chest radiographs, and an ECG. They started her on IV fluids and IV antibiotics.

Her leg was anesthetized and the vets pulled back a flap of shredded, fur-covered skin and irrigated her wound to remove as much dirt and shrapnel as possible. They drew the skin back over what was left of her leg and stitched it shut with temporary sutures so the wreckage was no longer exposed.

"There's not much we can do for her," one of the veterinarians said.

Rod stopped breathing and his chest tightened.

The vet continued. "We're going to have to send her on to Kandahar. They're much better equipped for this kind of trauma. We want to get her on a bird quickly. Why don't you grab some things? You won't be coming back."

Rod exhaled, felt the life rush back into him. He rested his hand on her soft fur and sensed her warmth and her breathing.

"I want to tell you," the vet said, "she would have bled out fast if you hadn't acted so quickly. You and the medic did an outstanding job."

Rod had been keeping stoic. But as he walked away, the reality of the situation came crashing down around him, and his emotions overwhelmed him.

THE AMBULANCE WAS waiting when the C-130 Hercules landed at Kandahar Airfield. Lucca lay on blankets in the lower half of a kennel crate. The top had been removed for easy access. Rod and some members of the Kandahar veterinary crew carefully hoisted the crate from the floor of the transport aircraft down to the ambulance. Lucca raised her head to look at what was going on.

"It's OK, Mama Lucca," Rod told her. "Rest easy."

The vet who had accompanied Lucca from Leatherneck briefed Lieutenant-Colonel James Giles III, senior veterinary surgeon in Afghanistan, and got back on the C-130 for the return trip. Giles, Rod, and a vet tech rode in the back of the ambulance to the other side of the airfield with Lucca. Giles did a cursory examination of Lucca. With the tech, he collected vital signs, inspected the bandages to see if there was any bleeding evident, and made sure her IV fluids and morphine drip were being delivered properly.

They parked just outside the veterinary tent, where veterinarian Captain Nathan (Shane) Chumbler, officer in charge of the veterinary clinic, awaited her arrival. The vets and techs did more blood work, inserted a urinary catheter, and switched Lucca from morphine to a fentanyl drip for pain control. Her leg was anesthetized again so they could assess the damage.

The front left leg had been blown off between the elbow and wrist. They couldn't simply make a neat cut in the antebrachium and let it remain as a partial leg. The muscles would atrophy and the leg would be vulnerable to complications such as decubitus ulcers—essentially, bedsores—which could lead to infections and further problems. With hind legs, there's usually enough muscle mass to leave part of the leg, but not with forelimbs.

Giles contacted the director of the Role 4 Veterinary Hospital at Lackland Air Force Base to discuss whether he should do a complete amputation or preserve most of her limb for a prosthesis—a procedure that was emerging in veterinary medicine, but not done routinely. The director wasn't against the concept of doing prosthetics in the future but in Lucca's case advised against it since there was no established plan or equipment in place.

The vets reassured Rod that dogs like Lucca do very well on three legs and that since Lucca is such a strong dog, she should be walking around in no time.

They wanted to arrange to do the surgery in the "human" hospital at Kandahar. The veterinary tent was a rustic structure that ran on a generator that went out on a daily basis. It wasn't the kind of place to do major surgery. The staff at the hospital had been very supportive of the vet staff bringing over their most serious canine patients. The procedure just needed a little planning.

Since Lucca was in stable condition and it was now late at night, they set her up with a vet tech to care for her until morning. Chumbler bandaged her using pinkish red and yellow vet wrap, the closest they had to the marine flag colors of red and gold. He wrote the marine motto, *Semper Fidelis,* on it with a Sharpie. Chumbler always tried to make the handlers of injured dogs feel at least a little better with touches like these.

The staff placed Lucca in the largest cage in the clinic. It was about four feet wide and three feet high, and at floor level. Rod could have spent the night in a room they provided for him, but he didn't want to leave Lucca, and he definitely didn't want to be alone.

He crawled in the cage beside Lucca, with his torso in the cage and his legs sticking out. The vet tech, who had seen loyal handlers like this before, grabbed him a blanket and pillow.

Just before dawn, when he grew too tired to worry about the complications of anesthesia, the possibility of deadly infections, the idea of his Mama Lucca's leg coming off, of her never working again, and of how Willingham would probably wish he'd chosen someone else for Lucca, he fell asleep.

WHEN HE AWOKE an hour later, Rod carefully maneuvered out of the cage so he wouldn't disturb Lucca. He left her sleeping and walked to the nearby military dog kennel office to write to Willingham. He figured Willingham already knew what had happened, since the dog guys at Leatherneck were going to try to keep him posted until Rod could contact him. As the dogs barked in the background, he sat down and wrote the most difficult e-mail he'd ever written.

Subject: Lucca urgent

Hey I got a second so i wanted to send you quick e-mail. I don't know if you were informed already but yesterday afternoon around 1400 Lucca found an IED and while searching for secondaries set off another IED. Initially she lost her left paw and had a couple of burn spots to her neck and chest. She is going through surgery soon. They will have to amputate her whole left leg. I'm very sorry and feel awful about the whole event. i know how much you care about her. I know you probably read this and have a lot of questions. You can write and I'll answer as soon as possible. I have pictures of her progress. If you like to see them just let me know. I'm very sorry, it was a very scary experience and i feel awful, I don't think i can express that enough. I know you gave me lucca with your trust and I hoped nothing like this to happen. I'll keep you updated as much as possible.

He kept it brief. He felt a need to get back to Lucca. He didn't want her waking up alone, and he was scared that in his absence, something could happen and he'd come back to bad news. When he returned, her eyes were open. She raised her head when she saw him coming. He fit himself beside her in the kennel again and stroked her head, and she relaxed and went back to sleep.

About an hour later, Chumbler came by and told Rod the hospital was ready for Lucca. Rod helped gently lift Lucca onto a gurney and carry her to the adjacent "human" hospital, the NATO Role 3 Multinational Medical Unit. Before surgery, she was given a full-body CT scan so the vets would know if there was further damage they needed to address. With her chest lacerations, they didn't want to take any chances. The scans revealed nothing serious.

The surgical staff assembled in the state-of-the-art operating room. Besides Giles and Chumbler, there were three "human" medical doctors—an anesthesiologist and two orthopedic surgeons. Many MDs at the hospital jumped at the chance to assist with military working dog operations. The dogs always seemed to bring a little bit of home with them, and it was a chance to help K-9s who had almost given their lives saving others.

Giles didn't think of dogs as truly separate from their handlers. He sometimes shared this insight with colleagues. "They're a dog *team*. They're kind of the same entity," said Giles, who had been a Special Forces soldier early in his career. He welcomed Rod to stay in the operating room during the surgery. It might be too much for some to handle, but Rod had been nothing but level-headed since arriving, and Giles thought he'd want to be there.

Rod changed into scrubs and stood out of the way, toward the foot of the operating table. The doctors, circulating nurses, and surgical techs scrubbed up to prepare for Lucca's forequarter amputation.

The operating room was warmer than typical hospital surgeries. Combat hospitals keep their operating rooms warm to help fight hypothermia, which can happen easily during anesthesia in patients with extensive blood loss. For added warmth, during surgery Lucca would also have a 3M Bair Hugger, an electric device that blows warm air through a hose and into a perforated blanket that's used to keep a patient warm. The Bair Hugger comes with various disposable paper and plastic perforated blankets. Sometimes staffers place the warm air hose under a traditional blanket, but they used a disposable blanket to create Lucca's warm microenvironment.

As she lay sedated on her right side, her leg, chest, and thorax area were shaved with battery-powered veterinary clippers and the site was swabbed with a chlorhexidine disinfectant solution. Blue surgical draping was placed over most of her body to create a sterile field around the surgery site.

To monitor her vitals during surgery, veterinary staff stuck adhesive EKG pads to her three paws. A pulse oximeter attached to her tongue, and a blood-pressure cuff wrapped around a hind leg. They set up a thermometer to track her temperature.

Once the analgesic, hydromorphone, had been administered via the IV catheter that the vets at Leatherneck had sutured into her leg, the anesthesiologist induced general anesthesia with intravenous propofol. He intubated Lucca with an endotracheal tube, which delivered both oxygen and the gas sevoflurane, which would help keep her asleep. An end-tidal carbon dioxide monitor measured how much CO_2 she was exhaling. The ventilator was activated with a switch, and the desired breathing parameters set. The ventilator would control the depth and rate of Lucca's respiration and make it easier to keep her at the appropriate anesthetic depth.

Rod knew that even with all the monitoring, there was always a chance of a complication with anesthesia, especially when inducing and recovering. He was relieved that so far it seemed to be going well.

Because Lucca was going to have a limb removed, Giles wanted her to have a brachial plexus block. The brachial plexus is a bundle of nerves that provides movement and sensation to the front leg. If those nerves were numbed with an anesthetic agent like lidocaine, Lucca would feel less pain during and after surgery. It also meant she wouldn't need as much anesthesia. Giles injected lidocaine directly around the leg nerves in Lucca's armpit area, explaining the technicalities to Chumbler, who was learning how to perform the procedure. The amount Giles gave her would provide about two hours of blocked pain sensation.

There are no saws in a forequarter amputation. No bones are cut. Surgeons remove the entire forelimb, including the shoulder blade, which is attached to the body by muscles. The trick is to cut through the right muscles with a minimum of bleeding. Giles took a sterile pen and marked out the areas where the incisions should be made.

Rod looked away when he saw a scalpel poised over Lucca's shaved leg. For the next ninety minutes, the team used scalpels and an electrosurgery device to cut through the muscle, ligating Lucca's arteries and veins with sutures to minimize bleeding. The area they were operating on was bright red from all the exposed tissue, but there was little blood.

The vets kept Rod in the loop by telling him everything that was going on. They were positive and optimistic, which helped improve Rod's outlook. He couldn't bring himself to observe the surgery in too much detail, though. Beginning medical students have fainted at far less graphic surgeries and had to be removed from the operating room. Rod was determined not to leave Lucca. He frequently glanced at the monitors, even though he had no idea what most of them meant. He took comfort in seeing

Lucca's steady heartbeat on the screen and hearing the short tone that accompanied each beat.

The electrical "hot knife" cut through tissue and controlled bleeding at the same time. As it did its job, little tendrils of white smoke floated up from Lucca's muscles. A light but noticeable scent of burning flesh reached Rod's nose, even through his surgical mask. It was slightly different from the smell of the burns to her fur and flesh caused by the IED, but it mingled with the disinfectant and some other odors he couldn't distinguish, and the ugly bouquet made the scene before him feel all the more raw.

THE SAME DAY the IED with Lucca's name on it exploded, Chris and Jill Willingham were out celebrating their tenth wedding anniversary. They had sent the children to stay with friends overnight and were enjoying a night on the town in Helsinki. Jill kept her cell phone handy in case of an emergency with the kids, but otherwise, the Willinghams had better things to do than monitor e-mails.

They checked into a hotel in downtown Helsinki and had a drink at the intimate Ateljee Bar atop the Hotel Torni. From the rooftop bar, they gazed at the sparkling city below, talking about how much they had been through together during all these years of war, nursing school, and kids.

"You're like a fine wine," she toasted. "You truly keep getting better with time. I love you, babe."

"Well, you *know* how much I love *you*, you wonderful woman."

They hadn't had much time to just sit and talk—especially about their relationship. So Jill took the opportunity to tell him how happy she was that he was doing so much better than after he returned from the Afghanistan deployment. She thanked him for sacrificing the dog career he loved so much so he could keep himself, and his marriage and family, on track.

As much as he missed the dogs, as much as he still identified himself as a dog handler, he knew he had made the right move. In the back of his mind, he was hoping there might be a way one day to get back into the military dog world, but he needed this calm after the storm. They all did.

Before leaving the bar for dinner at the Savoy, he presented his wife with a little blue box. She never asked for jewelry, but he wanted to show her how much she meant to him after this decade involving three deployments, two children, and a lot of moving. She opened the Tiffany & Co. box and gazed at the ten-year-anniversary band, with its row of diamonds set in platinum. She slipped it on her finger, and it fit her perfectly. It was much more than a piece of jewelry to her. It was a symbol of how everything they'd been through had just served to make them stronger. But she didn't say anything about that. That would be too sentimental. She just thanked him for the beautiful ring.

The next morning, as they were getting ready to check out of the hotel, Jill checked her e-mail on her Kindle. She saw one from Gunnery Sergeant Shane Green and clicked it open.

"Babe," she said, "Shane Green sent me an e-mail asking me to have you please get in touch with him."

He immediately knew something was wrong. Green, a long-time dog-handler friend of Willingham's, was now the kennel master at Camp Pendleton.

"Nothing good's going to come of that," Willingham said. Jill handed him the Kindle and he signed in to his e-mail account.

"Lucca's been hurt," he told Jill as he read the brief e-mails from a couple of the dog guys at Leatherneck. "I've gotta call Juan."

"She's such a sweet dog. She's got to be so scared and in pain." As a nurse, she didn't usually react like this about her patients. But there was something about a dog, about *this* dog . . .

The embassy where Willingham had been working for about four months had a DSN line he could use to contact Rod. They raced out of the hotel and Jill drove to the embassy to drop off her husband before picking up the kids. She didn't want the kids to see tears in her eyes, but there they were. At the embassy, Willingham had no luck reaching Rod. He got as many details as he could from Nuckles, who was now the kennel master at Leatherneck. He sent Rod a message on Facebook and then found the e-mail Rod had sent just before surgery. It tore at him as he read it. He knew all too well the gut-wrenching guilt Rod was probably experiencing. It was bad enough that Rod had to worry about Lucca, but Willingham hated to see Rod also feeling like he let him down. He wanted Rod to benefit from what he had learned in dealing with his own guilt. He dashed off an e-mail response, hoping Rod would see it quickly.

Subject: Re: Lucca urgent

Rod,

I got this message after I sent you the one on Facebook . . .

First, I'm just glad you're okay man. I just got off the phone with Nuckles and I received an email from Green too . . . I hear you saved her life . . . Thank you.

Please don't feel sorry man. Truth is, you were the right choice for Lucca . . . I had decided that way before you started handling her. I knew with your personality and experience mixed with her personality and experience, y'all would make a great team. I don't regret it for one minute and I don't want you to feel bad. You did a helluva job with her . . . I'm proud of you man.

I lost a dog handler in Iraq and then Max in Afghanistan . . . I know there is no certainty when you deployed in a combat zone. I'm just glad you're okay.

Lucca is a tough girl and I do love that dog and I know she will recover . . . after all she is mama Lucca Bear. If you don't mind, tell her I love her and I'm praying for her.

I can call DSN or cell phones and I'd like to talk to you.

Again, I'm glad you're okay and I know Lucca will recover. I would appreciate if you would keep me up to date with her progress and I would like to see the pics if you get a chance to send them.

Thanks for letting me know everything man. Keep in touch.

                                                              Chris

"YOU MAY NOT want to look, Corporal," Giles advised Rod. "We're ready to remove the leg."

Rod realized Giles must have seen him only indirectly observing the surgery. He appreciated the warning and turned his head and stared at a tray of medical supplies, reading their labels over and over again, trying not to focus on the reality of what was occurring a few feet away.

Giles lifted the leg away from Lucca's body. It came away

soundlessly, none of the popping or ripping Rod had expected. He handed it to one of the circulating nurses, who placed it in a biohazard container. It would later be incinerated.

The staff irrigated the wound bed using a large IV fluid bag connected to tubing. The sterile saline solution hosed off the dirt and sand that remained from the IED blast. They closed her up with absorbable sutures, stitching one layer at a time—first the muscles, then the subcutaneous tissue. Her skin was closed with staples.

The surgeons placed a Jackson-Pratt drain in Lucca's chest area so fluids wouldn't accumulate around the wound. Rod thought the soft plastic bulb that creates suction at the end of the catheter looked oddly like a grenade. They sutured a central line through her neck into her jugular. Unlike the leg catheter, which has one port, comes out easily, and needs to be changed often, a central line can remain in for weeks, is much more secure, and allows vet staff to run several drugs or fluids at once. It also makes it easy to collect blood for testing without another needle stick.

The anesthesiologist stopped the flow of anesthetic gas and monitored Lucca carefully until she was awake enough to try to swallow a few times. When the swallow reflex kicked in, that meant she was in control of her airway. Five more minutes of oxygen, and he removed the endotracheal tube.

"She's doing great, Corporal," he told Rod. "Came through like a champ."

Rod swallowed hard and got closer to Lucca, who by now was bandaged and cleaned up. She wore stretchy netting over the site. He thought she looked like she was wearing a tube top. Her eyes were still closed, and her mouth slightly open. Rod looked at the flat spot where her leg should be.

It hit him then that she would never again walk point, she would never do the job she loved to do—that Lucca's days of saving lives were over.

ROD WAS LYING with his hand on Lucca when she woke up in the veterinary kennel shortly after surgery. The first thing she did was try to get up and walk.

"Mama Lucca, no, it's too early," he told her gently as he coaxed her to stay lying down.

She needed to rest at least overnight before she started trying to walk, with assistance. A vet tech got her some water. She drank and fell back into a deep sleep.

Rod wanted to let Willingham know Lucca's progress. Lucca looked like she'd be out for a while, so he quietly slipped out of the cage and jogged over to the kennel office to use the computer.

There was an e-mail from Willingham. He clicked on it with fear and dread—and then came a rush of relief. At some deeper level, he still couldn't help but feel he'd let Willingham down. But—he took a breath and wrote back immediately.

Subject: Re: Lucca urgent

Thanks for your words I really needed to hear that. i'm doing fine. I did not receive any injuries from the blast. lucca saved me and everyone else on that patrol. Mamma Lucca bear did great on her surgery. has been a few hours after the surgery. she woke up and even tried to walk away. She's a tough dog, still putting smiles in peoples faces. I have been with lucca since the blast happened, I will be flying with lucca to Germany in a few days and eventually back to the states. Here's the DSN number to the kennels I'm located right now green line, and if I'm not there, I'm at the vets office and here's the number

Willingham phoned him right away.

"Rod! Hey, how are ya doing?" Rod knew Willingham was doing his best to sound casual, for his sake. He was touched that Willingham's first question was about him.

"I'm fine. They did the amputation. Mama Lucca did really good. She's sleeping now."

"I'm proud of you, man. You saved her life. I can't thank you enough for everything you've done for her."

Two NURSES CAME in the morning after surgery, while Lucca was asleep with her head on Rod's lap. Rod was asleep with his head and upper back on the rear wall of the stainless steel cage. He woke up to see two women in scrubs staring at him tenderly, with tears in their eyes. At first he thought something was wrong, but they reassured him.

"It's so sweet watching you two lie there. Just that bond you have, you can see how much you love each other," one said.

"She has the most beautiful, feminine face," the other observed, wiping her eyes quickly with the back of her hand.

Giles, who had seen this many times, had a theory.

"Every day, the human hospital staff deals with dead and dying and disfigured men and women with multiple amputations who are never going to be the same. They can't let in the pain or they couldn't function," he told Rod. "Sometimes it takes a dog to remind us of our humanity."

Word spread through medical staff at the human hospital about this patient and her devoted handler. Lucca and Rod had frequent visitors over the next three days.

THE DAY AFTER surgery, Lucca was allowed to take her first walk as a three-legged dog. The vet staff disconnected her from tubing and helped her stand up. Rod and a vet tech each held one end of a sling under her chest to steady her and support some of her weight. Chumbler and Giles accompanied them on the short jaunt out the front of the vet tent.

Lucca's loppy gait reminded Rod of a rocking horse. He was thrilled she seemed undaunted by this new way of walking. She found a spot and relieved herself, and wanted to walk some more.

The following day, after starting out with the sling, it became apparent she no longer needed it. They weren't having to hold any of her weight on it, and she was surer on her paws. Rod held her steady as the vet tech pulled the sling away. She walked without support. Rod couldn't believe it. He wanted to applaud.

She was already back on solid food—canned—and Rod noticed a little wag in her tail a couple of times. The pain meds seemed to be working well and weren't making her so groggy she couldn't function.

"She's so resilient," Rod told Willingham on the phone that afternoon, still in awe of her recovery.

"That's our Mama Lucca, Rod. You can't keep a good dog down."

The third day after surgery, Lucca was ready for the next step of the journey home. She and Rod would be flying to Dog Center Europe, in Ramstein, Germany, for a few more days of care and evaluation, and then flying back home to Pendleton to continue her recovery. He would be with her throughout.

At the flight line, Rod said his good-byes and thanked everyone for everything they had done for Lucca and for him. Giles leaned down to pet Lucca one last time. She was resting, leaning on her elbow. She looked at him and gave a single thump of her tail.

If Lucca had been injured at an earlier time in Giles's veterinary career, she would not be going home. There would have been no surgery. Since she could no longer serve her country, he would have had to euthanize her.

As he watched the air force medical flight take off en route to Lucca's new life as a soon-to-be civilian dog, he was grateful that policy had changed.

13

A Final Mission

LUCCA, C'MERE, GIRL! You like roast beef?"

Lucca bolted over from the other side of the kennel office at Camp Pendleton and stood on her three legs, looking up at the slice of meat dangling from the thumb and forefinger of the handler who was on overnight duty. Her tail swept wide and fast, and her dark brows gathered in concentration on the slice of meat he'd pulled out of his Subway sandwich.

"Here ya go!"

He let it drop. Without even a chew, she gulped it down. Then she eyed him to see what else he had to offer.

"That's enough, Lucca," he said. "Gotta watch your weight now that you're a tripod."

She sat down and stared at the remaining sandwich. Her ears were erect and turned fully forward, and her eyes were calm but conveying a message. It was the same kind of stare that had alerted her handlers to so many IEDs over the years. But now, in semiretirement, she was putting the look to new use.

The handler kept eating. So she pulled out all the stops.

Lucca reached out and gave him her paw. Universal dog language for *please*, and usually easy to dismiss if you don't want to give a dog what he or she wants. But when a three-legged gives a paw, it's another matter altogether. She sat there, one leg outstretched, her paw resting on his knee. The other leg was—well, the other leg was just not there, and it was painfully obvious to the handler. Instead of a leg, there was only a furless indent.

"Oh lord," the handler said. "OK, war hero. You got me. Just one more piece . . ."

As Lucca awaited medical retirement, her life at the Pendleton kennels was very different than it had been before her deployment. Already a kennel favorite, when she came limping home from Afghanistan she quickly became the unofficial Pendleton kennel mascot. She never had to stay in her locked, concrete-floor kennel again. Instead she spent her days and nights as a free-range dog in the large office, getting love, pats, and snacks from everyone who passed by. She slept on a mat, or on blankets in a portable kennel whose door was never locked unless a brute of a dog was coming through. Sometimes she hopped up and slept on the folding cot set up for handlers on night duty. No one minded.

Because she was no longer a working dog, she didn't have an assigned handler. But that didn't stop Rod from spending time with Lucca every day. While she was still in need of medical attention, he'd take her for her vet visits and tend to her wounds. She healed remarkably quickly. Within a couple of days of returning, she was running around in the same joyful way she used to. Even the veterinarians were surprised at her recovery.

Once she didn't need regular vet checks, Rod devoted more time to grooming her, taking her for walks, just chilling out. Sometimes he'd volunteer for night duty so he could sleep on the cot next to her mat. It was like old times falling asleep to the lullaby of her snores.

Rod wasn't sure how much longer he had with Lucca, so he tried to spend as much time as possible with her. Once her paperwork came through, she'd be heading to Helsinki to join Willingham and his family. He had no idea when—or if—he'd see her again.

Willingham, who was now a gunnery sergeant, was in touch regularly about Lucca's progress and about how Rod was doing. There was a question he felt he needed to ask.

"Hey, you know how we talked about me adopting Lucca after this deployment if she got dispo'd because of age," Willingham said. "I just want to see, you know, after what you guys have been through together, where your head's at about that. Are you OK with it? Have you given it any second thoughts?"

Rod didn't have to give it any thought. As much as he would have loved to keep Lucca, he was a single guy living in a barracks. He had no idea what his future held. He wanted to give Lucca the best home possible.

"I love Lucca. I owe my life to her. But she's your dog. I kind of took out a loan. It's time to pay up."

★★★★★

GUNNERY SERGEANT SHANE Green pulled Rod aside one day.

"Hey, Rod? Do you have a passport?"

"No, I don't."

"Everyone in the platoon needs to have their passport," Green told him. "Why don't you start the process of getting one ASAP?"

Rod didn't question this. Rules change over time.

He had no idea what was going on behind the scenes—that Willingham was trying to arrange for Rod to fly to Helsinki with Lucca and spend a week or two there to help with the transition. Willingham knew from personal experience the sting of having to part with Lucca, and he wanted to make it easier for Rod. He also thought it would be good for Lucca not to have such an abrupt change.

"How are you planning to get them here?" Nicholas Kuchova, regional senior commercial officer at the American embassy in Helsinki, asked Willingham one afternoon. Everyone at the embassy had fallen in love with Lucca—with military dogs in general—since Willingham's arrival five months earlier. Willingham felt it was part of his mission to explain the importance of military working dogs and the difference they make in the way wars were now being fought. The embassy employees were sold, and they began sending care packages to dog teams in Afghanistan. When Lucca was injured, everyone, even the ambassador, suffered and worried right alongside Willingham.

"Once we know Lucca is officially retired and Rod has a passport," Willingham told him, "me and Jill are going to look for the best fares and buy their tickets."

"Let me check into something and see if we can get you some help," Kuchova said. "You shouldn't have to pay."

Kuchova made some inquiries and found out about Air Compassion for Veterans, a not-for-profit organization that flies wounded warriors and Gold Star families around the world.

He updated Ambassador Bruce J. Oreck.

"That's excellent," Oreck said. "We might want to have a backup plan in case that doesn't work out. I'll be more than happy to pay for their tickets out of my own pocket."

"How about we split it?" Kuchova asked.

"It's important that we do this. Let's see how it plays out," Oreck said.

They never had to make those arrangements. The tickets came through.

"It would be an honor to reunite a wounded warrior dog and handler," said Jim Palmersheim, managing director of American Airlines Veterans and Military Initiatives programs. American Airlines had a long history of supporting veterans and those serving in the military. The company's first CEO, Cyrus Rowlett Smith, would go on to serve as the Air Traffic Command's chief of staff during World War II, eventually achieving the rank of major general in the army. American Airlines supported several key initiatives that benefited military members and their families. To help Lucca over to Helsinki, the company would partner with Air Compassion for Veterans, which helped with thousands of flights for wounded military and family members. Lucca definitely qualified as wounded military, and Rod was certainly a family member. . . .

In late May, once Rod had his passport and Lucca had her

retirement papers, Willingham called Rod to let him know the good news.

"I'd love you to escort Lucca to Helsinki. You can spend ten days with Jill and me," Willingham told him. "It'll give me a chance to personally thank you for saving Lucca's life, plus I think it'll serve as a great transition for Lucca."

Rod couldn't speak for a few seconds.

"That would be amazing. I'd love to hand over her leash in person."

When they hung up, Rod walked right over to the kennels.

"Lucca," he told her as they walked on their favorite path, on the grassy hillside with the beautiful views, "you won't believe who I talked to today, and where you and I are going. . . ."

They had a nice chat about the future.

AT 3:45 A.M. on July 5, Rod walked into the kennel office at Pendleton and set his bags on the floor. He wore a neatly pressed uniform—his service "Charlies"—with a colorful array of ribbons just above his left pocket.

"Good morning, Lucca. We've got a big day ahead," he said.

Lucca looked at him and yawned. She had been up late saying good-byes to everyone at the kennels and was in no rush to go anywhere.

"C'mon, girl, time to rise and shine! Let's go for a walk!" At hearing these magic words, she stood up, grabbed her Kong, and rocking-horsed over to Rod.

"Today's our last mission together, Mama Lucca," he told her solemnly. He clicked her harness around her and stroked her head. "It's an important one. Are you ready?"

He took her for her final walk at Pendleton. The overnight handler was the only person there at that hour. They said good-bye, and Rod and Lucca headed to the airport with a marine public affairs representative, who told him what to expect along the way.

"At your connecting flight in Chicago, the American Airlines veterans program is going to be doing a little ceremony honoring Lucca. You may be asked to do an interview, so thanks for wearing your uniform. There may be reporters there who want to talk with you."

"I'm very shy when it comes to that sort of thing," Rod told him earnestly.

"You'll be fine. Just talk about Lucca. You don't have to answer anything you're not comfortable with."

They arrived at San Diego International Airport at 4:30 A.M. He was surprised to find a couple of camera crews waiting for him. He felt the butterflies taking flight in his stomach, but he told himself that if he could deal with the Taliban in Afghanistan, he could handle the spotlight for a few minutes.

THE FLIGHT FROM San Diego to the connecting flight at O'Hare International Airport went quickly. They took off and were treated with sincere warmth by the flight attendants, and then they were on the ground in Chicago. Lucca, who had her own seat, dozed most of the way. Once in the airport, Rod and Lucca would change planes for the flight to Helsinki. He knew there might be some kind of acknowledgment of Lucca's arrival when he got to the airport but figured it would be pretty low-key. This wasn't even her hometown, after all.

The water cannon salute that welcomed the plane as it was

taxiing should have been a clue about what was to come. The two plumes of water from fire trucks on both sides of the taxiway arched over the plane. Rod looked out the window from his business-class seat as the water drenched the plane and came pouring down the windows.

"Look, Lucca!" he told his seatmate, who had woken up for the landing. "I wonder what's up with that?"

Just then a flight attendant made an announcement that the water salute was in honor of a marine hero returning home. She told Lucca's story and asked everyone to give Lucca and Rod a hand. He turned around a little and acknowledged the well-wishers with a smile and a nod.

"I wish you could do all the publicity, Lucca," he said under his breath to her as he slid back into his seat.

Rod shook some hands on the way off the plane, and a flight attendant escorted them up the ramp. He had prepared himself for a small gathering and maybe a quick interview and was relieved when there wasn't a throng of people. Just a few, and a waiting golf cart.

They hopped on and were whisked to another part of the terminal. The cart stopped and introduced them to the five-person color guard that would be leading the way down to Gate K9. Two women holding large photos of Lucca in front of a marine flag stood behind Lucca and Rod, and the little parade proceeded to the gate. As they got closer, the crowd grew thick on both sides of the walkway. TV cameras followed them, and passengers snapped away with their phones as they pointed and smiled.

Rod could feel his heart pounding faster as they moved closer to the gate. Combat missions were somehow more predictable, as crazy as that might sound. He looked down at the other end of the leash and watched Lucca moving along, grasping her Kong in her mouth, looking completely at ease. Her demeanor worked its way up the leash, and Rod felt calmer.

Pilot Tim Raynor, of American Airlines' Veterans and Military Initiatives, greeted them. Raynor flew F/A-18 Hornets during his eight and a half years' active duty in the marines and for a while in the U.S. Marine Corps Reserves. He was also an American Airlines 767 pilot. He told Rod that he'd be helping fly his plane to Helsinki. "I'm excited and honored to be doing this," he said.

Rod thanked him, feeling blown away that this important guy—a colonel, now in the reserves—who had flown the ultra-badass supersonic combat jet for so many years, would be in the cockpit to help get them to their destination.

As the ceremony unfolded, Rod stood by the podium at Gate K9, arms clasped in front of him, holding Lucca's leash while she chomped away on her Kong. An American Airlines employee sang "The Star Spangled Banner." Then Franco Tedeschi, vice president of the airline's Chicago airport operations, gave a short talk.

"This special event is a wonderful reminder that heroes come in all shapes and sizes," Tedeschi said. "A seventy-four-pound Belgian Malinois . . . has made numerous families extremely happy because their loved ones came back safe and sound from Iraq and Afghanistan."

Raynor took the podium, and when he announced it would be a little while until boarding, and invited people to come up and shake Rod's hand and Lucca's paw, Rod unconsciously wiped his forehead. He had begun to think he'd have to get up and talk to the crowd.

Rod did a few short interviews, changed into civilian clothes, and went back to the gate. The gate attendant announced that boarding would be starting and asked passengers Lucca and Corporal Rodriguez to please come to the front and board first. More clapping.

On the plane from Chicago to Helsinki, Rod reveled in his roomy, comfortable business-class seat. Lucca settled right into hers. He imagined how proud his mom would be if she saw him in such luxury on this international mission. He got a flight attendant to take a photo of the two of them in their seats together—it was easy getting the attention of a flight attendant at any point in the flight. From Chicago, across the Atlantic, and right up until they landed in Finland, they were always checking on Lucca.

"Would she like something to drink?"

"How about a blanket for the hero dog?"

"May I pet her? I miss my dog."

"Looks like she could use an extra pillow."

"Can we get her something to eat?"

Lucca spent most of the time on her own seat, except when she felt like stretching out for a snooze on the floor. When Raynor announced it was time to land and told the passengers about Lucca being reunited with her original handler, Rod patted the seat and she jumped back up. He leaned in and put his arm around her—partly to steady her and partly to have a few more minutes next to her before the end of their final mission.

"LADIES AND GENTLEMEN, we would like to announce that Lucca's flight has landed and will be taxiing to the gate shortly to drop off Corporal Juan Rodriguez and Lucca. The plane will be proceeding to another gate for the other passengers to disembark."

Announcing that any individual has landed at a major airport is almost unheard of. Announcing that a dog has landed, even more so. But this was a special occasion at the Helsinki Airport. A wing of the terminal had been closed off for the arrival of Rod and Lucca, so that the moment of reunion could be captured by the media without hundreds of people offloading around them. In attendance were the Willinghams, about fifteen Finnish television, newspaper, and web photographers and reporters, and several people from the embassy, including the ambassador and Kuchova.

When Claire Willingham, age four, heard Lucca's name announced, her mouth opened wide, as did her eyes. Then she smiled brightly and looked at her mom and dad. She was wearing a dress with big red and blue flowers on a white background, and her blonde hair was perfectly combed for the occasion. She held out the sign she and Jill had made for Lucca. It featured a photo of Lucca and her name and identification number.

"Not just yet, Claire. Your arms will get tired," Jill told her.

The Willinghams had been preparing for weeks. They had gone shopping and bought Lucca a cushy bed, two bowls, and dog food. Willingham had gone online and ordered her a new Alabama collar. "Roll Tide!" he'd said as he clicked on the "purchase" button.

Jill could sense the anticipation in the room and in her husband as the plane pulled up to the gate. He made his way to where Rod and Lucca would be coming off the walkway. Family followed, and photographers and reporters were right behind them to capture the moment the two saw each other again.

Willingham realized he was feeling something like an intensified version of the thrill he'd felt right before meeting her for the first time in Israel. He couldn't believe it had been more than six years since that day.

He had one concern. He'd brought it up to Jill the night before.

"What if she doesn't remember me?"

"Of course she'll remember you!"

"But she's been through so much since I saw her."

"That's *my* only worry. What if she's changed?" Jill said. "She could be one of those dogs who's scared of everything now. That would be so sad."

Post-traumatic stress disorder in dogs had finally been officially recognized by the Defense Department the previous year. Studies of military dogs revealed that about 5 percent of dogs were coming back from deployments with signs diagnosable as canine PTSD, including withdrawal, fear where there was none before, high anxiety, and depression. Most of the dogs diagnosed with PTSD were sporting breeds, primarily Labrador retrievers, but there had been some Mals and shepherds as well.

They'd talked about this possibility a couple of times. Rodriguez had assured them she was still the same dog, but they had known dogs who had been through so much less but suffered tremendously after deployments. Sometimes it didn't come out until the dogs encountered stressful events at home. The Willinghams hoped that moving halfway across the world wasn't one of them.

The crowd stilled when the announcement came that Lucca and Rod were making their way up the walkway. Photographers poised their cameras. Claire and Michael held up their signs. Willingham knelt down low, in front of the small crowd.

He saw them coming down the corridor through a glass wall. Seconds later Rod and Lucca walked through the open doors and into the terminal. Rod immediately spotted Willingham kneeling down.

So did Lucca.

She quickened her pace and gave a couple of wide wags of recognition as she sniffed toward Willingham to make sure it was him. Once she knew, she jumped up, put her front paw on his chest, and joyfully licked his face. She covered his face with licks, from his chin to one cheek, over his nose, to the other cheek. Lucca rarely gave anyone even a cursory lick, and Willingham couldn't stop laughing. He held her paw in his hand to make it easier for her. The cameras clicked away loudly, but he didn't even notice they were there.

He stood up and embraced Rod, then introduced the newest member of the Willingham family to Claire and Michael.

WHEN READING UP on visiting Finland, you will be counseled not to expect much warmth from Finns.

Ediplomat.com advises:

- "Never hug, kiss, or touch a Finn."
- "Do not show emotions in public."
- "Keep some physical distance from Finns. Respect their shyness and desire for privacy. Do not engage a Finn in conversation on a bus or in a line, restaurant or other public places."

A Wikitravel article on Finland states that "Finns are a famously taciturn people who have little time for small talk or social niceties."

Rod could not understand this reputation. For the ten days of his visit with the Willinghams, he met only outgoing, warm, friendly Finns. He, Willingham, and Lucca couldn't walk ten feet some days without someone recognizing Lucca from one of the TV programs or newspapers that covered her story. People always wanted to pet her, to find out more about her, to tell Willingham and Rodriguez their own dog stories. Often, they thanked her for her service.

Touring Helsinki took longer this way, but that was fine with Willingham and Rod. They were delighted with the attention she was getting. They noticed that the Finns approached the conversation very politely once they discovered the hero in their midst. It usually began with someone smiling broadly, pointing at Lucca, and asking them, "Lucca?!" or "Hero dog?!" After a couple of minutes of often animated conversation, most were hugging and petting Lucca, posing for a photo with her.

The travel website that came close to explaining the change of decorum Lucca inspired was Finland.fi, a site produced by the Ministry for Foreign Affairs of Finland and published by the Finland Promotion Board. In an article entitled "A Guide to Finnish Customs and Manners," the writer got to the heart of the matter: "Finns rarely enter into conversation with strangers, unless a particularly strong impulse prompts it."

It seemed to Willingham and Rod that Lucca was prompting strong impulses all over Helsinki.

"We're escorting a star here," Willingham told Rod as they took a break at an open-air restaurant.

They both looked down at her. She was asleep, snoring ever so quietly.

"Well, it's not going to her head, anyway." Willingham laughed.

From their table, they could see a man at an adjacent table engrossed in reading a newspaper article. The headline read, LIIKUTTAVA KOHTAAMINEN ("Touching Reunion"), and it was studded with large color photos of Lucca and the reunion at the airport.

"Watch this," Willingham told Rod.

He stood up and walked over to the man—not heeding the "Do not engage a Finn at a restaurant" advice. He realized that with Lucca around, such social counsel was unwarranted.

He got the man's attention and pointed to Lucca and then at the newspaper.

"Lucca! That's Lucca!" he said, pointing back and forth, eyebrows raised to help get the point across.

The man looked at her, and at his newspaper, and back at Lucca again.

"Lucca? This Lucca?!" He was overjoyed and asked, in broken English, if he could pet her, which he did.

Lucca was a particularly big hit at the embassy, where she seemed to impress everyone.

"She's been a member of the embassy family since we first heard about her from Chris," Kuchova told Rod. "Thank you for taking such good care of her."

Kuchova was very pleased with how well the reunion travel arrangements had worked out. He had gotten the ball rolling because he wanted to see the best outcome for Lucca and her handlers. But there was something else beyond the happy reunion. His father, a first-generation American from Albania, was a World War II combat veteran who earned a Bronze Star and the Combat Infantry Badge with three battle stars for action in the Battle of the Bulge and the Central Europe Campaign. When Kuchova was helping these marines, he felt he was honoring his father as well.

Lucca touched a chord with others in this way. To many Finns, no strangers to war, she provided a bridge of sorts to past generations who had served bravely.

Every day when craftsman Kalevi Soderlund went to the harborside market to sell the charming wooden bears he carved, he hoped to run into Lucca. She had visited the popular tourist stop on a day when he wasn't at his booth. Ever since, he had been on the lookout for the dog he had read about in newspapers and now heard about from fellow market vendors.

He had Lucca fever in a big way. He looked up articles about her online, and when he found Willingham's firsthand account of the reunion at an American military dog website, he left a comment. After stating his great desire to meet her at the market, he wrote:

"Lucca is well known here, and I and so many Finns are happy and proud of having Lucca here in Finland. One of my friends, having been drafted in 60's as I too was, met Lucca on Sunday and told me that he wouldn't have believed he would from full heart saluted a dog and feel so touched of it. Now I am going to wait for that moment as a lotto win."

After the editor of the site, SoldierDogs.com, wrote to thank him for his comment and wished him the best of luck meeting Lucca, he wrote again, revealing a deeper motivation for meeting her.

I am waiting to meet Lucca as for Santa Claus when I was child. I understand the big value of soldier dogs. I was born when bombs came down around here. My father was medic in WW2 for five years and his regiment lost about half of the men all from same area here. So many of them were my father's friends from childhood. I was a lonely boy but from my very early days I remember that I had a dog. Father was in the war (three times at home when he was recovering from wounds, great days for me because I had father). Well I could embrace my good dog friend. The first I remember well was Toti, a big black shepherd . . .

Finland, like so many other countries in the area, suffered deeply during World War II. It was a painful, tortuous path the Finns had to follow to make it through the war. But despite its losses, it held its own—valiantly and effectively—against insurmountable odds. When the Soviet Union invaded in November 1939, starting what would become known as the Winter War, the Finnish army was vastly outnumbered and outgunned. What should have been a slam dunk for the Soviet Union was anything but. The Finns made up for their lack of manpower and weapons by using clever tactics and sheer tenacity. In one battle more than 17,500 Soviets lost their lives, but only 250 Finns.

The welcome-to-school guide for Finland's University of Joensuu includes an explanation of something called *sisu*. It's a quality that may help explain some of Finland's past triumphs. It is considered to be a national trait, one the Finns are quietly proud of.

"Sisu is what makes a Finn grit his teeth against all odds; continue fighting against an overwhelming enemy; clear the forest with his bare hands; go on to win a race even after falling over. Sisu is 'what it takes': guts, determination."

When Willingham learned about *sisu,* he realized that this important Finnish characteristic might have been underlying the seemingly uncharacteristic reaction to Lucca.

WILLINGHAM HAD MISSED Lucca, but he hadn't realized just how much until she was back at his side. When he looked into her eyes he saw everything they had once seen together reflected back to him. No one else had been there for all that. Over her career, she had protected untold numbers of soldiers and marines on four hundred missions with no injuries other than her own. A war buddy like no other.

He was sure that when Rod looked into her eyes, he saw their own triumphs and tragedies reflected back to him as well. So Willingham hoped that the ten days in Helsinki had helped ease the transition for Rod, as it seemed to be doing for Lucca. She comfortably navigated between spending nights with Rod on the queen bed in the spare room and living among the family by day. Willingham wished Rod lived close, so he could visit all the time. So did Rod.

Willingham and Rod spent the days touring around, mostly with Lucca. Their main subject of conversation was Lucca, and everything they'd each been through with her.

They jokingly referred to themselves as "Lucca's two dads." They compared notes and bragged about their eight-year-old girl to each other as they could to no one else. Their bond with her had come to extend deeply toward each other as well.

On his last night with Lucca, Rod tried not to think about how much he was going to miss her. He put his hand on her side, felt the rhythm of her breathing, and eventually fell asleep.

The next morning, he went outside and threw the Kong for her. She raced back and forth, catching it on the bounce and bringing it back. Over and over, panting, tail wagging, full of life. She didn't lose her speed or gusto when she lost her leg. She just picked up and did the best she could with what she had, and she hadn't missed a beat.

Rod realized he was going to have to do the same. He felt that when he said good-bye to Lucca he would be closing a huge chapter in his life. It was like losing a part of himself.

He was going to be getting out of the marines in the next year. He'd seen too much tragedy and death, and he didn't want to be the guy on deployment who put others at risk by not wanting to be there. There would be no wartime bonding with another dog. He couldn't imagine another dog taking the place of Lucca anyway.

Before he left for his flight, he sat in the yard with Lucca and held her tight. She leaned into him and relaxed in his arms.

"I just want to thank you for being there to watch over me, Lucca," he told her quietly. "I don't think I can ever thank you enough for everything you've done.

"I don't know if I'll ever see you again, but if there's any chance I can, I will. I'll never forget you. But you're going to have a great life in this family. This is the future you deserve. Be good, Lucca Bear."

14

Pictures of a Dog
with Three Legs

O N A DAY trip to look at castles north of Helsinki, the Willinghams found themselves in a three-story brick building called Suomen Tykistömuseo. Willingham was delighted when it turned out to be an artillery museum. They walked into one of the rooms closest to the entrance, and Lucca tossed her head in the air, sniffed, and started wagging her tail—a familiar sight to Willingham. No one else was around, so he cut her off leash.

"Seek!" he said.

It was like the old days. She moved in on a ghost of a scent, bracketing left to right, moving toward a glass display case along the wall. She sniffed the seams with enthusiastic inhalations and lay down with purpose. She looked over to Willingham, who was hanging back with Jill and the kids about fifteen feet so she could do her job.

He walked up to check out what she had responded on. There, behind the glass and the wood, he saw a couple of rifles, some bullets, and an old artillery round from a bygone war.

"Woot, Mama Lucca! Gooood girl! You have no idea you're retired, do you?" He loved her up, talking like he used to when she found IEDs on deployments. She wagged and looked into his eyes. "You've still got it, Lucca Pie."

He fished her Kong out of his backpack and bounced it on the floor. She caught it and, in the midst of the war memorabilia, ran to a corner to enjoy it in peace.

Lucca lay on her dog bed, sleeping quietly next to Willingham's side of the queen bed he shared with Jill. He was on the verge of sleep when he heard Lucca's breathing become rapid, starting and stopping, almost as if she were trying to sniff in her sleep. He looked down at her. In the light that washed through the window from the city and the moonlit night, he saw that as she lay on her side, her three legs were moving as if she were running. The lower part of her right front leg pawed the air as it met no resistance, and her rear legs paddled in opposing rhythms.

Her breathing became more erratic. Her dream running stopped and started in fits. Then little sounds, more than breathing, high-pitched but muffled, then louder. Willingham heard distress in them. He thought she sounded like she was in pain, or scared, or both.

He realized he might be reading too much into it—that she might only be dreaming about chasing a rabbit that got away. But he didn't want to leave her in that dream, in case she was back on that farm field in Afghanistan again, her paw blown off and her chest and face freshly singed.

"Lucca," he said gently. He put his hand on her, in the middle of her torso. "Mama Lucca."

She stopped running. Then he saw her eyes open for a moment and close again. She sighed and fell back to sleep.

"I know how it goes, Mama Lucca," he told her, and fell asleep with his hand still on her side.

R OD HOISTED A small duffel over his shoulder as he exited the plane that had just landed at Dallas/Fort Worth International Airport. He had been looking forward to this trip for weeks. He still couldn't believe what was happening.

He had left Helsinki having no idea when—or if—he would see Lucca again. It had been a hard transition back to Pendleton without her. Everything reminded him of her. But now, only three months after parting from her, he was going to see her again.

Lucca had been flown in from Helsinki with Willingham to be a guest of honor—the mascot, no less—at Sky Ball in Dallas, Texas, a huge fund-raising event that supports programs that directly benefit veterans, active-duty military, and wounded warriors. A thousand volunteers help put together the event, which attracts thousands of attendees. The big bash, on Saturday night, is a $250-per-ticket extravaganza, held in the American Airlines Hangar at the Dallas/Fort Worth International Airport.

It was the first time Sky Ball had honored a military dog. Because of their involvement in Lucca's transport to Helsinki, Raynor, Palmersheim, and a few others realized how special military dogs were. They decided to shine the spotlight on military dogs, to give them the attention they felt they deserved. Who better as a mascot than Lucca, whose résumé—if she had had one—already bore the title of "mascot," for her pregame rounds with Special Forces in Afghanistan, and again at the embassy in Helsinki.

Rod, as Lucca's "other dad," had also been invited to take part in the week of festivities. As he was waiting for the luggage carousel to begin its rounds, something brushed up against his leg. He ignored it. Then he felt a dull poke. He looked down and he saw a dog nose by his leg and a pair of brown eyes staring up at him with the whites of the eyes showing beneath. They had dark little eyebrows that were raised in a way that made the face look expectant.

"Mama Lucca!" he said and dropped to his knees and hugged and nuzzled his old dog. He looked up and saw Willingham watching them with a big grin.

"Waddup, Rod?!"

Rod stood up and hugged Willingham.

"What a surprise," said Rod, who was now back down with Lucca, who hadn't stopped wagging since she saw him. "I didn't expect to see you 'til tonight."

"What goes around comes around," Willingham said. "As I recall, you came to the airport to give me her leash in Helsinki."

He handed Rod Lucca's leash.

"What do ya say Mama Lucca spends the nights with you in your hotel room, and we'll hang out together during the day."

"Sounds good to me! I've missed Lucca."

"I know. She doesn't make it easy to leave her, does she?"

What a week it was. With Willingham and Rod at her side, Lucca walked the red carpet at the gala event. She stood onstage as Ambassador Oreck told her story to the three thousand in attendance. She shook paws with Medal of Honor recipients including Sammy Davis ("the real Forrest Gump") and Bruce Crandall, and rubbed elbows with actors including Greg Kinnear and Gary Sinise. She also went to six schools, where Willingham told Lucca's story to auditoriums of mesmerized students. This was nothing like combat, but keeping cool in new situations is a transferrable skill that's second nature to marines.

Lucca seemed to be enjoying it all, and when she started looking tired, Willingham and Rod pulled her aside to let her rest, just as they did on missions.

What may have been Lucca's favorite part of the week was her afternoon at a doggy day spa before her red-carpet appearance. She splashed around a wading pool and got a massage, a bath, and full grooming. It reminded Rod of the characters in *The Wizard of Oz* as they were getting prepped to meet the wizard.

Willingham and Lucca returned to Finland. A couple of weeks later, they visited the Kauniala Hospital for Disabled War Veterans, in Helsinki. A veteran from the Winter War reached toward Lucca, who was lying beside him in his hospital bed, and rested his knobby hand on her head. He smiled a wide smile, even without his teeth, and said a few words in Finnish. Willingham, who was standing close to the man's bed, spoke back in English.

Neither knew what the other was saying, except that it was about this dog who was lying on his bed next to him. This dog with three legs.

"She was in wars, too!" Willingham said, smiling and gesturing to Lucca, who had jumped onto the bed effortlessly, only gently guided by Willingham. "She's a war veteran like you!"

"*Ahh, kyllä!*" the man said and nodded, rubbing Lucca's head with his fingertips.

"Mama Lucca, you transcend all languages," Willingham told her later as they walked to the room of another veteran.

The two were making the rounds at the hospital for a small Christmas party in honor of the veterans. Another visiting guest at this intimate event was the president of Finland, Sauli Niinistö. Earlier in the afternoon, the president had met Lucca and asked Willingham about her story. Lucca stood wagging as the leader of this proud Nordic country gave her a scratch behind the ears and told her what a good dog she was.

ON JANUARY 3, 2013, Marine Staff Sergeant Chuck Rotenberry was installing hardwood floors with his father in his Virginia Beach home when his wife yelled up the stairs.

"Chuck, come down here, quick! Hurry!"

He thought maybe one of their four children had gotten hurt or done something amazing. He ran downstairs.

"Look!" Liz told him. "Lucca is in the Rose Parade!" It was a busy day, and he'd forgotten that Willingham, his great friend, had been flown from Helsinki with Lucca to be part of a float honoring military working dogs and calling attention to the U.S. Military Working Dog Teams National Monument that was going to be installed at Lackland Air Force Base later that year.

The Rotenberrys watched as Willingham and Rod, all done up in their dress blues with covers and blouses, waved to the cheering throngs. Lucca sat placidly, surrounded by a bed of red roses. She looked so calm that she could have been sitting in someone's garden. The song "Born in the USA" blasted from the float's speakers. The first of the hundred or so times the song segment looped as the parade crawled along the five-and-a-half-mile route, Willingham told Rod he was glad Lucca didn't know the words to the song, since she was born in the Netherlands.

Rotenberry was proud of his friend. Even though Willingham was no longer officially in the military dog world, it was his mission, and clearly his passion, to let people know what these dogs bring to the fight. He wanted to tell the world how valuable these dogs are and would continue to be, even after the impending drawdown in Afghanistan. He did every media interview that was requested of him. Having Lucca at his side drove the point home.

Rod was committed to this new mission, too. He knew that simply by being her calm self, Lucca was helping more people become aware of how vital these dogs are. As he held her leash and looked at her in the pleasant Pasadena sunshine, surrounded by the carpet of red roses, he couldn't help but think how far they were from that day when she lay bleeding out on that Afghanistan field.

WHEN AUTUMN SWANK was hospitalized with brain cancer at nine years old, she received several teddy bears and stuffed animals from friends and family. Holding them lifted her spirits through radiation and, later, chemotherapy.

One morning as she was taking a walk down the cancer ward, she saw a child, alone in a room, without even a teddy bear for company. The sight saddened her, but she couldn't give the child one of her stuffed toys because of the possibility of transferring germs to someone who was immunosuppressed.

When Autumn was doing a little better, she asked her mom,

Crystal Fenn, if they could help other children at the hospital by giving them teddy bears. Her idea turned into Autumn's Angel Bears. It became so successful that she had more bears than she could use at the hospital. She and her mom then set their sights on Snowball Express, an annual event that had been taking place for years near their Dallas-area home. Every year more than twelve hundred children of fallen U.S. service members gathered for four days of fun activities and the chance to bond with other children who have lost a parent to war since 9/11.

American Airlines charters planes to pick up children and spouses from ten locations around the U.S. The party always started on the decorated planes, with gift bags, games, and special treats. Autumn and her mom asked if it would be possible to donate a stuffed animal to be put on the seat of every child. When they received a grateful thumbs-up, they started collecting new stuffed toys. For the 2011 event, they collected thirteen hundred. For the 2012 Snowball Express, they were on track for at least two thousand.

Because of her acts of kindness, the little girl with the inoperable tumor on and around her brain stem had been invited to attend Sky Ball. She was looking forward to it and to meeting Lucca. But in October, just before Sky Ball, she fell into a coma and was put on life support. She spent forty-five days in pediatric intensive care at Cook Children's Medical Center in Fort Worth. She emerged from the coma, which had been far from a sure thing, but still had a long stay ahead of her.

Not long after Autumn came out of her coma, Willingham and Lucca were in Texas again. They'd been flown in from Finland to once again help promote the Military Working Dog Teams National Monument.

Willingham had known about Autumn since Sky Ball and on this trip set aside time to visit the hospital with Lucca. Because of the delicate condition of some of the children in the ward, Lucca couldn't go upstairs. So Autumn's mother and a nurse got her ready for her first trip outdoors since the coma. They disconnected her from as many machines as possible, covered her with a colorful quilt, and wheeled her outside the front doors of the hospital.

Autumn still could not speak. Her mother had to cover the tracheostomy tube for her to get partial words out. But she didn't need to speak. When Lucca walked up to her and stood there wagging, with what looked like a smile on her face, Autumn lit up. It was the first time her mother had seen her this happy since before the coma.

Willingham told Autumn about Lucca and showed her how Lucca could be directed without a leash. "Forward, Lucca," he told her. Just like the old days, she moved forward. "Left," he signaled. He called her back, and as she stood close to Autumn, Willingham pointed his finger and raised his thumb to look like a little gun. He aimed it at Lucca and said, quietly, "Bang." Lucca dropped gently down and rolled to her side. Then, wagging at the joke, she stood back up.

Autumn couldn't laugh out loud, but it took just one look at her face to know that Lucca had made her happy.

"When that visit happened, I felt I was not alone," she would write a year later, at age thirteen. "She filled me with joy. I love that she was so brave in war. She inspired me more and I love her."

"So you know, like many of us here, Chris went to boot camp at Parris Island," Elden Willingham told a group of about twenty marine veterans and their twenty or so guests at a meeting of the Marine Corps League in Tuscaloosa. Willingham's time at the embassy in Helsinki had ended after one eighteen-month tour. He had done so well there that he had been selected to spend the second eighteen months in a new position, as recruiting and screening team chief at the Marine Security Guard School in Quantico, Virginia.

"I remember on the day he left, Martha and I were going to go to the recruiter's station to see him load the bus and tell him good-bye. Chris said, 'Okay, but no crying,' and Martha agreed. It was tough but she didn't cry. We told him good-bye, watched him load the bus and start his journey toward Parris Island and the Marine Corps. I reminded Martha to be strong and not cry.

"Once we got back in the car it was a different story. There was crying and boohooing and sobbing. And someone asked, 'Is Martha OK?' I said, 'I don't know how *she* was taking it, but that was *me*.'"

The room filled with laughter, and his son, who was visiting with his family for a few days, took the podium, with Lucca at his side.

After Willingham's short talk, the clapping, and the questions, a couple of board members presented Lucca with a Purple Heart plaque. The wooden plaque featured a Purple Heart in the center and stated that the award was "for courageous service for country and corps."

Willingham was delighted that Lucca was being recognized. The military doesn't officially bestow medals and ribbons on dogs. If any are given, it's usually because someone in a senior position happens to think the dog deserves one, or a group like this wants to do something special. But the Department of Defense is never behind it. Willingham knew that it didn't really matter to dogs whether or not they got awards. But it made handlers feel good, and that dumped down the leash to the dogs. So indirectly, at least, the dogs did benefit.

It was Lucca's first Purple Heart. The second came shortly after. Gunnery Sergeant Erik Housman, who also worked at the Marine Security Guard School, was a two-time Purple Heart recipient. When someone receives a second Purple Heart, it has a star on it. Houseman kept the original one, and an extra, in the little tackle box where he kept spare ribbons, medals, and insignias.

Willingham was bringing Lucca to the office once a week, and in exploring around, she wandered into Housman's office. Willingham came to check on her. Housman loved dogs and wanted her to stay.

"Has she got a Purple Heart yet?" he asked.

"She got a real nice plaque with one from the Marine Corps League down in Tuscaloosa."

"Well how about a Purple Heart she can wear?"

Housman pinned it on the back of Lucca's harness. When Willingham saw the purple ribbon on her black harness, he felt proud that she could wear something she deserved so much.

A few months later, after a barbecue at the Veterans of Foreign Wars post in Fairfax, Virginia, the men gathered underneath a tree, and three VFW officers presented Lucca with a plaque that briefly told her story and proclaimed that "Lucca is hereby given an honorary position at this post as Combat Veteran War Dog while in good standing with all the privileges and honors afforded her. Her actions brought great credit upon herself, the Marine Corps, the U.S. Military, and Her family."

The men told Willingham that to the best of their knowledge, Lucca was the first dog inducted into a VFW. They shook her paw and welcomed her to the club. She focused on them as they talked to her, but when they were done, she went back to staring at the barbecue grill, which had been the center of her attention that day.

THE SIGN THAT wounded Navy SEAL Lieutenant Jason Redman wrote in Sharpie on orange-red poster board is now part of a permanent display at Walter Reed National Military Medical Center, where he wrote it. It was signed by President George W. Bush and matted and framed behind glass.

> ATTENTION to all who enter here. If you are coming into this room with sorrow or to feel sorry for my wounds, go elsewhere. The wounds I received, I got in a job I love, doing it for people I love, supporting the freedom of a country I deeply love. I am incredibly tough and will make a full recovery. What is full? That is the absolute utmost physically my body has the ability to recover. Then I will push that about 20% further through sheer mental tenacity. This room you are about to enter is a room of fun, optimism, and intense rapid regrowth. If you are not prepared for that, go elsewhere. From: The Management.

It's a fitting sign to have hanging in the hospital's physical therapy room, which is a bustling place with amputees in various stages of recovery trying to get their strength back and learning to maneuver with prosthetics.

The morning Willingham brought Lucca to pay a visit, six amputees were going through physical therapy routines. Several family members sat and stood nearby, encouraging them, talking with one another, comparing notes. When Lucca walked through the door, everyone stopped what they were doing and all eyes were on her.

Brian Kolfage, a former Security Forces airman who lost both legs and his right arm after a rocket attack in Iraq on September 11, 2004, had brought them to the hospital with him. Kolfage had met Willingham and Lucca at Sky Ball. When Willingham contacted him again to see if he could help them get in to visit wounded warriors, he said he'd be happy to oblige next time he was in the Washington, D.C., area. It's where Kolfage had done his own recovery, and he visited whenever he could.

Kolfage was passionate about helping other amputees see the light at the end of the tunnel—that life can be great, even without most of your limbs. He was living proof, strolling in on his two microprocessor-controlled prosthetic legs, drinking from a water bottle he held in his high-tech right hand.

"You have to look forward to what you can do, not to what you cannot," was his message. He walked the walk. He was most of the way through architecture school at the University of Arizona and had married the love of his life a couple of years earlier.

As families and amputees gathered around Lucca to meet her and learn her story, Kolfage marveled at how quickly Lucca's presence brightened the room. Lucca made the rounds, at home among her fellow wounded warriors.

"They loved seeing her happy ending," Kolfage told Willingham after their four-hour visit. "It doesn't matter that she's a dog. She made a difference."

Kolfage loved dogs. And now that they were done with the visit, it was time to cut loose with Lucca. Using a combination of dog-play body language and an excited tone of voice, he got her fired up. She ran around the nearly empty lobby in tight circles, stopping suddenly, looking at Kolfage, and plunging into the puppy play position—chest down to the ground, hind end up, tail wagging like mad.

"Lucca, you want this?"

He was waving his hand. Willingham looked at what he was offering Lucca but didn't see anything in his hand. But Lucca looked like she wanted whatever it was. Willingham watched in amazement at what came next.

Kolfage pulled the lifelike cosmetic cover off his bionic hand prosthesis, waved it in his left hand, and tossed it to Lucca. The silicone rubber hand—it looked just like a hand, except it was almost pure white—bounced low, and she caught it, trotted a few steps with it, and lay down with her prize. Then she held it between her paws and began mouthing it.

It happened so fast that it took Willingham a few seconds to realize what had just transpired and that Lucca was now using Kolfage's hand as a Kong substitute. It wasn't the high-tech, robotic-looking hand itself, but no matter. He didn't want Kolfage walking around with holes in his hand.

He hurried over to Lucca, who looked up at him and wagged, proud of her fun new toy.

"Lucca, no, ma'am. Ma'am, let me have his hand."

Before she could consider negotiating, Willingham grabbed the hand. He didn't see any tooth marks, but it was coated with Lucca's saliva.

"Can I wash your hand?" he asked, realizing how strange that sounded.

"That's OK, I was going to wash my hands anyway," Kolfage said.

He gave Kolfage back his hand. Lucca didn't let it out of her sight until they parted.

IT WAS THE perfect backdrop for romance: The sun was shining, the grass was cool and green, the Lt. Dan Band was playing in the background, and the smell of grilled meat was in the air.

When Lucca laid eyes on Isaac, a yellow Labrador retriever service dog, at a wounded warrior fund-raiser, Willingham saw her excitement. After the mandatory standard dog greeting, she got down in the puppy position to play, but Isaac just stood there. She inched toward him, tail wagging, and he hightailed it under a table and hid behind the tablecloth.

Undaunted, she peeked under, then backed up. He poked his head out, and their eyes met. Eventually he came out, and they lay down close together.

Willingham had been talking with Isaac's owner, Army Captain (Ret.) Leslie Nicole Smith. While deployed to Bosnia, she developed a blood clot in her leg and was flown to Walter Reed, where she was diagnosed with a blood disorder, possibly caused by exposure to toxins in Bosnia. A severe reaction to the medication resulted in the amputation of her lower left leg, complete blindness in one eye, and 95 percent blindness in the other. She spent seven months at Walter Reed during her twenty surgeries.

Her challenges didn't keep her down. In her conversation

with Willingham, he learned that she was a spokesperson for several nonprofit organizations, including Canines for Veterans, the USO, the Fisher House Foundation, and the American Veterans Disabled for Life Memorial.

"Lucca, you always choose boyfriends with absolutely amazing parents," he told her later.

He thought about Billy Soutra and Posha. Soutra had received the Navy Cross the previous year, but Posha wasn't there to get it with him. He had lost a fight with cancer a year earlier. At the Navy Cross ceremony, Soutra was still in pain from the loss.

"Posha made me the marine I am today," he told reporters.

Soutra keeps Posha's ashes in an urn next to his bed, so he's never far away. Soutra has made it clear to his loved ones that he wants to be buried with Posha when his time comes, so they'll always be together.

He wrote a tribute to Posha after he died.

> *I wish I could tell you that it's going to be okay, but the truth is you've always been the one to pave the way.*
>
> *You were always two steps ahead making sure that the paths we traveled were safe.*
>
> *And although you've done enough already, I ask that you still watch over me, making sure the roads I travel without you are safe.*

LUCCA WAS USED to wearing eyewear. When boarding the helo after every air assault mission in Iraq, Willingham had her wear

Doggles so the sand and dirt kicked up by the rotors wouldn't hurt her eyes. She didn't seem to mind them at all.

But the eyewear she wore for the photos at Times Square the afternoon of New Year's Eve was another story. As her eyes peered out from circles cut into the colorful "2014" cardboard glasses Chris and Jill Willingham had bought her, she sat stone still. One ear stood up normally; the other angled slightly to the side. It had gone a little off-kilter after minor surgery removing a hematoma the previous month, and the vet had said it was probably always going to be a little wonky. They'd found it endearing, but now it added to her woeful expression.

"Poor Mama Lucca," Jill said. "Take the photo and let's end the torture."

"Aw, she knows we're just creating happy memories," Willingham said.

The photo session done, the glasses came off and she went back to looking like her usual confident self, angled ear and all.

Jill had never been to New York City, and before Willingham left for a six-week Marine Security Guard recruiting trip, he wanted to show her the town. He figured Lucca could be just as good a tour guide. It was her third trip to the Big Apple in four months.

In September, they'd come to Manhattan to receive the American Kennel Club Heroic Military Working Dog Award. It took them ninety minutes to make their way through the crowd at the end. That same weekend, they ran and walked with some 250 wounded warriors who kicked off the 12th Annual Tunnel to Towers 5k Run and Walk, in memory of those who were killed on 9/11. As they emerged from the 2.7-mile Brooklyn-Battery

Tunnel, they passed 343 firefighters lined up in dress-blue uniforms. Hanging around each of their necks, so their white-gloved hands could be free to clap for the runners, was a large sign with the name and photo of one of the 343 firefighters who died that day.

Willingham, who knew too well what it was like to have a brother in arms perish at the hands of the enemy, felt their losses sharply.

The next month, it was time to co-parent again with Rod. They had been asked to take part in the Veterans Day Parade, so for the fourth time in a year, Willingham handed over Lucca's leash to Rod, who couldn't believe his luck. Lynda Thompson, community coordinator for FDNY, which supports many veterans causes, saw to it they had a memorable visit.

Along with two other dog handlers from their old platoon, they got a VIP tour of 4 World Trade Center, which hadn't yet opened. She also managed to get them—four marines, two dogs—into the Foxwoods Theatre to see the musical *Spider-Man: Turn Off the Dark*. Lucca stretched out and slept through most of it. Willingham tapped her lightly with his foot whenever she started snoring.

As of early 2014, Kevin Wiens had been driving the same concrete mixer truck for nearly eight years. He could have gotten a new one from his company after three years, but he kept coming up with reasons why he didn't need one. This one drove better, or was more comfortable for his tall frame, or, simply, it was perfectly fine and the company didn't need to invest money in a new one.

What Wiens always left out was that on his way to a job on

July 5, 2007, his son Kory called from Iraq. He put him on speaker-phone, and the cab filled with his voice. The elder Wiens caught Kory up on family news, and Kory told him about his latest missions. Most of all, they talked about Cooper.

It would be their last conversation. The next day Kory and Cooper perished in the IED blast near the haystack. The cab of this truck was the last place Kevin Wiens had heard his son's voice. It had touched the cab's ceiling, the steering column, the seats, the upholstery. It was as if the cab contained the last precious molecules of his son. Even years later, when he climbed into the cab to go to a job, he felt like Kory was still there with him.

It was the same with Kory's 1972 Dodge Dart Swinger. Kory and his brother Kyle had worked on it just about every day, all day, when he came home for a couple of weeks before he deployed. He loved that green car and was determined to make it not only drivable, but every bit the hot muscle car he knew it still had the potential to be. It was a work in progress, and he'd continue when he came back for a visit after Iraq.

When he died, some friends, all girls, covered it with flowers.

Kevin Wiens was determined to fulfill his son's dream for that car. It was falling apart in the elements, even under the canopy Kory had put up to protect it. So Kevin Wiens built a large shop with the intent of devoting a good portion of it to the car and its parts. In lieu of flowers at the funeral, he asked for money for restoration. He got enough to buy a carburetor and some other parts, but the donations barely made a dent. He keeps chipping away at the project with a friend.

One day, when it's all done, he will put it to good use accompanying Patriot Guard Riders when they go to the funerals of other fallen heroes.

The living room of his double-wide, where he had thrown a shoe when the military casualty notification team came to tell him of Kory's death, has become a peaceful haven for him and his best friend, a yellow Lab named Cooper. Cooper is one of five yellow Labs he has acquired since Kory's death. Most of the others have Kory's initials, KDW. The first was Kitty Dog Wiens. He got her about three months after Kory died. He wanted something—something living—to keep the memory of Kory and Cooper as vibrant and within reach as possible.

The instant he laid eyes on Cooper a year or so later, he wanted to bestow him with the name of his son's beloved dog. There was something about him, an intangible quality that reminded him of the kind of dog Cooper must have been. They bonded quickly. Friends and family started hearing a great deal about Cooper, who achieved "best dog in the world" status within a few months.

There are qualities about Cooper, though, that have proven even more comforting than having a dog who reminds Kevin Wiens of the original Cooper. The dog, it seems, has many of Kory's traits.

Cooper loves walking from room to room holding on to something—a pair of socks, a newspaper, anything. When Kory was young, he did the same. It was usually his Batman doll, but it could be anything. Even rolled-up socks.

Then there's the bullying thing. Kory never liked it, and he stepped in whenever someone was getting picked on. Cooper does that, too, especially when Kitty hassles one of the other dogs. He'll physically block Kitty and hang out for a while with the other dog.

At night, after a long day of driving the concrete mixer,

Wiens likes to come home, put his feet up in the recliner, and watch a little TV. He gives the dogs turns sitting with him, but they generally don't stick around too long. But Cooper—he's another story. He drapes across Wiens's lap, or snuggles into his side, and stays for as long as Wiens stays.

Wiens doesn't believe in reincarnation. Really, he doesn't, he'll tell you. . . . Well, he never did before. He doesn't want to seem strange, and he doesn't like admitting it's something he would even really consider.

"But you never know," he says. "If there were a way he could do it, I wouldn't put it past Kory to come back to his dad as a dog named Cooper."

LUCCA STOOD ON the pavement and looked at the work that lay ahead. A row of about ten cars, parked with their trunk ends lined up with each other, needed her attention. She looked at the cars, then looked up at Willingham. He knew what she needed to do and cut her off leash to do her work.

She trotted from one car to the next, giving the back half of every car a few sniffs to make sure they didn't harbor explosives. She moved along with the grace and precision of a seasoned pro, dipping in between the cars and back out and around the next one. There was no dawdling over unimportant scents, and the candy wrapper by the passenger door of the fourth car was ignored.

In just over one minute, she was done. No bombs. No makings of IEDs. Nothing to report.

But she had done the work, and that always gets a reward. "Good girl!" Willingham cheered in the high voice she loved. He bounced the Kong on the pavement and she caught it and worked it in her mouth as they got into their car and drove away.

The people at Enterprise Rent-A-Car in Stafford, Virginia, will be glad to know that, at least on that chilly afternoon, when Willingham dropped off a friend to rent a car, their cars were all bomb-free.

CORNHOLE, THE OUTDOOR beanbag toss game known in some circles as "lawn darts for drunks," is purported to have been invented in Ohio, Kris Knight's home state. In hindsight, Willingham wished he'd known that before telling Knight how he was going to slaughter him at the game when he stopped by his house after an official visit to Yuma Proving Ground in early 2014.

Knight had been working there for years, first running the dog team predeployment program, and then being shifted to a non-dog job, taking it in stride because it's the best way to roll in the military. He and Willingham calculated they hadn't seen each other for four or five years. They'd each become gunnery sergeants in the interim, and they had a lot of catching up to do.

Willingham had brought along a fellow Marine Security Guard recruiter, and Knight invited an old marine friend he'd known since childhood in Ohio. Rinat Knight, his wife, whom he'd fallen in love with during his time in Israel, came home from school and brought with her a couple of large pepperoni pizzas from the YPG bowling alley down the street. The old friends washed it down with Bud Light and Coors Light.

After a while they set up the cornhole boards at opposite ends of the front lawn. Willingham recalled being quite the stud at cornhole when he and the other dog guys played it at Camp

Leatherneck in Afghanistan. But Knight's two-man team beat Willingham's more than handily.

"These guys got their asses handed to them ten out of ten times," Knight dutifully reported to Rinat.

Later, while sitting around the dining room, the handlers exchanged old stories. Willingham regaled the others with the tale of the time a nineteen-year-old Israeli dog handler who wanted Knight, thirty-four at the time, to spar with him. Knight tried to warn the kid about his martial arts black belt. Willingham tried to warn the kid not to mess with him. But there was no relenting.

"So Knight's there, almost twice his age and half his height. OK, not the height part. But he's standing in his Crocs and shorts, and the kid makes a move to hit him. Then boom, boom, boom, it's over in two seconds. Rib, armpit, ear! He could've made the kid meat, but he took it easy on him."

They also talked dogs. Willingham and Knight knew they probably would have talked dogs the whole time because that's what handlers—former or current—do when they get together. But the others were there, and they wanted to keep them in the conversation.

Bram's ashes rested in peace in the next room over, the military memorabilia room, in a polished wooden box. The urn sits beside a concrete square with an impression of Bram's paw print and his full name—BRAM K457—roughly engraved in the concrete, along with his birth and death dates, JUNE '03–JAN. '12.

Bram and Knight had to go their separate ways after their second deployment together, in Afghanistan. He hated to leave his dog, but that's how the dog program usually operates. When assignments don't mesh, and handlers are moved to another location or make a rank that precludes their working as handlers, teams are separated. Dogs and handlers don't usually get more than one deployment together, but specialized search dog handlers tend to have more time with their dogs.

It was rough on Knight, but worse was when he found out two weeks too late that Bram had been deemed unadoptable and euthanized at Camp Lejeune. Knight couldn't have adopted him because Bram couldn't be trusted not to bite Rinat or anyone else, no matter how much Knight worked with him. But he would have tried hard to find a single dog handler who lived in the country and could take him in.

"Bram was an amazing, crazy-ass dog," Willingham said. "He lived life to the fullest."

"That he did," Knight said.

CLAIRE WILLINGHAM, AGE six, loved all things princess and anything beautiful, really. The subjects of her drawings, when they weren't of her family, often involved flowers, castles, and rainbows. One evening while wearing her fluffy pink pajamas, she sat down at a little table in the living room and gathered four markers. Green, red, black, brown. Not her standard palette of pink and purple. They were slightly dried out, but fine for drawing a visitor a surprise on a piece of yellow construction paper.

As she drew, her brother, Michael, age four, played with his plastic Superman, running around the room holding him high, leaping tall cushions in a single bound.

Lucca moved closer to Claire and settled in next to her feet. From her first days as a live-in member of the Willingham family, it was clear she didn't have much patience for energetic boys.

When Michael and his friends came her way, she tended to get up and move somewhere else. Often, there was a sigh involved.

His parents didn't force the issue. Lucca had put in her time. They figured she'd eventually come around to him, especially as he got a little older.

Claire brought the visitor her drawing. It was a picture of a girl and a dog. They were both smiling. At first glance, they seemed like any happy girl and dog.

But if you looked carefully, you would notice something a little different about this drawing. The smiling dog with the pointy ears and the big brown tail had only three legs.

EVERYONE WAS IN bed except for Lucca and Willingham. His late night started when he got a hankering to see some videos of Lucca joyfully running through the snow in Finland. One video led to another, and then came the photographs. Family photos, but mostly photos of deployments with Lucca.

It got him to thinking about some old war gear that he kept in the garage. He went out to take a look, and Lucca followed. He flicked on a light and walked over to the sea bag and small backpack he had brought to Iraq. He hadn't opened them since his last deployment with her. Lucca watched with interest as he knelt down and unzipped the front pouch. He pulled out his old gloves and the bandana he sometimes wore around his head to catch the sweat.

Then he unzipped the main compartment. Lucca was now standing at his side, ears tipping forward as she looked down at it. Fast sniffs mixed with longer inhalations. He pulled out her portable water bowl, her canine medical kit, and her old harness. It was the original harness, the one with the BADASS name tape on the side.

Something in her look—he didn't know just what, but there was something different—told him that she was transported back to their time in Iraq. He realized that the scent of those days must have been everywhere. She looked almost nostalgic to him, like someone poring through long-lost photographs.

After giving the gear a thorough inspection, she sat and looked at Willingham, who was just a couple of feet away, still kneeling by the pack. Her ears were at attention, her eyes alert, her little dark brows slightly raised, and her mouth closed, serious. He thought she looked like a warrior remembering old times, and he knew exactly what she was telling him.

I used to be a badass. We had some good times together, didn't we?

ACKNOWLEDGMENTS

GETTING TO KNOW the Willinghams—the two-legged ones and the amazing three-legged one with the expressive eyebrows—has been a real joy. They welcomed me into their home, where, much to my amazement, Lucca chose to become my part-time roommate in the spacious basement guest room they generously provided during my eleven days with them. Living alongside this hero dog who canters about the house as if nothing has happened gave me a true insight into her character that I may not have had without this time we spent together.

That Lucca decided to hang out with me for hours at a time instead of constantly shadowing Chris Willingham, as is her tradition, made me think I must be pretty special. The doggy salmon treats I kept at my bedside table for her had nothing to do with her loyalty to me during my visit. The fact that every time she came in my room, she plopped down and positioned herself facing the bag of treats was mere coincidence. Same for when I ran out of treats and she ran back upstairs to be with Chris and family. Coincidence! No, Lucca was crazy about her biographer, and the feeling was mutual.

And yes, she snores, and it's endearing as hell.

It's hard to describe being in the presence of Lucca. You look into her eyes and realize how much this dog has seen, smelled, heard, and experienced: Her youth in the Netherlands, formative months in Israel, war in Iraq twice, war in Afghanistan, the death of her best friend, chaos and turmoil, night air assaults, the thrill of the Kong, the aroma of red chicken stew in Afghanistan, mortars, the scent of firefights and fear, IEDs and IEDs and IEDs, losing a leg, visiting wounded warriors, family life, waking up to the scent of pancakes and bacon on Sunday mornings. It's all inside this hero, and I'm happy to have had a hand in helping unlock her experiences for readers. Thank you, Lucca, for everything you have done in your life and for all the lives you have saved.

Jill Willingham, a devoted nurse, badass athlete, and great mom, was an incredible resource for this book. Her insights and her candor helped give *Lucca the War Dog* a depth it wouldn't have otherwise had.

She describes Lucca as a calm leader. Jill could just as easily be describing her husband, Chris. Chris Willingham is one of the most level-headed, nice, genuine, and positive people I've ever met. He cares deeply about family, including all his marine dog-handler brothers. He has a quiet confidence mixed with true humility. He says those same words about his father and personal hero, Elden Willingham. I am grateful that apple fell close to the tree. Chris's unwavering work ethic, patience, smarts, sense of humor, organizational skills, love of Lucca, and enthusiasm for telling her story are really at the heart of why this book is in your hands. Without him being there every step of the way—and almost every day—this book would not have come to be.

A salute to Elden Willingham for raising a fine son with Martha Willingham and for his service during the Vietnam War. I'm pleased that his own war story, which he has kept close to his chest for so long, can finally be told. In relating his story, I hope to honor others who served in the Vietnam War and to bring awareness to the kinds of experiences they had to come through with little or no support.

Juan "Rod" Rodriguez, Lucca's "other dad," was clearly a fantastic choice for Lucca's second handler. The first time I met him was via a three-hour Skype conversation with Chris and me when I was staying with the Willinghams. I could sense his deep devotion to this dog even through the grainy video. Like Chris, he is as humble as they get. Lucca, who was lying between Chris's chair and mine for most of the Skype conversation, seemed delighted to see Rod on the laptop screen and recognized his voice immediately, wagging her tail and angling her head when he first appeared. Despite his busy schedule of work and school, he managed to be there for me anytime I needed to interview him.

Hats off to Rod's mom, Elsa Nolasco, for doing what it took as a single mother who moved from Puerto Rico to Massachusetts to help make a better life for her children and help made Rod the great guy he is today. A book scene with her fell through, and I want her in this book, so here's to you, Elsa!

I've taken up a lot of book real estate to thank Lucca's immediate "family," so I'll try to keep the rest of the acknowledgments a bit shorter.

Jake Parker, the pseudonym for the Special Forces soldier who worked alongside Rod, was an immense help in putting together the scenes for Lucca's Afghanistan deployment. His experience as a Green Beret, with his knowledge of Pashto and insight into local culture, proved invaluable to the manuscript.

Kris Knight—what can I say? Larger than life, a main character in my book *Soldier Dogs,* and now a featured player in Lucca's story. You can't talk to this guy and not smile. He is a born storyteller and generously gave his time to our many interviews and countless texts. He and his wife, Rinat, visited my family in San Francisco right after the deadline for this book, and after they left, my daughter commented on his hug, which was also larger than life: "He's like a giant rock hugging you with two giant rock arms."

A huge thanks to army veterinarian Jim Giles, the head of the crack team that got Lucca through her surgery. He helped me understand every minute of the surgery and what happened before and after. We had an initial three-plus-hour interview about the surgery and several follow-ups. Lucca's surgery took less time than it took for him to painstakingly describe the details so I could make that scene come to life.

In a similar vein, I'd like to thank army veterinarian Shane Chumbler, who was in charge of the veterinary clinic at Leatherneck when Lucca showed up. He was an enormous help with descriptions of medical procedures. Lucca was in fantastic hands with everyone who dealt with her during this time, from the medic in the field onward.

I have great admiration for Danielle Roche, who was in charge of all the dog teams on Lucca's first deployment. She provided me with some wonderful details that enrich the book.

Retired U.S. Army Colonel Peter Mansoor, who served as

General Petraeus's executive officer during the troop surge of 2007 to 2008, was my go-to man for questions about the situation in Iraq from a military and historical perspective. I feel very lucky to have had Mansoor, the General Raymond E. Mason Jr. Chair of Military History at the Ohio State University, as my consultant on these matters. He has written some excellent books, and his book *Surge* was a valuable resource.

Also on my valued volunteer team of experts was marine EOD tech Matt Lenz. He fielded my inquiries about explosives, particularly as they pertained to explosive ordnance disposal. Matt: Get ready to buy the shop a case of beer, because someone there is bound to see this!

Pilot Tim Raynor, of American Airlines' Veterans and Military Initiatives, was always right there whenever I had questions about how the airline provided travel arrangements for Lucca, Chris, and Rod (most notably for the reunion) and about its support of many military and veterans programs. I applaud what this airline does for those who have served and for the families of those who have given their lives.

The staff at the American embassy in Helsinki provided excellent insight into Chris's devotion to Lucca and the U.S. Military Working Dog Program, and they helped me with details of the reunion. Thanks especially to Nicholas Kuchova for his at-the-ready assistance and for helping make the reunion a reality.

I'm also indebted to all the others who gave their time to interview with me for this book, including Danny Cornier, Kevin Wiens, Al Brenner, Billy Soutra, Brian Kolfage, Julie Schrock, Chuck Rotenberry, Liz Rotenberry, Autumn Swank, Crystal Fenn, Leslie Nicole Smith, Kalevi Soderlund, Branden Deleon, and Jim Palmersheim.

On the editorial side, my talented Dutton editor, Stephen Morrow, has once again been a hell of a lot of fun to work with, despite yet another tight deadline. Good on ya, mate! Enthusiastic and first-rate assistant editor Stephanie Hitchcock worked tirelessly to help all the pieces come together. I'm also grateful for my hardworking agent, Carol Mann, and a kickass freelance copy editor who I apparently shall know only by her Track Changes name of "COPY EDITOR."

Finally, my own family—husband, Craig, and daughter, Laura—for once again being hugely supportive as I disappeared into another book. Craig, you blew me away with your excellent editorial advice throughout. It's good to be back.

NOTES ON SOURCES

All interviews in this book were conducted between August 2013 and April 2014, either in person, by phone, via Skype, or by e-mail, with occasional questions answered via text or Facebook.

I spent about eleven days in November to December 2013 living with the Willinghams, who graciously opened their home to me so I could get to know Chris, Jill, the children, and, of course, Lucca. This is where the most extensive interviewing of Chris Willingham took place, but it continued for months afterward on an almost-daily basis via e-mail and phone.

Special Forces soldier Jake Parker's name has been changed in this book, as have the names of the two other Green Berets I wrote about. "Jake" asked not to use real names of the members of his Special Forces team, and I am honoring his request. There's a reason Green Berets are known as "the quiet professionals."

If I were starting to learn about military dogs from scratch, there would be a litany of sources I would cite in this section. However, I have become something of a civilian version of a subject matter expert on military dogs thanks to my previous book, *Soldier Dogs*. I keep on top of all things military dog on a daily basis and am in regular communication with many in the military working dog community. My knowledge of the topic meant I didn't have to pore over reams of papers and books, and interview countless dog experts, in order to gain insight into these dog teams.

That said, I did rely on dozens of articles, books, videos, websites, government documents, and PowerPoint presentations about various topics addressed in this book—particularly certain moments in the Iraq War about which I was not well versed. In this section, I cite primarily from sources that contain information that's not widely disseminated.

A word about dialogue in *Lucca the War Dog*. Since I was not there for most of the action, I relied on descriptions from those who were. They did their best to portray conversations, and I took it from there. Because of this, the book cannot always have exact quotes, but I did my best to capture the conversations and dialogue. The same with the scenes and settings. I was able to supplement the descriptions from those I interviewed with photographs and videos they provided, as well as finding details online and elsewhere.

This book captures the highlights of Lucca's story. She had numerous IED finds I didn't write about, was in more firefights, and had many other book-worthy experiences—even after retirement—that couldn't fit into the pages of this book. I'm sure she and Chris Willingham will go on to have many more, because that's how they roll.

CHAPTER 1

Interviews with former Marine Corporal Juan "Rod" Rodriguez, former Special Forces Sergeant Jake Parker, and Marine Gunnery Sergeant Chris Willingham.

CHAPTER 2

Interviews with Marine Gunnery Sergeant Chris Willingham, Marine Gunnery Sergeant Kristopher Knight, Jill Willingham, and Elden Willingham.

CHAPTER 3

Interviews with Marine Gunnery Sergeant Chris Willingham, Marine Gunnery Sergeant Kristopher Knight, and former Army Captain Danielle Roche.

CHAPTERS 4 AND 5

Broadwell, Paula, with Vernon Loeb. *All In: The Education of General David Petraeus*. New York: The Penguin Press, 2012.

"Department of Defense Bloggers Roundtable with Lieutenant Colonel Ken Adgie," transcript. September 27, 2007, http://www.defense.gov/home/blog/docs/0927adgie_transcript.pdf.

Interviews with Marine Gunnery Sergeant Chris Willingham; Army Colonel (Ret.) Peter Mansoor; Army Captain Nathan S. "Shane" Chumbler, DVM; and Marine Gunnery Sergeant Matthew Lentz.

Kagan, Frederick W. "Choosing Victory: A Plan for Success in Iraq." *American Enterprise Institute Online*, January 5, 2007, http://www.aei.org/papers/foreign-and-defense-policy/regional/middle-east-and-north-africa/choosing-victory-a-plan-for-success-in-iraq-paper.

Mansoor, Peter R. *Surge: My Journey with General David Petraeus and the Remaking of the Iraq War.* New Haven: Yale University Press, 2013.

MRE Info. "MRE Menus." Accessed June 17, 2014, http://www.mreinfo.com/us/mre/mre-menus.html.

Partlow, Joshua, and John Ward Anderson. "Troops Pushing South Through Insurgent Area." *The Washington Post.* June 22, 2007, http://www.washingtonpost.com/wp-dyn/content/article/2007/06/21/AR2007062100597.html.

Petraeus, David H. "CENTCOM Update, Center for a New American Security." Multimedia presentation. June 11, 2009, http://www.cnas.org/files/multimedia/documents/Petraeus%20Slides.pdf.

Rising, David. "U.S. troop buildup felt in Iraq hotspots." *USA Today.* September 4, 2007, http://usatoday30.usatoday.com/news/topstories/2007-09-04-3523744152_x.htm.

Roggio, Bill. "Arab Jabour: 'This Is al Qaeda Country.'" *The Long War Journal.* September 22, 2007, http://www.longwarjournal.org/archives/2007/09/arab_jabour_this_is.php#.

West, Bing. *The Strongest Tribe: War, Politics, and the Endgame in Iraq.* New York: Random House, 2008.

Chapter 6

"DoD News Briefing with Maj. Gen. Lynch from Iraq," transcript. July 6, 2007, http://www.defense.gov/transcripts/transcript.aspx?transcriptid=4007.

Interviews with Marine Gunnery Sergeant Chris Willingham, Marine Gunnery Sergeant Kristopher Knight, former Army Captain Danielle Roche, and Kevin Wiens.

Report on the death of Kory Wiens was merged information from two official military reports.

Chapter 7

Interviews with Marine Gunnery Sergeant Chris Willingham, Marine
    Gunnery Sergeant Kristopher Knight, Jill Willingham, and former Army
    Captain Danielle Roche.

Chapter 8

Interviews with Marine Gunnery Sergeant Chris Willingham, Elden
    Willingham, Jill Willingham, and Marine Sergeant William "Billy"
    Soutra Jr.
Lamothe, Dan, and Andrew deGrandpré. "MARSOC team honored for
    breaking Taliban ambush." *Military Times*. December 4, 2012, http://
    www.militarytimes.com/article/20121204/NEWS/212040324/
    MARSOC-team-honored-breaking-Taliban-ambush.

Chapter 9

Interviews with Marine Gunnery Sergeant Chris Willingham, Julie Schrock,
    former Marine Corporal Juan "Rod" Rodriguez, former Marine Sergeant
    Alfred Brenner, Megan Brenner, and Marine Sergeant Branden Deleon.

Chapter 10

"A Birthday Message from the Commandant of the Marine Corps." Accessed
    on June 19, 2014, https://www.mca-marines.org/leatherneck/birthday
    -message-commandant-marine-corps.
Interviews with Marine Gunnery Sergeant Chris Willingham, Marine
    Gunnery Sergeant Chuck Rotenberry, former Marine Corporal Juan
    "Rod" Rodriguez, Marine Gunnery Sergeant Kristopher Knight, and Jill
    Willingham.
Sgt Grit Staff. "Marine Corps Birthday Message." Accessed June 19, 2014,
    http://www.grunt.com/corps/scuttlebutt/marine-corps-stories/marine
    -corps-birthday-message.
Yount, Shannon. "Mark Wahlberg visits troops in Afghanistan." *DVIDS*.
    December 19, 2010, http://www.dvidshub.net/news/62281/mark
    -wahlberg-visits-troops-afghanistan#.U5OrsZRdUZ2.

CHAPTER 11

Burton, Janice. "Game Changers: ANA Special Forces Impact the Course of Afghanistan." *Special Warfare*. October–December 2011, http://www.soc.mil/swcs/SWmag/archive/SW2404/SW2404GameChangers.html.

Foreman, Jonathan. "The Meaning of 'Green on Blue' Attacks in Afghanistan." *National Review*. September 18, 2012, http://www.nationalreview.com/corner/322428/meaning-green-blue-attacks-afghanistan-jonathan-foreman.

Gentile, Carmen. "In Afghanistan, special units do the dirty work." *USA Today*. November 9, 2011, http://usatoday30.usatoday.com/news/world/afghanistan/story/2011-11-09/special-forces-key-in-afghanistan/51145690/1.

Interviews with former Marine Corporal Juan "Rod" Rodriguez, former Special Forces Sergeant Jake Parker, Marine Sergeant Daniel Cornier, Marine Gunnery Sergeant Matthew Lentz.

Training Developers of Training Development Division 1, "Inside the SFCQ," http://www.specialforcesassociation.org/inside-the-sfqc.

CHAPTER 12

Department of Health and Human Services. "Explosions and Blast Injuries: A Primer for Clinicians." Accessed June 19, 2014, http://www.cdc.gov/masstrauma/preparedness/primer.pdf.

Interviews with former Marine Corporal Juan "Rod" Rodriguez; former Special Forces Sergeant Jake Parker; Marine Sergeant Daniel Cornier; Marine Gunnery Sergeant Matthew Lentz; Army Lieutenant-Colonel James Giles III; Army Captain Nathan S. "Shane" Chumbler, DVM; Marine Gunnery Sergeant Chris Willingham; and Jill Willingham.

UXO Info. "Ordnance Hazards." Accessed June 19, 2014, http://www.uxoinfo.com/uxoinfo/ordhazards.cfm.

CHAPTER 13

Alho, Olli. "A guide to Finnish customs and manners." November 2002, http://finland.fi/public/default.aspx?contentid=160036.

eDiplomat. "Finland." http://www.ediplomat.com/np/cultural_etiquette/ce_fi.htm.

"Finland," http://wikitravel.org/en/Finland.

Goodavage, Maria. "Dispatches from Helsinki: Hero Dog Amputee Reunites with First Handler." *Soldier Dogs*. July 12, 2012, http://www.soldierdogs .com/2012/07/12/dispatches-from-helsinki-hero-dog-amputee-reunites -with-first-handler/.

Interviews with former Marine Corporal Juan "Rod" Rodriguez, Marine Gunnery Sergeant Chris Willingham, Nicholas Kuchova, Jim Palmersheim, Marine Colonel Tim Raynor, Jill Willingham, and Kalevi Soderlund.

Orchard Group Productions. "American Airlines Sendoff for Lucca." Accessed June 19, 2014, http://vimeo.com/46908687.

"Welcome to the University of Joensuu!" http://www.mendelu.cz/dok_server/ slozka.pl?id=39552;download=41541.

CHAPTER 14

American Airlines. "In Support of All Who Serve." http://www .airlinereporter.com/wp-content/uploads/2013/08/INITIATIVES -BROCHURE-2013_Final.pdf.

Interviews with Marine Gunnery Sergeant Chris Willingham, Jill Willingham, former Marine Corporal Juan "Rod" Rodriguez, Marine Colonel Tim Raynor, Nicholas Kuchova, Marine Gunnery Sergeant Chuck Rotenberry, Liz Rotenberry, Autumn Swank, Crystal Fenn, Elden Willingham, former Security Forces airman Brian Kolfage, Army Captain (Ret.) Leslie Nicole Smith, Marine Sergeant William "Billy" Soutra Jr., Kevin Wiens, and Marine Gunnery Sergeant Kristopher Knight.